ENCOUNTERS WITH GREAT PSYCHOLOGISTS
Twelve Dramatic Portraits

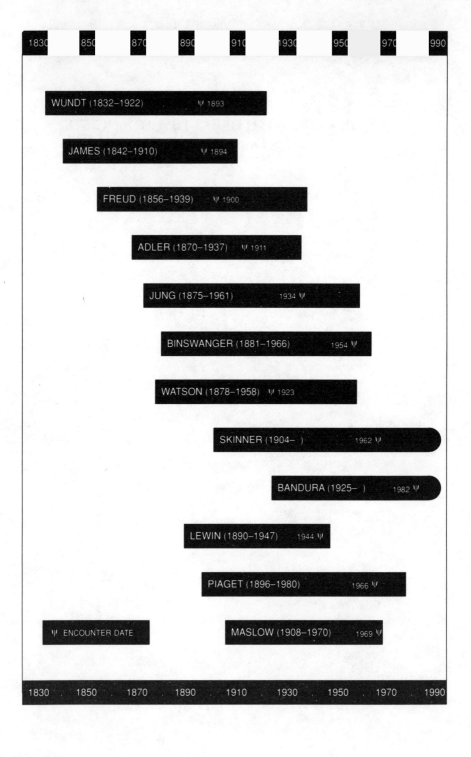

Encounters with Great Psychologists

Twelve Dramatic Portraits

By
JOHN H. KUNKEL
University of Western Ontario

With a Foreword by
ERNEST R. HILGARD
Stanford University

Illustrations by
Alice M. Mansell

WALL & THOMPSON
Toronto

Requests for permission to make copies of any part of the work should be mailed to: Wall & Thompson, Six O'Connor Drive, Toronto, Ontario, Canada M4K 2Kl.

SALES AND DISTRIBUTION:

In the United States, send orders to:
University of Toronto Press
340 Nagel Drive
BUFFALO, NY 14225
Telephone: (716) 683-4547

In Canada, send orders to:
University of Toronto Press
5201 Dufferin Street
NORTH YORK, ONTARIO
M3H 5T8
Telephone (416) 667-7791

The dialogues in the encounters are based upon historical sources. Permission was kindly given by Brooks/Cole Publishing Company to quote words attributed to Abraham Maslow from its publication, *Abraham H. Maslow: A Memorial Volume,* International Study Project, Inc., Menlo Park, California; compiled with the assistance of Bertha G. Maslow. Copyright © 1972 by Wadsworth Publishing Company, Inc.

Canadian Cataloguing in Publication Data
Kunkel, John H. (John Howard), 1932-
　Encounters With Great Psychologists
Includes bibliographical references.
ISBN 0-921332-14-9 (bound) ISBN 0-921332-09-2 (pbk.)
1. Psychologists - Biography. 2. Psychology -
History. I. Title.
BF109.A1K86 1989　　150'.92'2　　C88-095304-7

ISBN 0-921332-14-9 (hardcover)
ISBN 0-921332-09-2 (paperback)

Printed in Canada.
1 2 3 4 5　　93 92 91 90 89

TABLE OF CONTENTS

FOREWORD

Psychology as we know it is a product of the work and thought of those who are identified as psychologists, with contributions from its close relatives in the other social sciences and psychiatry. Surely one way to cut through the breadth of topics studied and the numerous theories offered is to become acquainted with the lives, interests, and accomplishments of some exemplary psychologists.

John Kunkel, himself a seasoned social scientist, has chosen a unique method to provide this acquaintance with twelve significant psychologists by offering "encounters" with each of them. While such a small number cannot cover everything, he has included a broad enough spectrum to produce a feel in the reader for what psychology has become over its first century of claim to be a science.

To produce the encounters, Kunkel first introduces a psychologist with a brief account of his career and theory, so that he can be understood in the context of the time and culture when he was working. This is then followed for each by the longer and more innovative feature of the book: an extended conversation that occurs in a plausible place with plausible participants. Although the conversation is fictional, it serves as a vehicle for making the psychologist come alive as he explains and defends the view that he has come to hold about human nature—the central problem of psychology as the author rightly perceives it. While "listening in" on these conversations, the reader comes away with a vivid impression of what the psychologist must have been (or is now) as a person. The final chapter attempts to find the common threads that give some coherence to the mosaic of viewpoints.

Limiting the selection to twelve psychologists could not have been easy. Selecting Wundt and James as the prominent pioneers was pretty obvious, and Freud, Adler, and Jung were the evident names early in the history of psychoanalysis. Ludwig Binswanger may come as something of a surprise to represent later developments, not because he was not important in the history of psychology but because he is better known as an existentialist than as a psychoanalyst. Still he, as only six years younger than Jung (the youngest of the original three), remained on good terms with Freud despite naming his position existential analysis. Kunkel chose him in part to show the amount of room there is for original theories at the boundaries of conventional psychology. By including Binswanger, the existential movement, so strong in Europe, and recognizable in America, is given a hearing.

Only two of the encounters are with psychologists alive today: B.F. Skinner of Harvard University, and Albert Bandura of Stanford University, classified along with John B. Watson as experimenters. Skinner is an appropriate choice to represent contemporary behaviorism, and Bandura was selected because his social learning theory, although not a behavioristic theory, meets many of the issues raised by behaviorism in its search for objectivity. At the same time, Bandura gives a more human view than behaviorism does through his emphasis on cognition, in line with the current prominence of cognitive psychology.

Categorizing psychologists is always somewhat arbitrary, and Kunkel recognized this when he decided not to list Lewin as a derivative of Gestalt psychology, not to list Piaget as a developmental psychologist, and not to list Maslow as the father of humanistic psychology, but instead grouped them as "the free spirits."

The "encounters" come off very well indeed. *Encounters with Great Psychologists* is to be recommended to those who are overwhelmed by the detailed substance of introductory psychology texts which emphasize the nitty-gritty of psychological research, its varied topics, its apparatus, procedures, and statistical methods of assuring the reliability and validity of its data. Such features are not to be despised as part of becoming acquainted with psychology as a science, but it is a pleasure to have this supplementary approach which keeps the larger issues of human nature in the forefront.

Many teachers of psychology may wish to assign this book in addition to a standard text. *Encounters with Great Psychologists* will also be attractive to a general audience of those who are not students of psychology, or are no longer in college, but who share a curiosity about what has been happening in psychology.

Ernest R. Hilgard
Stanford, California

PREFACE

Psychology is more than laboratory and consulting room, experiment and observation. As a scientific discipline, it contains a great variety of concepts and propositions, ideas and theories. All of these embody the labor of many researchers whose efforts have spanned decades. It will be interesting to meet some of the individuals whose work exemplifies the field's vigor and continuity.

In this book I introduce the human element through dramatic portraits of twelve psychologists who have been influential in the discovery of human nature. Each chapter presents a sympathetic view of an individual's unique character and lasting contributions. Together, these encounters provide a vivid picture of the major perspectives and methods of modern psychology.

Any selection of twelve significant psychologists—or twenty—may appear somewhat arbitrary, especially to admirers of those not included. Perhaps one might hold back until the field reaches its full maturity, so that time will have ample opportunities to render judgment. But psychology is too vibrant and dynamic a science for such a wait.

I have selected the researchers on the basis of three criteria. First, since a major goal of psychology is to increase our understanding of human nature, I have emphasized explorers who focused their attention on human beings. Thus we encounter Watson rather than Pavlov. Second, I have chosen investigators who are generally recognized to have made significant contributions to their special fields. Third, I have tried to cover a wide range of topics and interests within the whole of psychology. Hence we will venture from simple reactions to intricate deeds, from plain thoughts to complex mental processes, and from single individuals to social interactions.

In the course of these discussions we also participate in some of the major debates that enliven modern psychology. While there is general agreement that psychology is a science, there are many questions about appropriate methods. Is psychology limited to laboratory experiments and their results, as we see in our encounters with "The Experimenters," or does it include the broader concerns of Jung and Maslow? The encounters elucidate the whole range of possibilities, from the experiments of Skinner to the observations of Binswanger.

These twelve researchers represent most of the areas, perspectives, "schools," and methods of modern psychology. The structural and functional approaches of the early years appear in Part I. Psychoanalysis, Individual Psychology, Analytical Psychology, and Existential Psychology, constitute Part II. In Part III we encounter Behaviorism, Neobehaviorism, and the Cognitive approach. Social, Developmental, and Humanistic Psychology make their appearance in Part IV. We also become acquainted with various methods of collecting and analyzing data, ranging from personal introspection and the insights of therapists to systematic observations from daily life and conclusions from laboratory experiments.

Each chapter comprises three sections. I begin with a sketch of the psychologist's life and times, and trace the development of his ideas. I also describe the methods he employed and assess the information on which he relied.

Then I outline the researcher's major contributions to our knowledge of the human mosaic. I do not describe the whole theory but emphasize only those principles and insights that have a solid basis and are likely to stand the test of time. I also include a few ideas which suggest intriguing hypotheses, even when they go beyond the facts we have today.

The third and longest section consists of an imaginary conversation between the psychologist and various real and fictional individuals in a setting of actual events. I have chosen the dates to reflect a time at which the psychologist had formulated his major ideas, though not necessarily in published form. Each encounter portrays the atmosphere and general spirit of an occasion that was typical of the researcher's life. The conversations illuminate the character of the man and the significant events of his life, and highlight the vitality of his contributions. While the discussions focus on the researcher's major ideas, they also raise many of the critical questions and express the qualifications that are suggested by ongoing research.

I hope that readers will be caught up in the spirit of constructive debate and raise their own questions about the ideas and methods of the twelve researchers. The variety of views regarding psychology as a discipline, and its "proper" methods and subject matter, should help us clarify our own position.

Some of the later chapters contain a few references to earlier material, but each chapter is an independent unit that can be understood by itself. Together, the chapters give us a sense of continuity and show that psychologists are making progress in their efforts to discover human nature. Today's knowledge, summarized in the last chapter, should enable us to comprehend ourselves better, and to reduce the individual difficulties and social problems we meet in daily life.

In the "Notes" at the end of each chapter I sketch the background of the encounter and indicate which parts are real and imagined. I also provide references for the material that appears in the conversations.

The seeds of this work developed while I held a year's fellowship at the Center for Advanced Study in the Behavioral Sciences. In the serenity of the hills above Stanford University I first saw the possibility of bringing together the elements of so many diverse and seemingly conflicting views of human nature.

As a social psychologist, it is perhaps inevitable that I consider some experiences of daily life as indirect tests of various hypotheses. For many years now, my friends, students, and colleagues have demonstrated repeatedly that psychological theories have some validity and some definite limitations. Most important, my family has shown in no uncertain way that individuals are considerably more complex than any one theory would have us believe. The fascinating questions raised by these experiences provided the impetus for writing this book.

Over the years, a number of individuals have extended their help, and much of what follows is due to their encouragement. In particular, I wish to thank Albert Bandura and B. F. Skinner for their critiques of "their" chapters, Douglas Cann for comments on the Jung chapter, and Charles Levine for suggestions on the Piaget encounter. The kindly advice of Benjamin Singer, Byron Wall, and of Orrin and Evelyn Klapp, has improved several chapters. Finally, I gladly acknowledge my debt to three friendly but severe critics: Mary, Katharine, and Michael.

John H. Kunkel
London, Ontario
September 6, 1988

INTRODUCTION

1
THE QUEST FOR PSYCHOLOGICAL KNOWLEDGE

Psychology gives us a kaleidoscopic picture of human beings: a wondrous array of intriguing facts and beguiling theories. But a coherent image has not yet emerged. Hence we may well ask: what do we really know about human nature, and what are the roots of psychological knowledge?

Today it is fashionable to emphasize the great variety of psychological theories and methods, and to deplore their conflicting explanations of human behavior. But such diversity can also be beneficial, for it leads to productive tensions. Investigators confront new problems and search for solutions, they become dissatisfied with existing answers and look for better ones. In the early stages of its development the character of a science—such as psychology even today—is to some extent a reflection of the individuals who work in that field.

The imaginary conversations of twelve significant psychologists in this book portray the links among ideas and the controversies that invigorate the field. These investigators devoted their lives to the careful study of human beings and helped make psychology what it is today. Most of them were either physician-therapists or academics working in laboratories. All were astute observers of human beings, honest in their analysis of data, ready to test their insights, and eager to disseminate their conclusions to the world.

The individuals we meet investigated human phenomena from a variety of perspectives and focused on different aspects of the human condition. We should not be surprised, therefore, that they came to rather different conclusions about human characteristics, possibilities, and limitations. While these researchers developed and defended sharply contrasting views, however, they all contributed to a comprehensive, dynamic conception of human nature.

In the encounters we will see that the perspectives which guide psychologists in their work have several roots. First, a researcher's *personal interests* focus attention on one or another topic, give rise to certain questions, and channel the ways in which answers are sought. A person who is primarily interested in memory or motivation, for example, is likely to view human phenomena rather differently than someone who wishes to use effective methods to help people solve personal problems. A psychologist's interests are not always clearly evident, however, and they may change over time. Sigmund Freud, for example, was actually more interested in discovering the unconscious aspects of human nature than he was in the welfare of his patients. B. F. Skinner, on the other hand, began with an interest in the general laws of behavior (of any organism) and thereby laid the foundation for programs that have benefitted a wide range of human beings.

Second, the perspective of researchers is affected by their *intellectual environment*. The "great questions" and "important problems" that surround young psychologists during their formative years tend to provide the impetus for later work. The generally accepted definitions of "proper procedures" (and even of the "scientific method") indicate what can be done, and how. We will see in the twelve encounters how contemporary questions, problems, and methods compelled psychologists to follow new paths—and also limited their efforts. Thus Freud, Adler, and Jung discovered different "facts" and argued about the various "explanations" they inferred. Because they could not agree, however, they eventually went their separate ways. Watson sought to overcome these and other methodological problems by concentrating on behavior and avoiding any inferences at all.

Third, the *values and customs of a society* affect a researcher's work—and indeed the choice of career. The cultural milieu within which psychology developed, for example, deemed both science and therapy to be largely male provinces. Until the 1930s there were very few women psychologists, and most of the early discoverers were men (hence the major figures in the following chapters). One cannot help wondering what psychology would look like if women had entered the field earlier so that some of them would be recognized as pioneer contributors to the field. Several of the best known neo-Freudians were women (e.g. Melanie Klein and Karen Horney), and during the 1920s women wrote many of the intriguing dissertations supervised by Lewin (e.g. Bluma Zeigarnik). Women did not begin to work in Wundt's laboratory until the 1890s, and only a few of Watson's students became well-known researchers (e.g. Mary Cover Jones). In the years since then, women have played increasingly significant roles in the development of all branches of psychology, and today their numbers are proportional to the general population.

On the individual level, the culture in which psychologists grow up influences the nature of their work and affects their data—as well as the larger implications they see in the results. In every encounter we will notice examples of this. Freud's patients, for example, reflected upper middle-class European culture and its restrictions, while today's laboratories in North America are largely populated by middle-class college students. The four analysts' European cultural tradition was rather different from the three experimenters' North American background.

During the last hundred years, psychologists have been divided on a number of hotly debated issues. As we will see in these encounters, there are major disagreements about the scope and limits of the field, the best methods that might be used, and the need for experimental research. These debates continue to this day, and the divisions within psychology run as deep as ever.

Other debates center on psychologists' discoveries of major human characteristics, which eventually raise divisive questions about "who is right?" and "what is valid?" But as we will see in the encounters, it is too early to give definitive answers. The complexity of human beings is such that researchers must employ several perspectives. If psychology were to limit itself to only one point of view, one method, and one set of elements, its description of individuals would be rather partial and distorted, to say the least.

Consider what happens when we meet a person we do not know very well. Our understanding is based on what we see and hear, what we remember of past meetings, and some implicit comparisons with other people we have known. We use several methods, we look at small items and larger events, and we "add everything up" in some way (which may well be incorrect). If we want to be certain, we are likely to ask our friends for their opinions.

How much would we know about any person, or human beings as such, if all our information came from an AM radio or a 4-inch black-and-white TV set? How much would we know about the human race's creative capacities if we used only one ear or only one eye? What if "art" were limited to miniature sculptures, "literature" to fairy tales, and "music" to the first recording of the Beatles? Surely we would have no more than an inkling of mankind's grandeur and potential.

It is reasonable to expect that psychologists analyze their extremely complex subject matter from several perspectives, use different methods, and concentrate on numerous elements. We should not be surprised, therefore, that psychologists have come to several different conclusions, even when they study ostensibly similar individuals. Furthermore it is understandable that researchers who study parts have a different view of "the human being" than do those who consider only the whole.

As we meet experimenters and observers of daily life, professors and therapists, theorists and practitioners, we will get a feeling for psychology's wonderfully broad range of topics, methods, and conclusions. While the early theories may appear outmoded in the light of today's knowledge, some of their parts still make sense and often provide useful insights. The following encounters, therefore, do not describe the whole fabric of a psychologist's work. Instead, we will become familiar with well grounded principles and with the concepts and ideas that are likely to increase our understanding of human beings. We will also consider intriguing hypotheses and insights which appear plausible and may well turn out to be supported by future investigations.

All of the psychologists we meet sought to discover basic human characteristics, either for the sake of knowledge alone, or for various practical applications. All thought of themselves as scientists (except, perhaps, William James), and believed that they used proper methods. But what are "proper methods?"

In essence, the proper methods of psychology are the procedures and attitudes which have been effective in various other sciences. These include as a minimum the reliance on empirical data, observable (or at least measurable) events, objective analysis, falsifiable propositions, and the replication of investigations by several researchers.

But "science" and "proper methods" are matters of degree and even perspective. The experimenters we meet in Part III used methods which by any standard would be called "scientific." The analysts (in Part II), on the other hand, often used methods which were less rigorous. Their poorly defined concepts and vague measures made it very difficult and frequently impossible to test hypotheses and replicate each others' results. These problems, combined with the different people they studied, led to rather different and even contradictory conclusions that could not be reconciled.

As we will see in Parts III and IV, experimenters have also produced inconsistent results, and explanations of human behavior often appear to be contradictory as well. But in the encounters it will become evident that many of these differences in discoveries and explanations are more apparent than real. Since the experimenters and "free spirits" (as well as many others) focused on different aspects of human beings and were interested in rather different questions, we should expect the results of their work to diverge as well. And since researchers came to their work with a wide range of perspectives, we cannot really expect their conclusions to be identical.

In these encounters it will become apparent that there is agreement as well as disagreement among psychologists, that some of the discoveries made by quite different researchers do fit together reasonably well. Conflicts and questions remain, of course—but these spur psychologists on to further investigations.

We begin with two individuals who earned medical degrees but never practiced medicine. Today Wilhelm Wundt and William James are recognized as the pioneers of psychology and the founders of the two major intellectual and research traditions within the field.

Wundt established the experimental emphasis which has been the foundation and hallmark of academic psychology for the last hundred years. James's approach has been followed by those who emphasize daily life, whole individuals, and introspection. Two other traditions, which cut across the first two, have contributed to the creative diversity of psychology. Some psychologists devoted their lives to more or less "pure" research to discover new principles, while others were mainly interested in applying existing knowledge to solve various problems.

In the second group of our encounters we meet four famous analysts who were originally physicians: Sigmund Freud, Alfred Adler, Carl Jung, and Ludwig Binswanger. They were interested in discovering human characteristics but spent much of their time dealing with the mentally disturbed, from whom they obtained most of their data. Each analyst constructed a theory of human nature which became the foundation for a therapeutic movement of considerable vitality.

These (and most other) analysts relied heavily on introspection, and frequently made inferences about complex internal processes. By their very nature, the conclusions were hard to test and substantiate. Hence the investigators often produced inconsistent results, which led to the growth of different "schools." Yet the analytic tradition and its methods have exerted considerable influence in psychology, and today their appeal is as strong as ever.

The analysts (and William James as well) had considerable difficulty with their procedures and overall conclusions. As we will see in the encounters, it was extremely difficult to check one's inferences about actions and thoughts, and it was equally hard to test one's explanatory hypotheses. Both Adler and Freud, for example, relied on inferences from their patients' stories to support conflicting hypotheses about the causes of neuroses. Such methodological problems led many psychologists to consider other procedures.

The most popular choice was an emphasis on experimental methods and observable actions. The laboratory became the favorite locale, but from the very beginning experimenters also ventured into the world of daily life. While some investigators explored various aspects of human nature (such as perception, motives, and intelligence), others outlined the practical implications of major discoveries (e.g. behavior modification).

The three experimenters we encounter (John Watson, B. F. Skinner, and Albert Bandura) devoted their university careers primarily to laboratory experiments. But they were also concerned with the practical applications of their discoveries. Since these researchers were mainly interested in objective and measurable aspects of human beings, they necessarily concentrated on overt behavior and its determinants.

But there is more to human life than visible behavior. During the last few years, experimenters have become increasingly interested in the various mental processes which occur as part of most human actions. Bandura exemplifies the transition from behavioral to cognitive perspectives. Indeed, the combination of such interests is likely to be the hallmark of psychology during the next twenty years.

Not all researchers who have contributed to modern psychology can be easily categorized. Some we may call "free spirits" because they ventured beyond the traditional range of interests and methods. They shunned both the mentally disturbed clients of therapists and the laboratory subjects of professors, and worked primarily with normal individuals in the natural environment of daily life.

We will encounter three of these "free spirits" who do not fall into the major categories. Kurt Lewin analyzed how individuals are enmeshed in complex situations that affect their actions. Jean Piaget devoted his life to the study of children in order to discover the ways of cognitive and moral development. Although Abraham Maslow began his work in the laboratory, he soon entered the real world and spent decades studying a wide range of human characteristics.

If one takes a narrow view and considers the complete works of these pioneers, analysts, experimenters, and free spirits, the result is a rather confusing picture of human beings. But when we take a broad perspective—as in this book—and consider only the viable propositions in each man's work, coherent and meaningful features emerge. Several psychologists, for example, describe the importance of goals, schemas, and equilibrium. The melding of discoveries from various sources and the broadening of earlier narrow views leads to a deeper and more complete understanding of human nature. In chapter 14, I outline how information from disparate sources enhances our comprehension of the human mosaic.

As we will see in the following chapters, all of these researchers, each in his own way, contributed to the quest for psychological knowledge. They pursued their own interests and used the methods they deemed most appropriate. To varying degrees, each recognized the contributions of his forebears and peers, and tried to correct their shortcomings. The result of their efforts is modern psychology.

Notes

In the encounters that follow, just about all participants other than the major figures are invented. All conversations are fictional, and most of what the major psychologists say is imagined as well. In each chapter, the main character's substantive statements regarding psychological ideas, propositions, and methods are for the most part summaries and paraphrases from various publications. The sources are described in some detail in the notes that follow each chapter. Only a few statements are actual quotations; when these are lengthy, I give the relevant bibliographic reference.

Because all of the encounters are imaginary conversations, one should not assume that the words I have the main characters speak are in fact their own. Even well-written paragraphs in books do not "sound" the way people talk—hence I have adapted the material to give it a conversational tone. Readers who wish to follow up any of the ideas presented in these encounters should consult the books, chapters, and articles cited in the "Notes" section of each chapter.

In all chapters I have relied on one or more of the following general books which summarize and assess the works of most psychologists we meet in these encounters. The general histories of the field include:

Edwin G. Boring; *A History of Experimental Psychology*, 2nd ed. New York: Appleton Century Crofts, 1950.

Gardner Murphy and Joseph K. Kovach; *Historical Introduction to Modern Psychology*, 3rd ed. New York: Harcourt Brace Jovanovich, 1972.

Duane Schultz and Sydney Schultz; *A History of Modern Psychology*, 4th ed. San Diego: Harcourt Brace Jovanovich, 1986.

Robert I. Watson; *The Great Psychologists*, 4th ed. New York: Harper & Row, 1978.

There are several books which focus on personality theories and their assessment. I have relied on two classics:

Calvin S. Hall and Gardner Lindzey; *Theories of Personality*, 3rd ed. New York: John Wiley & Sons, 1978.

Salvatore R. Maddi; *Personality Theories: A Comparative Analysis*, 4th ed. Homewood: Dorsey Press, 1980.

We must not forget that psychological phenomena do not operate on their own but are intricate manifestations of complicated physiological processes. A very readable introduction to this area is Melvin Konner's *The Tangled Wing: Biological Constraints on the Human Spirit*. New York: Holt, Rinehart and Winston, 1982.

PART ONE
THE PIONEERS

2
WILHELM WUNDT
A Laboratory in Leipzig, 1893

Until the 1860s the field of psychology was considered to be a part of philosophy, and many of the early psychologists were officially housed in the philosophy departments of universities. From the very beginning of psychology's independence as a science, researchers followed two quite different paths. One focused on the objective study of certain aspects of human thought and behavior; the other took as its object of study nothing less than the whole person. The former approach emphasized laboratory experiments employing objective measurements that could be repeated by other researchers. In our first encounter we meet the pioneer of empirical laboratory research who set the pattern for much of what today is known as "academic" psychology.

Wilhelm Wundt was born on August 16, 1832 in Mannheim, Germany. A few years later his father, a Lutheran pastor, moved to the village of Heidelsheim, where the boy spent his childhood and went to school. His brother who was several years older lived at a distant boarding school, and Wundt grew up virtually as an only child, with very few friends. When he was eight, a vicar joined his father and became Wundt's private tutor. The boy read many books, especially novels and histories, but came to prefer daydreams to studies; indeed, the first months of high school were a disaster. When his father died the following year, his mother's relatives took him into their home in Heidelberg. Despite his average school career he was ready for university at the age of nineteen.

For a year he studied anatomy and physiology at the University of Tübingen. Then he returned to Heidelberg and continued his studies there, as had several Wundts of earlier generations. In the following year he published his first article—on the salt content of urine—with himself as the subject. In the summer of 1855, at the age of 23, he received his medical degree and was ready to practice. Within six months, however, he realized that he would not make a good physician and decided to continue his physiological studies at the University of Berlin. After a year he returned to Heidelberg where he became a *dozent* (instructor) of physiology.

When the famous physiologist Hermann von Helmholtz joined the Heidelberg faculty in 1858, Wundt became his assistant, helping in the laboratory and demonstrating procedures. Even before Wundt left that position five years later, he had begun to give his own courses on psychology as well as public lectures. He also wrote several books on physiology and philosophy. In 1872, Wundt married, after the university at last offered him a paid teaching position.

A year later he published the book that made him famous. The *Outline of Physiological Psychology* describes in more than 800 pages the several areas and goals of scientific psychology. At that time, the word "physiological" indicated what we today would call "experimental," for psychology was still considered a part of philosophy and not a laboratory science.

In 1874, the outside world finally recognized him when the University of Zürich asked him to become professor of "inductive philosophy." Wundt had taken only one philosophy course in his life, yet he had studied the field well enough to consider himself a philosopher; indeed, his inaugural address paid homage to Hegel, Schopenhauer, and Kant. His stay in Switzerland was short, however, because in 1875 Wundt moved to Leipzig, again as a professor of philosophy. In that inaugural address he expressed the belief that "philosophy must assert its old influence among the empirical sciences"; yet his work eventually resulted in the severance of that tie.

Wundt remained in Leipzig for more than forty years. Soon after his arrival, the university gave him some small rooms and an old auditorium, and there he established a psychology laboratory. He quickly became the most popular lecturer at the university, for he had a gift of presenting complex and difficult material in understandable and interesting form. His classes on ethics, the history of philosophy, and especially his courses in psychology, regularly filled the largest auditorium.

For more than three decades Wilhelm Wundt headed the first and most famous psychology laboratory in Europe—and indeed the world. Students came from all over Europe and America to study experimental psychology under him. Some of these students remained for only a year, but many stayed for two or more years and received their doctorates. By today's standards, the laboratory equipment was rather primitive: chronoscopes to measure small intervals of time, kymographs to measure muscular contractions (and record these on rotating drums), and tachistoscopes to measure memory and attention by flashing images on a screen for split seconds. These and other more specialized instruments were used by students in their investigation of topics assigned by Wundt. The subjects were other students, sometimes the professor himself, and Wundt lost part of the vision of one eye in an experiment. The reports of these experiments were published in Wundt's own journal, *Philosophical Studies*.

Most of the new PhDs returned to obscurity, for the doctorate was mainly a ticket to permanent positions in the German high school system. A few PhDs became famous, however, and a generation of American psychologists received their training, directly or indirectly, from Wundt's Institute for Experimental Psychology. The first American laboratories—at Harvard, Yale, Chicago, and Cornell—initially reflected Wundt's shop, but within a few years they broadened their investigations to include new topics and theories. The Leipzig laboratory and the work done there established psychology as an independent scientific discipline with a strong experimental, or at least observational, basis.

Wundt was a prolific author; he wrote four major books on philosophy and six on psychology, plus several others on such topics as physiology and anthropology. Many of these books were expanded and revised in successive editions, some as many as six times. During his active academic career—which spanned about six decades—he also wrote more than four hundred articles, edited a journal for more than two decades, and supervised several dozen doctoral dissertations. Edwin Boring estimates that Wundt wrote more than two pages every day, from 1853 until 1920 when he died, soon after finishing his autobiography. His critics complained that it was difficult to pin him down, for by the time they had made a telling point, Wundt had either written more or revised his position so that the critics were once again left behind. In the following pages I outline those of his ideas which still have relevance today, sometimes in formulations which appeared after 1893.

BASIC HUMAN CHARACTERISTICS

Wilhelm Wundt's major contribution to our understanding of human nature is not so much substantive as methodological: most of his ideas about the human mind have been superseded, but the general approach he outlined for the study of human characteristics is still with us. He insisted that psychology is the science of experience rather than an area of metaphysical speculation, and in his laboratory he investigated what he called the structures of the mind. Yet he frequently engaged in speculations and considered himself a philosopher.

While it is true that philosophical interests lay behind some of his theories and experiments, his basic procedures were scientific, involving careful measurements, empirical data, and replication by different researchers. Indeed, his major approach is still followed today: most experiments are designed to test a hypothesis, and the outcomes determine whether or not we accept the proposition. If an experiment does not support a hypothesis, and if we are sure that the experiment was done properly, then the proposition—and also the theory from which it is derived—must be re-evaluated, modified or rejected. Wundt revised many of his hypotheses and books precisely because new experimental data showed that earlier formulations had been wrong or at least inadequate.

Much of the work he supervised in the laboratory was what we today would call "behavioral" (for example, the studies of reaction-time), and most of the data were objective measurements of perception, sensation, and attention. His interpretation of results, however, often proceeded along a subjective line associated with his theories about mental life, with special emphasis on the structure of the human mind.

Along with gathering objective data, the major procedure within the laboratory involved the individual's "internal perception" (or introspection). This consisted of the subjects telling the experimenter just what they experienced during the performance of a laboratory task such as recognizing complex light patterns. This procedure required not only awareness of oneself but considerable training in describing the results of that awareness. Indeed, a person was not deemed to be an adequately prepared subject until several hundred hours of training in introspection had been completed. Wundt fully realized what problems haunted this method: faulty memory, inadequate description, and a host of unknown factors that might affect an individual's awareness of what was going on inside.

Wundt sought to overcome these difficulties by rigorously controlling the laboratory situation and stimuli, and by repeating the experiment several times. He believed that when the experimental conditions are replicated, the inner experiences are repeated as well, leading to a series of internal perceptions that eventually provide an accurate account of conscious mental processes involving the perception of size and distance, for example, or the evaluation of intensity and duration of various stimuli.

Wundt was quite aware of the limitations of laboratory experiments, but many of the lines he drew were too strict and narrow. This was only partly due to the rather simple instruments available to him; in larger part the limits he saw reflected his view that the "higher faculties" such as thinking and feeling were not amenable to laboratory manipulation and objective measurement. He believed that in order to learn about these one would have to study groups of people in various natural situations. Wundt had always been interested in history and anthropology, and eventually he turned to these fields for data about higher and more complex aspects of mental life. In his eighties he published a ten-volume work on ethnic psychology, which extended the scope of psychology far beyond the limits of laboratory experiments.

Most of Wundt's elaborate system of psychology, and most of his ideas about human nature, have not withstood the test of time and new data. He would not be surprised by this, for he himself continually updated and revised his major books; and since he believed that theories must be rejected or modified on the basis of new information, he would no doubt accept the fate that befell his work.

Yet a few of the major ideas he proposed are still with us, albeit in rather different form and dress. Some of these ideas had also been proposed by others—they were "in the air," so to speak—but regardless of their origin they were part of Wundt's system. The major ideas still relevant for us today are:

First, Wundt emphasized the motives, drives, and goals underlying human actions (or "voluntarism" in his words). He believed that actions and psychological processes can be understood only when we view them in terms of goals and the general consequences a person expects.

In daily life, for example, people engage in selective perception and construct in their minds certain images of the situation and its future (Wundt called this "apperception"). Experience is a building block of this image, but later experiences are molded and interpreted by that very image as well. Motivations and expectations are other building blocks.

When I am hungry on a Saturday morning, for example, my thoughts frequently turn to food, and perhaps on seeing a round, red pin cushion I may momentarily mistake it for a tomato. I may arrange to have lunch early, and hurry home. When I finally open the refrigerator and see a lonely wrinkled slice of old pizza it actually looks good to me, for I think of it as it will smell and taste after I warm it.

This type of "psychological causality" is rather different from the mechanistic "physical causality" commonly found in the natural sciences, and Wundt concluded that psychology is essentially different from the so-called "hard" sciences. Today, many people consider that distinction rather debatable, but the importance of goals, motives, and anticipated consequences is generally recognized. We cannot say, however, that *all* psychological processes involve these factors.

Second, Wundt held that the significance of mental events is defined by the circumstances in which they occur. An isolated phenomenon is meaningless, both to the individual and the psychologist. When I looked into the refrigerator after a good breakfast I only glanced at the old pizza slice and hardly realized it was there—it "did not register" until the circumstances changed. Today we would say that Wundt's point is often true, but not always.

Third, his "principle of mental growth" states that we integrate our experiences into progressively more complex and longer-lasting images or conceptions. Over the years, for example, "our world" becomes larger as it includes more people and events, and it gains a time dimension as we become aware of history and look ahead—first to college, a job, then marriage, and eventually retirement.

Fourth, Wundt pointed out that voluntary actions (as distinguished from reflexes) involve more than goals and anticipated consequences. When we have reached a goal, or when the effect we desired has occurred, there will be other results as well, which we are usually unable to anticipate. My daughter is short with me that Saturday afternoon and I become annoyed at her behavior; but only in the evening do we discover that she had been looking forward to a warmed-up pizza lunch herself. Again we would say today that unanticipated consequences often occur, but not necessarily or always.

These basic principles proposed by Wilhelm Wundt have been modified and refined by subsequent research, and their applicability and limitations have been outlined by later psychologists. Indeed, these ideas seem rather commonplace to us, simply a part of human nature and social life, and we certainly do not connect professor Wundt with them. But in the 1880s and 1890s these formulations were new, and the syste-

matic effort to examine them with careful laboratory experiments was a
revolutionary step forward.

Ψ

An Evening in the Laboratory

Late in October 1893, soon after the beginning of the Fall term, Wilhelm Wundt settled into his accustomed routine. He was a methodical man and looked forward to the smooth operation of the university after the first boisterous days of the semester.

He spent the morning working on his newest monograph, which he planned to call "On Psychological Causality." After an hour of thinking and writing—still with that customary two-inch pencil stub—he put the pages aside and began to look over the proofs of the next issue of *Philosophical Studies*. He was pleased that the eighth volume of this journal would be as full of significant articles as the others had been and would continue to enhance the reputation of his laboratory. Just before noon he decided to take a glance at the manuscript of the forthcoming English translation of his *Lectures on Human and Animal Psychology*. The paragraphs seemed reasonable enough to him, but he could not help worrying that this book, like some of his others, would be misunderstood. Confound that language! Whereas in German he was careful to distinguish between *selbstbeobachtung* (self-observation) and *innere Wahrnehmung* (internal perception), for example, English translators usually employed only one word for both: introspection. He shook his head in dismay: how could he convince the Americans that the first method was useless while the second was essential to psychology? Even Titchener, his American translator who had studied with him some years earlier, often did a poor job.

Wundt sighed and arose. He rubbed his fingers to relieve the chronic writer's cramp. How he missed the typewriter another American student, James Cattell, had given him some years before—how many, seven or eight? He smiled when he remembered the comment a newcomer from America had made after dinner last Sunday: Cattell's infernal machine enabled the professor to write more quickly than his critics could answer—leaving the last word always to the Leipzig Lab.

After lunch he put on the black suit he regularly wore to lectures and prepared to leave the apartment. He decided on a light overcoat, for as yet there was no frost in the air. "Sophie, my dear," he asked his wife at the door, "please remind the shop to hurry up with Cattell's machine. I do miss my typewriter." She smiled and nodded, and handed him his old floppy hat. In the street he put on this hat from his student days—so very much out of keeping with his prim and proper figure—and headed toward the university.

He spent barely ten minutes at the laboratory, taking pleasure, as always, at the sight of work tables, instruments, and students in whispered conversation about experiments.

Then he began his usual afternoon walk through the streets of the town that would take him to the auditorium in time for his 4 o'clock lecture. As he walked he outlined his presentation, careful to remember the illustrations from experiments and examples from exotic cultures that would support his arguments. As he climbed the steps to the auditorium his sparse figure seemed barely equal to the task, but when he entered the hall he felt eager and fresh. He nodded to the porter who opened the door for him. Hardly aware of the three hundred-odd figures in the hall, he clambered up the steps of the stage and shuffled to the podium. As usual, he arranged his notes with great care, even though he knew he would not use them, and placed his elbows on the lectern. With his chin in his hands he began to speak, oblivious to the hall that had not one empty seat. He hardly moved until he had finished his presentation.

After the lecture, his chief assistant Oswald Külpe met him at the building's main entrance. Külpe was in his early thirties and had been at the Institute for Experimental Psychology since he had received his doctorate at Leipzig seven years earlier. He had originally studied history, but Wundt's psychology had fascinated him, and even after some months' historical studies in Berlin the excitement of laboratory work brought him back to Leipzig. Wundt returned the younger man's greeting and said:

"I must tell you again, Dr. Külpe, how much I like your new book. Your *Outline of Psychology* is just what our new students need. As I was coming down the stairs I was happy to realize that in this year's lectures I can finally skip some of the basic materials. Thanks to you. But, you know, I am *still* unhappy with your reservations about apperception."

Külpe nodded. "But that's only in a few places here and there. Many students won't notice... Professor Wundt, there is something else... May I go with you to the laboratory?"

"Of course," Wundt answered. And after a while he continued, "What's on your mind?"

The young man hesitated, and the two walked in silence. Külpe had thought about his position for quite a while. Wundt was still vigorous and no younger man could hope for a permanent position here for several years. The Würzburg offer was something he could not really refuse, yet he did not want to hurt his old professor. And then there was the fact that his own views on some aspects of psychology would soon be noticeably different from the old man's...

"Don't be embarrassed," Wundt interrupted his thoughts. "The University of Würzburg finally came through with a definite offer?"

Külpe nodded. "Yes, Professor Wundt...a laboratory, equipment, some assistants, a good salary..." his voice trailed off.

Wundt stopped and extended his hand. "Congratulations, Dr. Külpe," he said with genuine pleasure. They shook hands, and Külpe smiled, relieved.

"I'll miss you, of course," Wundt continued. "The students will miss you, the laboratory will miss you. But you'll continue to do good work...as long as you follow my procedures and don't listen too much to other people."

"I won't leave until summer next year," Külpe said slowly. "There will be enough time to get my successor settled."

"Of course," Wundt agreed amiably. "I'm glad you told me so early...Yes...I'll miss you. Seven years is a long time..."

The two men continued their walk in silence, until Külpe opened the laboratory's door. "Everyone is expecting you, as usual."

Wundt smiled at him and greeted more than a dozen students who rose as he entered the large room. Some of them had been working at instruments on several tables, others had been in conversation around a large pot of coffee warming on a bunsen burner, and some advanced students had been working on reports at desks along the walls.

A young man approached with a cup of coffee while another helped Wundt with his coat. "Some coffee for you, Professor Wundt?" he asked with a heavy American accent. Wundt smiled and accepted the cup. "Thank you, sir," he said in English. Then he continued in German, "Please remember, I understand English very well, but I do not speak it well at all. So you may talk to me in your tongue, and I'll talk to you in mine...You have heard of my problem with Shon Locker?" He laughed, and the others joined in. The American shook his head.

"A few years ago, at a lecture, Professor Wundt was talking about Shon Locker," a student with a British accent said brightly. "The English students didn't guess until much later that 'Shon Locker' was actually John Locke."

"Since then I'm careful not to say too much in English," Wundt said good-humoredly, "Or the foreigners might think I speak Lilliputian."

Wundt slowly made his way to an easy chair between two draped windows. "My sixty-one years show, but only after a long lecture," he said to students who pulled up chairs around him or moved equipment to sit on nearby tables.

"This is a lot better than his office," Stolberg, an older German student, whispered to the American. "In his office, only the professor sits. Even Külpe stands. And Wundt assigns topics depending on where you stand in line. Just like a lottery."

"Really?" the American was astounded.

"Yes, but it's not all that bad," Stolberg continued. "All the topics are interesting. So everyone wins in this lottery."

"Professor Wundt," a student began with some hesitation. "Would you mind if Miss Corbin came to the laboratory some afternoon? She would like to see us here, at work."

"She is welcome, of course," Wundt replied. "I allowed her to attend my lectures last year because she is so intelligent. *Of course* she should come to the laboratory if she wishes. And on top of everything else, she plays the piano so very well."

"Do you still have time for music, with all your writing?" a new student asked, naïvely.

Wundt laughed and motioned that he would like another cup of coffee. "Of course I have time for music. But I *am* glad that I'm no longer a music critic. My evenings are non-psychological, you might say. I read, I go to concerts, I discuss politics with my friends, I talk to my wife, my son, my daughter. The well-rounded man...almost Plato's ideal," he added jokingly.

"And your dinners for students last year, don't forget those," Francisco Gomez added. "They were memorable. Better than at home in Madrid."

Wundt smiled happily. "They get better each year. Have you heard Miss Corbin on the piano? A few days ago I heard her. She was superb. When she played that old English song...what's it called? Oh yes, 'Flow Gently, Sweet Afton'...I was really moved. And I am again convinced that those higher mental processes—thoughts, emotions, feelings, inspiration—cannot be studied in the laboratory; they are beyond ordinary psychological methods."

The students nodded. Külpe, who sat near the coffee pot and watched a student prepare a kymograph for recording data, looked at his watch and turned to Richard Hagood who was correcting a manuscript page. "I'm keeping track of how long it takes Professor Wundt to get back to psychology," he mused. "Today it was six minutes."

Hagood smiled.

"Someday you can write a paper on that, " Herbert Gennin whispered from his kymograph. "The stuff is measurable..."

"Psychology is the study of *conscious* processes," Wundt said in response to another question. "All of you here are part of a new movement.

The projects I assign over the years all fit into a great scientific enterprise—the discovery of the structure of mental life."

The students nodded and Gomez spoke up: "The projects you assigned us last year are interesting, but it's hard to see how they all fit together."

"The ones I assign next week to the new students are also interesting," Wundt replied. "And they all do fit together, even if it's hard for you to see." He rose and walked over to one of the tables. He gently caressed a tachistoscope and continued:

"A subject, someone like you," he turned and pointed to a new student, "has an objective experience, perhaps he sees a very short flash of light. We can measure that in this laboratory. Then the subject describes what goes on within him while he has that experience. We tell him what to do and what to watch out for. And he reports to us—that is introspection, as you all know. But there are hundreds, thousand of different experiences. We must study all of them. We start with light flashes, sounds ... and go on from there to more complex phenomena."

"I understand that, I think we all do," an older student said. "But I see a problem. You told us last year that all experiences are composed of sensory images... But when I did some experiments on myself this past summer, I could think without images."

Wundt shook his head. "Impossible, Herr Stempel. You were not paying enough attention to your internal processes. You need more practice with introspection. How many hours have you had?"

"I've had about 400 hours," Stempel answered.

"Obviously that's not enough practice for you," Wundt said with some irritation. Then he turned to the other students: "Gentlemen, psychology must be objective, experimental. It must rely on physiology and laboratory instruments. But it cannot do without introspection. We teach you how to use instruments." He pointed to the tables and his hands swept across the room, "But only *you* can learn introspection. That is the key."

"I have problems with the actuality principle," one of the new students ventured. "Don't we all impose categories on our experiences?"

Wundt nodded. "Yes, when we describe what goes on inside us, we use words and categories—such as the statement: 'I notice two spots of green light about two centimeters apart.' But these words may have nothing to do with psychological reality. Unfortunately, there is no other way of transmitting information. My actuality principle simply states that we must not confuse actual psychological processes with the categories and words we use to describe them—such as a motive, feeling, or sensation. The human mind is one whole, and it is intimately related to the underlying physiological structure."

"So, what we describe is not necessarily what actually happens?" the student continued.

"That's quite possible," Wundt replied. "And that's why we use experimental procedures. In the laboratory we can vary the stimulus, or we can repeat it as often as necessary. When we have repeated an experiment dozens of times, there is a high probability that our information about the process we study is valid."

Külpe turned to Gennin beside him and said softly, "always remember that Wundt's favorite word is 'probably.' The sign of the true scientist— one can never be certain of anything."

"Your actuality principle makes sense to me," an American student said, choosing his words with some difficulty. "But how then can one know that behavior is determined? I mean, we can't be certain of it, can we?"

Wundt shrugged his shoulders. "Yes, that's where I and your William James differ. And that's where Professor James is absolutely wrong. Psychological causality works in everyone—including William James."

"Just as physical causality operates throughout the physical universe," another student interjected.

"The big difference is purpose and motivation," Wundt said with complete conviction. "Physical causality is mechanical—the causes lie in the past and present." He banged the table with his hand. "The sound you hear is caused by my hand hitting the wood."

"But you *wanted* to hit the table, for emphasis," Gennin volunteered.

"Yes, that was my purpose. Or you could say that I was motivated to make a point regarding William James's error." After a pause, Wundt continued, "People have drives that lead them to do things; their actions have a purpose; all of us anticipate the future and act accordingly. That is the essence of voluntary—of human—action."

"How significant are reflexes?" a new student asked.

Again Wundt shrugged his shoulders. "Reflex actions occur, of course, but their numbers and proportions are small. Indeed..." He hesitated for a moment, deep in thought. "Perhaps one should make a study of how many behaviors during an ordinary day are clearly a matter of reflexes."

"When you banged on the table, I winced," Stempel said, "But I don't think that's a significant part of my life today."

Wundt nodded. "Precisely. So one would have to count important actions and insignificant actions separately."

"It might not be a worthwhile problem for investigation," suggested a student with a slight Italian accent.

"You are too brash, like Americans," Wundt replied. "Don't jump to conclusions, Signor Martinello. We have to experiment or make other studies whenever a theory requires testing, or whenever there is a question without a clear answer. That's what separates psychology from philosophy. At this stage, all psychological theories need testing. We need continuing tests of hypotheses so that we can tell when a hypothesis needs to be changed, or must be rejected. That's the only way to improve theories. Isn't that the most pragmatic course, Mr. Hagood?" he asked with mock seriousness and turned to the American.

"I don't know what Professor James would say," Hagood replied, "But your position makes sense to me. There's nothing more useless than a wrong theory."

Wundt applauded and said amiably, "If your thesis is as logical as your words, you won't have problems this year. How is your work coming along?"

"Quite well," the young man replied.

"Good," Wundt said. "Tell me about it, please. And after that, I'll talk to anyone who needs advice on his project." He accompanied Hagood to his table. A few students followed, while most returned to their work.

Hagood stopped at a table where a chronoscope rose from a confusion of papers. He searched for two large sheets and handed them to Wundt, who murmured: "what a messy table."

"As you know, I measure reaction times to various stimuli. But not just the one light Albrecht studied last year. I show a pattern of several lights on the tachistoscope. And I find that the more complex the pattern, the longer the reaction time."

"Ah," Wundt exclaimed, "an excellent example of mental chronometry. This has always been a good way of studying how fast people think. How long it takes for apperception to occur."

"Yes," Hagood said and smiled. "The experiment is turning out just as you thought it would."

"According to my theory of mental structure, a more complex pattern requires a longer reaction time," Wundt said. "But that theory needs to be tested several times. As you are doing this year."

"There is only one problem," Hagood said slowly. "I didn't tell you about it last Spring, because I thought I might come up with a solution during the summer. But I've worked for a couple of weeks now, and the problem is still there."

"What is it?" Wundt asked. "Your data here are just what I expected. My theory is probably correct."

"Yes," Hagood agreed, "but the data don't form a straight line." He pointed to a series of dots on the sheets.

"What do you mean?" Wundt asked with some concern.

"Well," Hagood began, "a simple pattern of three dots takes a certain fraction of a second to recognize. But a pattern of six dots does not take twice as long, and a pattern of nine dots does not require three times as long."

"Is that what you would expect?" Wundt asked.

When Hagood nodded, Wundt continued: "A pattern of six dots is not necessarily twice as complex as a pattern of three. It could be more complex, or less, depending on the pattern. And that goes for nine dots, or fifteen." He thought for a moment and continued: "your measure of complexity is probably not very good. Why don't you try another?"

Hagood looked doubtful. "Perhaps geometric figures?" he asked.

Wundt nodded. "Sure. Try that approach. And keep good notes while you work with figures. You might talk to Mr. Zimmer."

"I already have," Hagood said. "he's just getting started on his color-reaction project. But he doesn't know much about psychology yet."

"That's just what I mean," Wundt said. "He is bright and he still has a fresh mind. When you discuss reaction times with him you might both get some good ideas...At any rate, I think you have to find another way of measuring complexity...By the way, two years ago Mr. Wetzler studied the reaction times needed for words in different languages."

"I have already looked at his article," Hagood said.

"Fine," Wundt said. "But read his thesis. It is much more complete. Anyway, I'll think about your problem, and if I come up with anything, I'll let you know."

Hagood thanked the professor, who turned away and followed another student to his table. On the way, Wundt stopped to fill his cup and turn down the bunsen burner under the coffee pot.

"Perhaps Mr. Hagood is close to the limits of what a laboratory experiment can show?" the student asked timidly when they arrived at his table.

Wundt shook his head. "Not at all, Herr Martens. We simply have to find a better way of measuring complexity. That's all. A laboratory can tell us about objective, conscious processes. And reaction times involve just such objective processes. Entirely different processes, as we find in thought or emotions, those can't be studied in the laboratory setting."

"But where is the line?" Martens asked. "Don't those areas, or processes, shade into each other?"

"That's often true," Wundt agreed. After a pause he continued, "To some extent the line depends on the instruments we have. But the location also depends on the experimenter's ingenuity, perhaps even his optimism. If Mr. Hagood, for example, feels optimistic about solving his problem, he is likely to find a solution and do good work. In spite of all good intentions and excellent instruments, however, much...ah, so much...voluntary behavior cannot be studied in the laboratory. And..."

He turned to Külpe who had stepped to his side. "Don't you agree, Dr. Külpe?" he asked.

"Some voluntary behaviors clearly are beyond the laboratory's power of analysis, Professor Wundt," the assistant said. "But it is probably too early to draw the line. This laboratory is not even twenty years old." He turned to Martens, "When I came here to start my doctoral work we knew much less about the human mind and its structure than we do now."

"That's true enough," Wundt said. "But in this kind of experimental situation we cannot go beyond conscious processes."

"Probably not," Külpe agreed. "But it seems to me that we have to let the future decide. There is so much of daily life that has not yet been tested—in this laboratory or any other. For instance..." Külpe hesitated.

"Go on," Wundt encouraged him and leaned against a table. "I value your ideas."

"Well," Külpe began with some hesitation. "As I mentioned to you before, we have not yet asked people to perform mental tasks, for example, judging the weight of stones. At least, we haven't done this carefully, and systematically, with many different people."

"Because it cannot work," Wundt replied with some agitation. "Such a job would require a person to think rather abstractly, and that cannot be described. No one can think without images. Weight has no image. No, I'm sure, introspection would not get us anywhere in that case. The work I assign here goes to the very limits of experimental psychology. I've shown that in the twenty years we have worked here."

"You may be right—and you probably are," Külpe said, but there was no conviction in his voice. "It seems to me, however, that one ought to try out new ways of experimenting, or experimenting on new aspects of mental life."

Wundt shrugged his shoulders and turned. "Not here," he said with finality. "It would be a waste of time. Now I'll have a look at some more projects." He followed a student to his work place, leaving a half-empty cup on the table.

Ψ

Notes

In this encounter I describe an ordinary day in Wundt's extremely busy life. His hours were devoted to research, writing, lectures, and dealing with students from all over the world. Oswald Külpe, who became a famous psychologist himself, is the only other actual person in the encounter. I have chosen the year 1893 because by then Wundt was world famous and had developed most of his ideas. In that year, too, Külpe was about to leave and pursue a research career somewhat different from that of his mentor.

For all three sections of this chapter I have relied primarily on Robert W. Rieber's *Wilhelm Wundt: and the Making of a Scientific Psychology* (New York: Plenum Press, 1980). The article "In Memory of Wilhelm Wundt" in *The Psychological Review* (May 1921) provides much interesting personal information, based on recollections by his former American students.

3

WILLIAM JAMES
A Study in Cambridge, 1894

The other pioneer of modern psychology fought many of the battles for independence that Wundt did: the separation of psychology from philosophy, and its recognition as a respected empirical science. But the second pioneer was interested in understanding the whole person rather than various parts, and employed quite different procedures. Since the totality of a person could not be analyzed within a laboratory, other methods had to be used, such as careful observations of daily life. He, too, established a tradition which flourishes to this day.

William James was born in New York City on January 11, 1842. His family was wealthy enough so that his father did not need to earn a living. The elder James travelled widely, wrote several religious books, and devoted considerable attention to the education of his children, particularly William and his brother Henry who became a famous novelist.

Two patterns of James's life were established rather early: journeys and poor health. The family travelled through Europe when William was barely a year old, and prolonged bouts with various illnesses haunted his childhood and youth. The boy was educated by his father and private tutors in Europe and the United States, and initially wanted to become a painter. But after six months of study with William Hunt he realized that he would never be an important artist. He therefore entered the Lawrence Scientific School of Harvard University to study chemistry, without any clear idea of a future occupation. Laboratory work did not appeal to him, however, and thus he eventually decided to study physiology and medicine. But on a year-long expedition to Brazil as an assistant to the naturalist Louis Agassiz, James realized that he could never be a biologist, perhaps not even a physician.

His medical studies at Harvard were interrupted by another lengthy journey to Europe, and it was not until 1868 that he received the medical degree. Because of his delicate health he could not practice, however, and decided to continue his study of various psychological subjects.

Depression and insomnia, back pains, and eye and stomach troubles plagued him for several years, so that he could not live a normal life. His travels rarely helped and sometimes increased his suffering, but he met writers and scientists, observed life in several countries, and continued to read widely in physiology, psychology, and philosophy.

In 1872 James became an instructor of physiology at Harvard, and his health improved—partly because he now had a meaningful job and was quite successful in the classroom. After one year, however, he took a leave of absence and spent several months in Europe. On this and earlier journeys he had become interested in the work of Helmholtz and Wundt, and in 1875 he gave a course in the new field of psychology. That first year the topic was the relationship between physiology and psychology and relied heavily on the work of European researchers. In the same year James also established a laboratory in which he demonstrated the physiological processes he discussed in his courses. A year later he became assistant professor of physiology, and in 1878 he married a Boston school teacher whose interests were similar to his. She was a devoted wife who read to him when his eyes bothered him, wrote his letters when he could not handle a pen, and took good care of a growing family that eventually included five children.

In 1880 James was appointed assistant professor of philosophy, even though some of his colleagues objected to psychology being taught by a physiologist rather than a philosopher. Five years later he was promoted to full professor in spite of the fact that he had written only a few articles. In 1889 his title was changed again, to professor of psychology.

His major book and the work that made him famous in Europe and America, was published in 1890 after a dozen years of labor. In *The Principles of Psychology* James discussed other people's theories and research findings but emphasized his own ideas regarding psychological processes. This work epitomized the American interpretation and critique of European psychology, mainly German laboratory work, and anticipated many of the topics and ideas that psychologists would investigate in later decades. Here and in his later writings, James showed himself to be open-minded and tolerant, while he proposed his own definite ideas. He advocated a scientific and experimental psychology, even though he considered himself a philosopher and was not enamored of laboratory work. *The Principles* was well written and widely read (the "James" to generations of students); and a shorter version (the "Jimmie") brought in substantial royalties when it became popular with general readers. But this culmination of his interest in psychology also marked a decided shift toward philosophy, a field to which he devoted the next twenty years of his life.

During the 1890s he still taught psychology, but philosophy courses took increasing portions of his time and interest. During the academic year he typically averaged ten lecture hours a week, read several books and worked on his manuscripts, and carried on a voluminous correspondence with scientists and authors all over the world.

James was a good teacher with a great sense of humor, and students flocked to his classes. But he had no disciples in psychology, and few psychologists have called themselves his followers. He respected experiments but disliked the actual work involved, and arranged for Hugo Münsterberg, an experimental psychologist from Germany, to take over the Harvard psychological laboratory. He himself showed decreasing interest in actual experiments, although he continued to make some use of other researchers' findings.

In 1897 James no longer considered himself a psychologist, and his title was changed once again, to "Professor of Philosophy." By 1910 James had become the best-known American philosopher, famous for his contributions to the doctrine of pragmatism. Indeed, today he is known primarily as a philosopher rather than as an early psychologist, and he no doubt would be quite happy with that reputation.

Throughout his life James was interested in facts, regardless of their origin. Initially he was concerned mainly with laboratory data, but later he came to believe that careful observations of daily life were equally good sources of information. During the last twenty years of his life his interest in para-psychology and philosophy led him to consider still other phenomena—an indication that he was broad-minded indeed.

BASIC HUMAN CHARACTERISTICS

Today most people think of William James as a philosopher, as the chief exponent of pragmatism. Yet even the books he wrote in his last ten years—*The Varieties of Religious Experience,* and *Pragmatism*—are not all that far removed from the kind of hard-nosed empirical psychology he had championed earlier.

Throughout his life he displayed an open mind and intellectual tolerance that allowed him to consider and appreciate a variety of viewpoints and methods. Thus he thought well of Wundt's experimental work, although he eventually became disenchanted with the narrow emphasis on descriptive data that emerged from the laboratories of Europe and America. He considered psychology a natural science, but he thought it should gather information from a variety of sources.

James accepted the data that Wundt and others discovered in their laboratories, yet he rejected many of the conclusions these researchers drew. He believed that psychology includes the whole range of human experience and mental life, not just those few aspects that are studied in the laboratory. He admonished psychologists to go beyond the gathering of facts and try to *explain* those facts. At the same time, James was very much aware of psychology's infancy: he was not satisfied with existing theories but always sought improvements, and while he did not do this work himself he believed that others would come up with better explanations in the future.

What is important for us today is not so much James's substantive contribution as his general approach to psychology: broad-minded, humane yet objective, interested in all aspects of psychological life.

James's position is evident in the first two sentences of *The Principles*: "Psychology is the science of mental life, both of its phenomena and their conditions. The phenomena are such things as we call feelings, decisions, and the like; and, superficially considered, their variety and complexity is such as to leave a chaotic impression on the observer." That confusion disappears, however, when the several aspects of mental life are carefully analyzed. The proper starting point of any psychological investigation is experience. Upon reflection we discover that life is a never-ending stream whose parts produce a whole that is quite different from the sum of its parts, for each component influences the others. Mental processes, rather than mental elements, are the proper focus of psychology. He considered habits—ranging from speech patterns to intellectual views—to be the major components of the individual.

James's conception of the human being reflects his overall view of psychology, usually called functionalism since it emphasized mental processes and operations. The individual adapts to the social and physical context through consciousness (today we would say cognition), which enables us to make choices and guides us to do whatever is necessary for survival. Indeed, James thought of consciousness almost as an organ, which is needed by human beings because they have such a complex body that lives in a complex and changing world.

Behavior always involves purpose and choice, and a preceding mental state (such as feelings and thoughts). The general goal of continued existence takes the form of the mundane goals of daily life which guide our selection of activities. Through behavior we adjust to the world. James held that experiences produce changes in the mind, which accumulative over time. Hence no mental state can ever recur. Every repetition of an experiment will be slightly different because the subject's mind will be slightly different.

According to James, the individual is made up of at least three different kinds of selves: the material self consists of our body and possessions; the social self is made up of what people think of us, and there are as many social selves as there are individuals or groups whose opinions of us we value. The spiritual self includes our psychological faculties, states of consciousness, and the subjective opinions we have of our various characteristics and skills. But while James distinguished several aspects of the self, he was convinced that psychologists must study the whole human being in reciprocal relationships with the environment.

James was partly a determinist, who believed that behavior is greatly influenced by anticipated consequences. But he also believed in free will—as it is expressed, for example, in the selection of one or another action or the choice of a goal. He thought that mechanistic interpretations fail in the analysis of the human will, and that introspection would probably be more successful. He believed, for example, that he could will to improve his health, and indeed after that decision he did get better (for a while).

James was convinced that the "immediately given data" of human existence form a continuous, flowing stream of consciousness. Mental life consists of such streams of consciousness, it is not a collection of separate elements that somehow fit together. The stream of consciousness is personal—mine differs from yours—and changes constantly as new experiences become part of it. The stream is also selective, for not all past or present experiences are integrated. In order to understand this essentially indivisible stream of consciousness, which is often quite vague, incoherent, and intangible, we often use introspection. When psychologists dissect the stream and analyze its elements (as did Wundt, for example), they look at a cross section that has been arbitrarily torn from the stream, a cross section that tells us little if anything about the continuing stream itself.

While James talked much of self, mind, and streams of consciousness, he also stressed the nervous system, the senses, and the organism as a whole in relation to the environment.

Many of James's ideas foreshadowed the work of psychologists in later years. Behaviorists and members of the Gestalt school, for example, have been busy elaborating James's suggestions. But he did not found a school himself, in part because he did not wish to build a comprehensive theoretical system—he believed that premature structures are dangerous. Another reason was the acknowledged difficulty of studying the will, the mind, and the stream of consciousness. Introspection could only go so far, and empirical measurements of these phenomena were not available at the time.

In the Study

The house at 95 Irving Street was large and barely five years old. William James had designed it himself to make sure that there would be enough comfortable space for his family—his wife Alice, their five children, a maid and a cook. On the ground floor was his study, a large sunny room with bookshelf walls, a fire place, and a triple window overlooking the garden. He also had a smaller room upstairs, where he could write in complete solitude.

When he lived in the earlier house, on Quincy Street, he had sometimes held his classes, such as the famous Philosophy 9, in his home. The new house, too, was open to visitors; students frequently came for chats or longer discussions and sometimes were invited to stay for dinner.

On a pleasant Spring day in April, a week after the Easter holidays had ended, James left his house at the usual hour, about half past eight. He attended the short morning service at the College Chapel, as he always did during the academic year, and then taught two classes. On the way to the library, he met some of his students on the front steps and talked with them. The conversation turned to the relationship between philosophy and psychology and whether one might aspire to be a philosopher *and* a psychologist. It depends on the views one has of the two fields, James contended, and the students were divided on the issue. When the clock struck twelve-thirty, James indicated that he had to leave, but he invited the students to continue the discussion at his home that afternoon. They gladly accepted, and James hurried to the faculty club.

When he entered the dining room, the colleagues with whom he had made arrangements to eat had already begun—they knew his habits and could not be sure when he would finally arrive. So he ordered a sandwich and ate while they talked about the university's library budget and the probable support for the Harvard Psychological Laboratory, now under the direction of Hugo Münsterberg. James would have liked to discuss another subject—almost any other—but his colleagues were concerned about a laboratory interfering with the acquisition of books.

Back in his office, James wrote some letters; philosophers, psychologists, and acquaintances all over the world eagerly awaited his replies to their notes. James did not mind the burden of fame brought on by *The*

Principles of Psychology; he liked to write letters and could write them even during conversations with other people. But the bright sunshine and the gentle breeze that swept the fragrance of lilacs into his office soon persuaded him to take a leisurely walk through Cambridge.

As he turned onto Irving Street half an hour later he saw the students he had met that morning, waiting for him on the sidewalk in front of his house. They entered together, and James showed them into the library. In the hallway he patted his wife on the shoulder; "I knew you wouldn't mind, Alice," he murmured.

"Of course not," she smiled. "But don't forget, we eat soon after six."

James promised to remember and followed the maid with the tea cart into his study. The room was still cool, for the windows were shut. He put on his favorite old jacket and opened a window to the garden. The students were standing around the room, awkward with their tea cups and respect. James motioned them to find seats and chose his favorite armchair near the fire place. Some of the students were now relaxing, for they had been invited before and were used to the room and the philosopher. Two sat upright and rigid, ill at ease, for this was their first visit to the house, their first meeting with Harvard's most famous professor.

One of the new students had told James earlier that he would soon have to choose a career. He was interested in pursuing work in experimental psychology, but he was also attracted to philosophical questions. That morning he had asked whether these two interests might be combined.

The silence over tea was ended by the new student who said nervously: "I...hope you do not mind...that I come to ask your advice...but my friend here thought that your opinion...would be most...valuable."

James smiled and nodded. "I do not mind at all, Mr..."

"Hoyt," the student said and blushed at his oversight, "Timothy Hoyt."

"What else is experience good for, Mr. Hoyt, if we don't use it, pass it on? But it will take me a few minutes to consider an answer. After all, some very complex issues are involved."

"I suppose twenty years ago the answer would have been much easier," said Alan Perrod, one of the older students. "Today philosophy and psychology are indeed quite different."

"But equally fascinating," James said enthusiastically. "Indeed, I often introduce philosophical considerations into psychological analysis, as you know. But I always make sure that students—or readers of my books—are aware of what is psychology and what is philosophy. Philosophy makes a contribution to the study of mental life, but the two fields are quite different and must be kept apart. As you know, I easily go from one field to the other. My university appointments change as I change my interests. But I always know who I am!"

The students joined in his laughter, and one said, "my elder brother came here to study psychology with you, but you were then a professor of philosophy."

"And I read your *Principles of Psychology* and was fascinated by the book," said Perrod. "So I came to study with you, but I understand that you are planning to become a professor of philosophy."

"Which I will remain in the foreseeable future," James said emphatically. "I have found my place. Especially now that Professor Münsterberg has taken over the laboratory."

"I am taking a course from him, and he is very good," said Laurence Gilman. "Experiments come alive when he talks about them and demonstrates physiological principles."

"That's good," James said. "I should congratulate you. Experiments never seemed very alive to me...They are necessary, of course."

"They provide us with data," Hoyt added.

"But we must also get other kinds of facts," James continued. "There are more significant data in other places, perhaps. Actually,..." He hesitated and searched for words. "Actually, brass-instrument and algebraic-formula psychology fills me with horror. Sometimes I think that I naturally hate experimental work. And I must admit that logic and mathematics are repugnant to me."

"But in *The Principles* we get a rather different view of your position," a student interjected, surprised.

"In the book I'm just being polite," James replied. "We want facts, of course. But I think that we get the most important facts from our experience, as it comes to us through senses and perception."

"Then...what do you think of Professor Wundt's immense work?" a student asked.

"Many of Wundt's results are interesting and important," James answered, "but I don't know what they add up to...if anything. Wundt himself—well, one of the finest examples of how much mere education can do for a man."

"Mere education?" Perrod asked and wrinkled his brow.

"Yes, mere education," James replied. "No feeling, no deeper understanding, no insight into the marvelous complexity of mankind's nature and work. No wish to discover the real truth about the human being's wholeness, the human character."

James stroked his beard and looked at his tea cup. "About your earlier question, Mr. Hoyt," he continued after a while. "Let me put it this way. As you know, there are two kinds of experimenters: those who demonstrate what is already known, and those who try to make new discoveries. Which type appeals to you?"

"The latter, of course," Hoyt answered. "I don't find the demonstration of old knowledge very interesting...or exciting."

"Hmmm..." James commented.

"But where would psychology courses be without such experiments?" Perrod asked.

James waved him aside and said to Hoyt: "Today we have about as many laboratories in America as we need. Frank Angell experiments at Stanford, and soon Berkeley will have someone, too. Why do you want to torture your brain to devise new varieties of insipidity for publication? It's quite enough to show students the physiology of brain, senses, and psychophysic methods in general...I always enjoyed that much of psychology...But I was burdened with weight of woe that I couldn't invent original investigations or find the patience to carry them out...What about you?"

"I'm just beginning my studies," Hoyt replied lamely. "I have much interest but little experience. Actually, no experience. So I can't tell you whether I'll have ideas to investigate..."

James smiled good-humoredly. "Of course. I understand. But even at this stage you must have a feeling...Do you like to tinker?"

The student nodded. "I like mechanical things—and philosophy, too."

James paused and then said slowly: "My impression is that a person who has caught the metaphysical fever is not likely to grow into a successful laboratory psychologist—in the long run. Unless he also happens to have a lively mechanical and experimental turn of mind. I think that otherwise he would drift away from the laboratory...and find it quiddling and irksome. Book work...the kind of work I do...would absorb his attention more and more as he grows older."

"That is true of your life, Professor James, isn't it?" a student asked.

"Yes," James nodded. "Perhaps I am influenced too much by my career and predilections. But I am sure that if a person does not love to tinker anyhow, he is not likely to be successful in the laboratory. To be sure, there are tinkerers and metaphysicians in one, but the combination is rare indeed. Wundt and Münsterberg are the only ones I know."

"What would you suggest, then?" Hoyt asked guardedly.

"You might give up the notion of original research," James replied. "Do experiments to demonstrate psychological principles. But make discoveries of your own by being very observant of life, as I have been. Then you'll have plenty of time and opportunity to follow your philosophical bent as well."

"I suppose that's one advantage of living today," Perrod said. "Psychology is such a broad field that one really has a choice of careers."

James nodded with enthusiasm. "Absolutely. When I started, now more than twenty years ago, there was very little, if anything. The first psychology lecture I ever heard, I gave myself." He chuckled, and the students smiled even though they had heard that story before.

"And what about the future?" Gilman asked.

"Ah, the future…" James stroked his beard. "I think that psychologists will continue to experiment in laboratories—as well they should. But I hope that they will place more emphasis on *explaining* the facts of mental life they discover. Facts by themselves aren't half as interesting as theories that explain them. And I should hope that the new discoveries—and the old ones, too—can be applied to help solve human problems."

"That would also test the theories, would it not?" a student suggested.

James nodded, and Gilman replied "As you said in class a few days ago, a theory that doesn't work is of no use, but we don't know whether a theory works unless we apply it."

"You have great faith in the psychologists of the future," Hoyt said. "I hope this generation will live up to your expectations" and he gestured to the group.

James smiled. "Of course. And why not? Look at how far we have come in just twenty years. Now we know, for example, that psychology includes the whole abundance of human experience, all aspects of mental life, and not just those few aspects that can be dissected and desiccated in the laboratory. Today's theories need to be modified, tested, applied—and even transformed. That includes my own theory of emotions."

"Will your next book present a complete psychological system?" Hoyt asked.

James laughed. "Of course…" he paused for a moment,"…*not*. I'm not going to build a complete theoretical system…*ever*…because it is much too early for that. A complete system invites the mediocre to worship it and the brilliant to find faults and reject it. So…I rather do a bit of philosophy."

"But what will psychology be without you?" Perrod asked. "Isn't there a sequel to *The Principles*?"

James shook his head. "Psychology—that nasty little science—will get along without me. Besides…" he paused, and the room was quiet for a while.

The students looked at him expectantly. "Besides," James continued, "sometimes it seems to me that psychologists do little more than elaborate the obvious."

"Let's be serious for a moment, Professor James," an older student said. "Here I can't separate your humor from your real thoughts."

"But I *am* serious," James replied earnestly. "When I glanced at *The Principles* for the first time—that is, when I first held the book in my hands and leafed through it—I thought to myself: 'I'm not sure that psychology is a science, or can be one, with or without this book.' Those doubts still come to me on occasion."

"Can you give us an example of why you have doubts?" Hoyt asked with some concern, and the others voiced their agreement.

"I don't want to frighten you off," James replied. "But take habits, for example. I think our explanation of these must be essentially physiological. When we understand the nervous system and how it works, we'll understand habits as well. Psychologists by themselves can go only so far and sometimes it's not far at all."

"It seems to me..." Gilman began and stopped.

"Go on," James urged. "There's no reason to be shy."

"Well..." the young man continued with some hesitation, "it seems to me that even when psychologists elaborate the obvious they can still make discoveries. What you said this morning about the causes of behavior, for instance, was quite new to me..."

"Only because you are a freshman with limited experience," Perrod interjected with a laugh.

James chuckled with the others and said: "When you really think about it, doesn't it seem obvious that mental life is primarily directed toward the future? Our various ways of thinking and feeling have grown to be what they are because of their utility in shaping our *reactions* to the outer world. All mental states are followed by bodily activities of some sort. And the end result is that life goes on—we solve the many little problems of daily life and the big problems, too."

"I'm still not sure that's obvious, at least not immediately," Gilman persisted. "Hindsight is one thing..."

"Good heavens, Laurence," Perrod interrupted. "It's not a matter of hindsight at all. It's a matter of careful and deliberate introspection." He looked at James. "At least, that's what I gather from your lectures. And it's true. I've tried it myself. And you should, too" he ended with emphasis, turning to Gilman.

"Yes," another student added. "When we think deeply about our actions, any old experience, we gradually discover its causes, and they usually take the form of goals we want to reach. I've discovered that many times during the last few months."

"That's right," James nodded. "But there is a problem. What we experience is quite simply *there*. Experience is not some grouping of elements, as Wundt thinks. When a psychologist describes such elements—as Wundt's students always do—that does not prove the existence of those elements. After all, psychologists always interpret their experiences. They read into their facts, you might say, whatever their theory tells them should be there. I think that's one of the greatest dangers of psychology—indeed, I think that's a grave psychological fallacy."

"That would be another good reason for not building a complete theoretical system," Hoyt added.

James smiled and nodded. "Precisely. But even in my case there is a danger. I believe that behavior is greatly influenced by the ends we want to achieve, especially our inborn desire to continue living. I'm convinced I'm not reading anything into the facts of mental life...but people who disagree with my explanation of behavior will probably say that I do—and that my students do."

"That seems to be true of Wundt's concept of apperception," Perrod said. "But it's not true of the stream of consciousness. That simply exists. Or so it seems to me."

"But you know how experimenters react to my concept of the stream of consciousness," James said. "I don't know *how* many of them have told me that my notion of the stream is vague and intangible and therefore quite useless. But it's not really a concept. It's a fact."

"Professor Münsterberg,...in his lectures...points out that the stream of consciousness is just about impossible to analyze...even by introspection," Perrod hesitated.

"And he is right," James said with conviction. "But consider this: in the laboratory, the researcher artificially divides the stream of mental life into several components, and then he makes a mosaic from the pieces in some way. But those pieces are not natural. The result does not tell us much about human nature. In fact, it tells us nothing about human nature. All those pieces are based on artificial, sophisticated insights which reflect a particular theory... which one learns gradually, over the years. Wundt's students spend hundreds of hours practicing their introspection, but I am sure their efforts are worth very little. Why not simply admit the existence of the stream of consciousness in all of us? Then challenge the next generation of psychologists to analyze it—without chopping it up into bits!"

"And do the same with 'will'?" Hoyt asked.

James nodded. "Of course. 'Will,' as we know it now, as we experience it, cannot be studied with brass instruments. But it exists nevertheless. When I read Renouvier many years ago I became convinced that there is such a thing as free will. My first act of free will was to believe in free will. Later I willed to get well. And that worked, too. At least to some extent."

"Are there other methods, besides observation, experiment, and introspection?" a student asked. "It seems to me that the new psychologists will need new methods to discover the true nature of the stream of mental life, for instance."

James shrugged his shoulders. "There is also the comparison of people from various cultures, but I can't foresee what additional methods there might be. Perhaps our descendants will elaborate our methods as well as our theories, or come up with completely new ones. Perhaps we will simply apply present methods—improved, of course—to new phenomena."

"Such as parapsychology?" Gilman asked.

"Perhaps," James agreed. "But there are other facts, still beyond the realm of experiment or introspection."

"Could you give us an example?" Perrod asked.

"Well," James said slowly. "I have the feeling that our lives are like islands in the sea, or like trees in the forest which commingle their roots in the darkness underground, and the islands also hang together through the ocean bottom. Just so, there is a continuum of cosmic consciousness, against which our individuality builds but accidental fences, and into which our several minds plunge as into a mother-sea or reservoir."

The students were silent, trying to follow the implications of these words. After a few seconds, James continued: "I am rather intrigued by the possibility that there are some mental events which seem to be outside the sphere of our awareness."

"But if some mental events are outside our sphere of awareness, how can we ever know them—or even be aware of them?" Perrod asked, with a puzzled look on his face.

"A good question," James replied. "I can't give you a perfect answer, but I'll give you a hint..."

Before he could do so, however, his wife opened the door to the entrance hall and said: "Professor Münsterberg is here to see you."

The students rose quickly and prepared to leave. As Gilman approached the door, he whispered to Hoyt: "I never thought I'd see Professor James saved by an experimentalist." They both chuckled at the thought.

In the entrance hall James shook Münsterberg's hand and opened the front door for the students. Upon his return to the study he invited his colleague to be seated and opened another window.

"I can only stay a moment," Münsterberg said. "I just wanted to tell you that my stay in Freiburg for '95–'96 is definitely set now. Everything is arranged."

"I'm glad to hear that," James said pleasantly. "I hope to have you back the following year, on a permanent basis. I simply don't want to head the laboratory or guide experiments. These last two years, with you in charge of the work, have been heavenly for me."

"I'm glad to help you out," Münsterberg said. "The equipment here is as good as at home, and the students, too."

James smiled. "It helps to be a friend of President Eliot. And God puts good students into every country."

Münsterberg nodded and laughed. "Of course. A statistical fact. By the way, this year I have a very good student in my laboratory class. A lady,

no less. I recommend her to you. She is very good—a first-rate mind from
Radcliffe."

"Excellent," James said with enthusiasm. "Perhaps she will take my
seminar next year. Put in a good word for me."

"I already have, as if that's necessary," Münsterberg said. "You'll appreciate her intelligence and wit. Her name is Gertrude Stein. From a place
called Oakland."

James gave him a blank stare and shrugged his shoulders. "It doesn't
matter where students come from, as long as they head in the right direction," he said.

Münsterberg rose. On his way out he said: "I'll suggest to her to see
you before the holidays."

James saw the young man out the door and was about to close it when
his wife emerged from the living room. She was followed by Mrs. Cummings, the minister's wife from across the street. The ladies were beam-
ing, and after an exchange of greetings, James inquired about their
happiness.

"Oh Professor James," Mrs. Cummings exclaimed, "Come October
there will be a little Cummings in the house. His name will be edward
estlin cummings."

"Congratulations," James said and shook her hand affectionately. "I'm
so happy for you, and..." he hesitated and smiled. "...And so amazed
that you already know the baby will be a boy."

"I always hope and pray," Mrs. Cummings said as she left. They exchanged farewells, and James gently closed the door.

Notes

William James was fond of students and frequently invited them over to his
house for lengthy discussions. I have chosen the year 1894 because he was in
good health. He still gave psychology courses, but was preparing to make his
final switch of professorial titles. Within a few years he would be a famous philosopher. All participants in the encounter, except for James and Münsterberg, are
fictional, and the whole conversation is imagined.

I have relied primarily on three books: *William James: a Biography*, by Gay Allen
(New York: Viking Press, 1967); *The Thought and Character of William James*, by
Ralph Perry (Boston: Little, Brown, 1935); and James's famous *The Principles of
Psychology* (Cambridge: Harvard University Press, 1983).

PART TWO
THE ANALYSTS

4

SIGMUND FREUD
A Congress at Achensee, 1900

A major reason psychology became popular at the turn of the century was the desire to understand the roots of human actions and thoughts, including such difficulties as hysterias and neuroses. No wonder that so many of the early psychologists originally had been physicians. The first analysts developed large-scale theories of human nature to account for a wide range of normal activities as well as mental illness. Such grand theories were difficult to test, however, and from the very beginning there were questions about their validity.

More than any other psychologist, Sigmund Freud has fascinated professional and layman alike. Ernest Jones's official biography, which appeared in the mid-1950s, has been followed by several others. The book by Ronald Clark, for example, provides a much fuller account of Freud's life, and gives a more comprehensive picture of his times and character. Freud's postulate that early experiences leave an indelible imprint on adult character, life, and views has been a major reason for this interest. After all, it *would* be fascinating to see how his theories, or which portions of them, were affected by various experiences in *his* early and later life.

Yet Freud insisted that the development and nature of psychoanalysis were not affected by his own life experiences—making him the only exception to the rule. At least three times during his life he destroyed a mass of personal papers because he did not want his intimate life and thoughts to end up in biographies or as factors in the critical assessment of his theories. Many of his personal papers were originally published in censored form—such as his letters to Wilhelm Fliess. Yet when the complete versions have appeared, the censored parts turn out not to be all that detrimental. While it is true that a final and complete biography remains to be written, the course of his life and the major characteristics of Freud the individual are quite well known. The details which have been cut from various records, letters, and papers are not likely to change the picture we have today: neither hero nor charlatan, but a decent, hardworking, and insightful psychologist whose work affects us all.

Sigmund Freud was born on May 6, 1856 in Freiberg, a small town in Moravia, the northern part of the Austro-Hungarian empire. His father was a merchant who moved to Vienna three years later in order to improve his business. But he did not do well, and his large family of five girls and two boys had difficulty making ends meet.

Sigmund Freud was the eldest son, the favorite of his mother, who from the beginning expected that he would accomplish great deeds in the world. He was a quiet, pleasant, and studious youth who received a normal classical education—Greek, Latin, modern languages, and mathematics. Freud was the best student of his high school class for several years, and graduated with honors in 1873.

That fall he entered the University of Vienna without a definite career in mind. Initially he attended courses in zoology and physiology, as well as in philosophy, for his interests inclined toward scientific research. After a journey to England in 1875 to visit his two much older half-brothers, he decided to prepare for a career in medical research.

During his years of medical study he maintained an active interest in physiology, and especially neurology. He spent two summers on a research grant at the Trieste Zoological Experimental Station, which resulted in his first scientific paper, on the testes of mature eels.

Early in 1877, Freud became a research student at Professor Ernst Brücke's Institute of Physiology, where he stayed for six years and became an excellent neurologist. Here he published several papers and gained the reputation of a first-class researcher, but he also realized that there was little hope for advancement. Indeed, during his eight years of medical studies—longer than usual because of his research interests—he frequently had to live on borrowed funds. He enjoyed the scientific work in Brücke's laboratory, and it soon was abundantly clear to him that he was more interested in research and discoveries than in medical practice and cures.

Freud received his medical degree in 1881. Upon his engagement to Martha Bernays a year later, he became convinced that marriage would require financial security—such as the practice of medicine could provide. He therefore became an intern at the Vienna General Hospital and spent three years in the hospital's several departments. Meanwhile, his fiancée had moved with her family to Wandsbeck, a town near Hamburg, hundreds of miles away.

In 1885 Freud was appointed *dozent* (instructor) in neuropathology—an unpaid university position which allowed him to give lectures on various physiological topics. That fall he also received a six-month travel grant to study neurology in Paris with the French physician Jean-Martin Charcot at the Salpêtrière hospital. In Paris, Freud soon became interested in mental illnesses, particularly hysteria, and Charcot's treatment involving hypnosis.

Soon after his return from Paris, Freud set up his medical practice, specializing in nervous diseases—that is, neuroses, especially hysterias. The practice grew only slowly, and at times he had to borrow money again. In these years Freud continued to follow his two-pronged interest: to discover the structure and workings of the human mind, and to cure the patient if possible.

In September 1886, Freud was finally able to marry, settle down to a normal social life, and raise a family. For the next five decades he lived in straight-laced Victorian Vienna, a city he often said he hated, but which he probably liked and appreciated. Eventually there were five children, and Martha's sister, Minna Bernays, also became part of the family. Martha ran the household quietly and efficiently, primarily for Freud's benefit and comfort. But she insisted that his theories and methods not enter the family's quarters at Berggasse 19, and in later years several visitors commented on how little she knew about psychoanalysis.

During the 1890s Freud continued to work with hysterics, but his practice soon broadened to include a range of neurotics. His first book was written with the physician Josef Breuer: *Studies on Hysteria*, published in 1895. The seminal book of psychoanalysis, *The Interpretation of Dreams*, appeared in 1900. Here he outlined his major ideas about the internal processes that operate in normal and sick individuals, and the methods used to study them. In later years these ideas and methods were elaborated, modified and improved in a number of theoretical works and case histories. These were so well written that Freud received the Goethe literature prize in 1930.

Freud's theory of the human mind and behavior was a very complex array of concepts and propositions about instincts, internal processes, and the unconscious. The theory itself and Freud's applications to anthropology, history, art, and biography—along with his numerous comments on current events and daily life—are contained in the *Complete Psychological Works* of some 23 volumes. The kernel of fundamental ideas is surrounded by a complex theoretical structure and a layer of speculations which Freud used to explain most aspects of social and cultural life.

It is difficult to evaluate Freud's work, because it is so vast and complex, and because few people approach it from a neutral perspective. Furthermore, it is sometimes difficult to separate the theory from its applications, both legitimate (as in psychoanalysis) and illegitimate (analyzing people from a distance, perhaps even without meeting them). Indeed, some of his applications, especially to social systems and individuals long dead, seem rather inappropriate. Thus we can do justice to Freud's basic ideas only if we consider single propositions and accept those which are valid, and if we look at concepts and retain those which increase our understanding.

BASIC HUMAN CHARACTERISTICS

Sigmund Freud's work consists of two major parts: a rather complex conception of human nature, and an associated set of procedures for dealing with mental illness, especially neuroses. Since our interest lies in Freud's contribution to knowledge about human nature, I will not be concerned with therapeutic methods, except insofar as these tell us something about human characteristics.

Freud's major contributions are three ideas which seem commonplace today but were new, exciting, and rather disturbing a hundred years ago: 1) behavior is determined, often by factors unknown to us; 2) within every person there exists a realm of complex forces, some of which may be unknown (in "the unconscious"); 3) the normal and the abnormal (i.e. neurotic) lie on a continuum, they have many aspects in common and differ only in degree.

These ideas have their roots in the work of several earlier writers. But whereas Saint Augustine, for example, wrote about the unconscious in a rather haphazard fashion, Freud painted a systematic and comprehensive picture of the human mind, its structures and processes.

Freud's work has aroused considerable controversy, and the debates among orthodox Freudians, neo-Freudians, anti-Freudians, and other psychologists show no signs of abating. Over the years there have been many attempts to test—and to support or refute—Freud's theories, using laboratory experiments, systematic observations, and cross-cultural comparisons. But the results are inconclusive, and their interpretations are greatly influenced by the researcher's theoretical affiliation and philosophical predilections.

Most psychologists agree that Freud's complex system of propositions is very difficult to test. Indeed, many hypotheses cannot be tested at all and are therefore irrefutable—as well as insupportable. Hence the scientific status of the work remains in limbo. Yet the precarious position of the theories has not damaged their credibility in the eyes of those who are fascinated by complex and comprehensive explanations of individuals, behavior, and historical events.

It is far from easy to determine just what valid contributions Freud has made to our understanding of human nature. His many books are full of interesting ideas, fascinating insights, and captivating hypotheses—which may or may not correspond to reality. Here I describe only those major contributions which have a reasonably firm basis or provide useful suggestions that are likely to gain increasing acceptance.

The basic principles which Freud formulated and applied to a large variety of situations reflect a materialistic and mechanical 19th-century view of science. The hydraulic imagery of giant waterworks pervades Freudian theory, where psychic energy flows, rises and fluctuates, is stored, dammed, channeled, reduced and transformed, and does work within the person and through behavior. That imagery, however, is not necessary, and the hydraulic conception is out-dated and inadequate.

First, Freud postulated the existence of largely sexual and aggressive energy (called libido) which has its basis in the individual's physiology and results from a person's fundamental instinctive and genetic constitution. When the normal energy level increases or decreases for any reason, this is experienced as tension, and the individual attempts to reduce this tension by bringing the energy level back to normal. This he called the *pleasure principle.*

Second, Freud postulated that a person's instincts and needs require some accommodation to the social and physical context which limits the means by which satisfaction, (or the discharge of energy), may occur. Individuals learn the values and customs of their society, which define the ways in which instincts can be expressed and needs can be satisfied. This is the *reality principle*.

The first postulate is troublesome: what is psychic energy, and how is it related to instincts? The hydraulic imagery certainly leads us astray. The other postulate makes intuitive sense; most people have experienced these processes themselves.

These internal processes are performed by systems which Freud called id, ego, and superego. Over the years, he described the structure and operation of these systems—or personality components—in great detail. Although he sometimes indicated that these systems are hypothetical constructs, he often treated them as if they were real, and most people today think of them as entities rather than hypotheses.

Freud was not content to say simply that people learn the ideals and customs of their culture. He tried to explain this "learning" by describing other processes such as internalizing, introjection, and identification: all are complex series of events which occur within the person. In similar fashion, he described in great detail the workings of id and ego, the gradual development of personality as the ego strengthens and the superego takes form.

Yet new concepts and verbal explanations by themselves do not enlighten us. As we will see in later chapters, psychologists even today are not agreed on just what goes on when people learn simple tasks, let alone their culture's ideals. Saying that a child "introjects" her parents' standards adds little if anything to our understanding of the process.

We find similar elaborations in Freud's descriptions of other internal processes, and these elaborations are in turn explained by other words. Introjection, for example, is said to involve incorporating another person—virtually becoming the other person. The additional explanatory steps Freud provided, however, do not necessarily lead us closer to an understanding of *how* a person learns.

Much of Freud's fame rests on his proposition that individuals develop through a series of stages, beginning with the *oral* stage, followed by the *anal, phallic,* and *latency* stages, and finally by the mature *genital* stage. During the phallic stage children are assumed to encounter the Oedipus situation, which plays a major role in the development of a normal personality and the learning and acceptance of a culture's norms. Freud postulated that the boy comes to love his mother and hate his father (as a rival), but eventually comes to identify with his father and accepts his way of life. Girls also go through such a stage, but the particulars are different and involve other factors, such as penis envy. The outcome for girls, however, is similar: identification with the same-sex parent and her norms.

Freud considered his discovery of the Oedipus situation in families a major accomplishment of his career. He first saw this sequence of events in his patients and in himself, and then generalized its existence to all of mankind. Yet there is considerable evidence that the Oedipus situation is not universal—its existence and form depend on the culture in which the child grows up.

While the "Oedipus complex" is often dismissed these days, "the unconscious" has become a widely accepted aspect of human nature. Freud postulated an unconscious which consists largely of biological urges but also contains our memories, forgotten events, and thoughts we have repressed. The repressed materials are still "there," however, and produce tensions and reactions in the form of behaviors that often seem inexplicable, inappropriate, and in extreme cases are neurotic. Again, however, there is only limited empirical support for hypotheses regarding the unconscious itself or of the ways and factors of repression.

Freud postulated that the activities of daily life—as well as the unique behaviors of artists and neurotics—are determined by a variety of causal factors, many of which lie in the past, and often the distant past. Childhood experiences, and especially the traumatic events of early years, play a significant role in adult life, even when they are unconscious. He saw defense mechanisms, and errors in writing or speech—the famous Freudian slips—as manifestations of unconscious factors. The wishes presumably contained in dreams, and the behavior of neurotics, he considered to be the results of more complex unconscious processes.

A major reason for the widespread skepticism of Freud's ideas is the rather flimsy empirical evidence he produced to support his concepts and propositions. Most of his patients were members of the upper middle class, living in Central Europe at the end of the 19th century. Clearly, this was not a random sample of the population, and it would be dangerous to generalize from these few neurotic individuals to mankind as a whole.

Freud's published work contains only a few complete cases, a small number of partial case histories, many anecdotes, and much material based on his own experiences. Most of the important dreams in *The Interpretation of Dreams*, for example, are his own, and he had faith in other people's evidence only if he himself had had similar experiences. But one must admit that it would be difficult to have experimental evidence, or large samples of the kind of material he worked with; and medical ethics do place a limit on the amount and kind of intimate case material that can be published. More telling, however, is the fact that even the few cases he published can be interpreted quite differently.

Finally, it is disconcerting that so few people were treated successfully. Indeed, most of the individuals whose treatment he described were not cured. Perhaps the therapy was not handled well—but the master himself was the therapist. Or perhaps the case was too severe—Freud admitted that his procedures would work only on neurotics. Or perhaps the convoluted theoretical structure from which the therapy was derived, did not reflect human reality.

With Fliess at Achensee

Psychoanalysis developed gradually during the 1890s as Freud's practice attracted an increasing number of neurotics (mostly women with hysteric symptoms) whom he tried to understand and help. He was fascinated by the improvements brought about through the "talking cure"—simply letting the patient talk about past events that were traumatic or otherwise significant, but had been largely forgotten. It seemed that re-living these traumatic events and coming to terms with them frequently relieved hysterical symptoms. Why should this be? Evidently one would have to understand the innermost workings of the human mind, and Freud set out to do just that. He spent several years developing a theoretical schema that would explain the "talking cure," the causes of neurotic symptoms, and the repression of traumatic events.

During these years he was professionally quite alone. The other physicians in Vienna did not understand his work; they distrusted his explanations and therapeutic methods (which initially included hypnosis). Yet he desperately needed someone with whom he could discuss his seemingly outrageous hypotheses, someone who was sympathetic and open-minded, a person who was willing to listen and question, who might even be a bit hard-headed in a supportive and constructive manner. There was no colleague in Vienna who could fill these requirements, and no relative. But there was such a person in Berlin, with whom Freud had an intense emotional and intellectual relationship for about fifteen years.

Wilhelm Fliess was a physician specializing in diseases of the nose and throat. He was two years younger than Freud and came to Vienna for a few weeks in 1887 to take some postgraduate courses. There he met Freud, and a close friendship developed rapidly—for years they called each other by first name, and each took great interest in the life and work of the other. Upon Fliess's return to Berlin, where he had a growing practice, they began a correspondence which lasted until 1902. Freud sent Fliess his discoveries and hypotheses, including a long essay, the "Project for a Scientific Psychology," which foreshadows his later description of psychodynamics. Fliess kept Freud informed about his theory that many events in a person's life, including diseases, follow rhythms of physiological, and especially sexual, periods—28 days for females, 23 for males.

The two friends commented on each other's work, made suggestions, and in general supported each other's intellectual efforts.

Freud and Fliess met a few times in Berlin, more frequently in Vienna, and several times in other places. These latter "congresses," as the friends called them, lasted two or three days and were the intellectual highlights of Freud's otherwise mundane life. For weeks he looked forward to a congress, and for weeks thereafter he pined for the companionship and intellectual stimulation provided by his friend. Their first congress was held in Salzburg in 1890, and the last one in Achensee in 1900. There was a gradual estrangement even before 1900, but the differences between them became especially evident and profound at the Achensee congress. Two years later their correspondence ceased.

Ψ

Freud's practice had not been very extensive in the spring of 1900. In later years he often analyzed patients for nine or ten hours a day, beginning at 8:30 in the morning, which left him with little time for correspondence and manuscript preparation. He always looked forward to the summer holidays.

By May 1900, it was evident that the family's vacation would have to be modest. Freud made arrangements for his wife and children to spend the summer at the Bellevue, a tourist-oriented mansion near Vienna. As usual, Freud worked into July and late that month joined his family. Early in September he set out for Achensee, a lovely Alpine lake a few kilometers northeast of Innsbruck.

He had arranged to spend three days with Fliess at the Hotel Seespitz, near the southern end of the narrow lake with its cold blue waters surrounded by steep mountains. Freud boarded the night train in Vienna and arrived at Kufstein early the next morning. An hour later, just after breakfast, he left the train at Jenbach and hired a carriage to take him to the Hotel a few kilometers to the north.

For months now he had been looking forward to this meeting, and from the carriage he eagerly surveyed the countryside for suitable places where the two of them could take their long walks. How he anticipated the hikes with his old friend: along the lake, up the mountains, and across the meadows near the southern shore! He looked forward to the support he would receive from a friend who would commiserate on the poor reception of his book, *The Interpretation of Dreams*. Freud wondered whether the carriage driver might be interested in that book, whether *anyone* he passed on the road that morning would ever be interested in psychoanalysis. What would Fliess say about the book he was writing for next year, about the psychopathology of everyday life? As always, Freud was confident about the future, but for the present he could depend only on Wilhelm Fliess. No one else understood his work, no one else seemed to be interested or even care.

Fliess arrived at the hotel just before lunch, and the two friends had their meal together on the terrace overlooking the lake. Afterwards Freud suggested that they climb the wooded slopes toward the Bärenkopf; they might see some ferns there and perhaps even find mushrooms. But Fliess indicated that he had had a bad night on the train from Berlin and was too tired for such strenuous exercise. They agreed, instead, to follow the path along the southern shore and then cut across the meadows toward the village of Maurach. Fliess promised that he would join Freud the next day to "tickle the bear's head."

At first they walked along the narrow beach, and Freud commented rather bitterly that the day's food bill would just about equal the royalties he had received so far. "The dream book has sold 141 copies," he said. "Not a leaf has stirred to show that the interpretation of dreams means anything to anyone. That silence...has once more destroyed any budding relationship with the world. Even the press has hardly noticed it."

"Well, now, wait a minute, Sigmund," Fliess interrupted. "There was a good review in *Die Gegenwart*. Your book was described as 'epoch-making.' Isn't that enough so far? After all, your book has been out for only half a year."

"I don't care about the general public," Freud replied. "I want the medical profession...university people...to accept me and my theories."

"Didn't you tell me that *Die Umschau* also reviewed your book?" Fliess asked.

Freud nodded. "Yes," he murmured. "It was a short and friendly piece—but showed no understanding."

"Real comprehension will come, Sigmund," Fliess encouraged him. "I hear that Paul Näcke is reviewing your book. The famous old psychiatrist is quite positive, I understand. So you see, acceptance will come. And then fame."

"I can't wait long," Freud said sadly. "I'm going to die at 51, and that's only seven years away."

"Nonsense," Fliess said firmly. "Quit smoking and you'll feel fine and live to be eighty."

"You're not as sympathetic as you used to be, Wilhelm," Freud wrinkled his brow. "You know I can't stop smoking for long. I tried that once and it didn't work out. And I do have the key to mankind's future, even if nobody accepts it. What will happen to that key?"

"Part of that key comes from me, Sigmund, please remember that," Fliess replied somewhat testily. "The ideas of bisexuality, biological rhythms, and so on."

Freud nodded. "Your biological work puts me to shame. I'm beginning to be envious...almost. It's a good thing we are friends. Otherwise we'd be rivals...But what bothers me most is that nobody seems to be listening to me...I mean us."

"It takes a while for new ideas to take root," Fliess said soothingly. And then he added with a smile, "I've met two more people who have read your book. In all of Berlin, that makes...let's see...fourteen."

"And another fourteen next year makes twenty-eight, your magic number," Freud muttered and shook his head. "It'll take ten years to sell the 600 copies Deuticke printed."

"Any movement begins small, Sigmund," Fliess said and put his hand on Freud's shoulder. "And just think of how much more you know now than you did ten years ago. In another ten years, who knows? There are many people out there in the world, waiting for your message." After a few steps he continued: "All these years I have admired your courage and tenacity...After that seduction fiasco you immediately saw how to use your discovery that patients had lied to you—I mean, told you fantasies. You came up with the question: why such fantasies? And it led you to new discoveries."

Freud stopped and looked at his friend. Then he put a hand on Fliess's shoulder and said warmly: "Thank you, Wilhelm. You are the only person who has stood by me. You and Minna have helped sustain my faith in myself."

"Courage is part of your constitution, Sigmund," Fliess said with conviction.

"Ah yes," Freud smiled wistfully. "In that sense I'm lucky. If a man has been his mother's undisputed darling he retains throughout life the triumphant feeling, the confidence in success, which often brings actual success along with it."

"Perhaps birth order is more significant," Fliess interjected.

"Well, anyway," Freud sighed, "my teachings aren't becoming more popular."

"In your next book—the one you described to me in the spring—will you take back your words about childhood seduction? That would help a great deal, Sigmund."

Freud was silent and used his walking stick to draw patterns in the sand. "The new book applies my psychology to daily affairs. It offers no occasion to make a retraction."

"But Sigmund," Fliess sounded alarmed. "For three years now you have known you made a mistake. Isn't it time you publicly admitted you were wrong? Or, are you no longer sure about absolving parents?"

Freud shook his head. "How can I tell people that—simply by chance—my sample happened to include a disproportionately large number of cases in which sexual seduction by an adult or by older children played an important role in the patient's childhood? No wonder I overestimated the frequency of such events! The numbers were so shockingly high. So many fathers, uncles, friends would be involved! So many child victims! And how about my own father? It was hardly credible that perverted acts against children were so frequent." His voice trailed off.

"Well..." Fliess broke the silence.

After a moment, Freud murmured: "No, eventually I realized that these scenes of seduction had never taken place. It simply must be so. These memories were only fantasies which my patients had made up, or which I myself had perhaps forced on them." He stopped and anxiously looked at his friend. "How would that sound, Wilhelm? Tell me! And I don't believe that I forced these fantasies on my patients, or even suggested them."

But Fliess was relentless: "You told me all about this a couple of years ago. Why not wipe the slate clean at the next opportunity? Why not write what you just said? You aren't the first physician who's been deceived by patients—or by himself, for that matter."

"Good heavens, Wilhelm," Freud exclaimed. After a few moments of stunned silence, he whispered "Well—actually, I'm glad to be rid of that theory. It no longer fits into the rest of my ideas. But I wish I could abandon it quietly. Just let it die."

"The theory is too outrageous to die quietly, on its own," Fliess said. "...You are big enough to admit an error."

"In '96 Krafft-Ebing said that my lecture on childhood seduction as a factor in neuroses sounded like a scientific fairy-tale," Freud exclaimed. "And now he turns out to be right! It's hard to admit he was right, and I won't do it. I can't!"

"You don't need to admit anything of the kind, Sigmund," Fliess assured him. "If there is a chance in your next book, just write that the stories your patients told you were fantasies, and you didn't realize that until much later...In science, honesty always pays off."

"That's true in principle, Wilhelm," Freud replied. "But you know how much trouble you've had with your ideas about biological rhythms and periodicity. An admission of error on my part would only strengthen my enemies."

"Not in the long run," Fliess said slowly. "When you set the record straight it would put sexuality in its proper place. I mean, in the sense that one differentiates between sexual behavior and sexual fantasies."

"I'll think about it, Wilhelm," Freud smiled wanly. "But how can I convince my critics—and especially my enemies—that this is my only error, that there are no others?" After a moment he said wistfully: "The hope of eternal fame was so beautiful. And so was the hope of certain wealth, complete independence, travel, and removing my children from the sphere of the worries that spoiled my own youth."

"Just let the evidence speak," Fliess suggested. "It's not the end of the world. A physician lets his recovered patients speak, a surgeon can point to successful operations. But we all know that errors are made. That's accepted—by patients and by the medical profession."

"As in your case of Emma," Freud whispered.

There was an uncomfortable silence. Then Fliess nodded. "Right," he said and looked out over the lake.

They walked along the shore until a path turned south across the meadows toward Maurach. "Shall we go a bit further?" Freud interrupted the silence. Fliess nodded. After a hundred yards or so, Freud again spoke up. "In your last letter...you mentioned finding the physiological basis of life's rhythms...Is there anything new you can tell me?"

Fliess shook his head. Then he said: "I think I was too optimistic. Today's knowledge is very limited. I'll need at least five more years of research to come up with an answer." After a few moments he turned to Freud and smiled: "How about you?"

"The same problem," Freud answered. "I assume—I always have and I always will—that mental processes are linked to physiological events. But I don't know yet what the link is..." his voice trailed off.

"For more than a decade I've tried to help you find it, Sigmund," Fliess broke the silence. "Our knowledge of the nervous system, and especially of the brain, is not sufficient. We simply must wait for the neurologists."

"I have no desire at all to leave my psychology hanging in the air, without an organic basis," Freud said. "But beyond a feeling of conviction, I have nothing to go on, either theoretical or therapeutic. And so I must act as if I were confronted by psychological factors only. I have no idea yet why I cannot relate the psychological to the organic."

"Perhaps the linkage is not yours to discover," Fliess suggested. "After all, it lies within the realm of physiology, not psychology. You simply have to pay tribute to biology, Sigmund. Bisexuality and periodicity are the most significant biological aspects of human beings; everything else, all the psychological aspects, are derived from them...Don't you agree? You used to."

Freud pursed his lips. "Perhaps," he said at last. "As so many times before, you may be right, Wilhelm. I just don't like the thought of some overpowering physiological factors. There *are* psychological processes. I just haven't found the links between them. I think your...reduction of everything psychological to biological...goes too far."

"We'll see," Fliess said firmly. "The future will tell." They spoke little on the way back to the hotel.

Ψ

The next day the two friends started early. Fliess carried their lunch in his knapsack, while Freud's was empty but ready to hold whatever interesting finds they might make. They followed the winding path through the forested hills toward the Bärenkopf peak, but by noon it was evident that they would not reach it. So they sat in the shade of some large boulders and unpacked their lunch. Freud commented on the view of the lake below, the silence, and the absence of people.

"Nature is meant to be enjoyed in solitude," he said. "With a good friend, but far away from the crowd."

"Perhaps," Fliess replied. "But aren't people a part of nature?"

"That's my worst attribute," Freud said slowly. "A certain indifference toward the world. Just as powerful as my best attribute..."

"Which is..." Fliess encouraged him.

"A defiant courage about truth," Freud continued, and his friend nodded emphatically.

"Just be sure it *is* the truth," Fliess said after a while. "Many people..."

Freud interrupted him: "In the depth of my being I remain convinced that my dear fellow-creatures are, with individual exceptions, good for nothing. Worthless."

"You are the great pessimist," Fliess said with an edge to his voice.

"No, just a realist," Freud countered. "After all, I have looked deeper into the human mind than anyone else. And what I see is not pretty."

"But Sigmund, is what you see—all that ugliness you describe to me— is that really there? In the psyche that no one can measure? Or is what you see just a reflection of what you put there?"

Freud was startled: "How can you say that?" he demanded.

"With biology we always have data, observations," Fliess replied. "But when you deal with psychological factors—so much more amorphous— I wonder...Perhaps I should say that I have started to wonder since your seduction mistake."

"My new methods will solve your problem, Wilhelm," Freud said sharply.

The rest of the lunch was silent. After the meal, the two friends descended the Perchertal and then made their way along the lake back to the hotel. They talked a little about their families but most of their conversation returned to the topics they had touched on the previous day.

After a refreshing bath—Freud valued comfort and cleanliness very highly—they had coffee and cake on the veranda in front of the restaurant. A well-dressed lady in her sixties sat at a nearby table and observed them closely. After a few minutes she walked over and asked Freud whether he was the well-known physician from Vienna. He admitted this and she introduced herself as Theresa von Königsrath, a long-time resident of Vienna and the mother of two daughters. She proudly said that they had married Viennese physicians, one a well-known surgeon and the other an internist who taught at the university. The lady also mentioned that she had read *Studies on Hysteria* some time ago and had discussed it with her friends. Fliess invited her to join them, which brought him a reproving glance from Freud.

While she returned to her table to fetch her parasol, Freud whispered: "We must be careful. Every word we speak will make the rounds in Vienna next week."

Fliess laughed and shrugged his shoulders. "She seems nice enough, Sigmund. Don't worry so much."

Freud ordered coffee for the three of them and Fliess asked for another piece of cake.

"The scenery is heavenly, but I miss the Viennese cooking," Frau Königsrath said pleasantly. "What do you miss, Herr Doktor Freud?"

"Nothing, madam," Freud replied. "I'm not all that fond of Vienna."

"Really?" She raised her eyebrows in surprise. "With all the music, how can you not like it? You know..." she leaned forward and whispered, "I have always been an admirer of Brahms, and I went to hear all of his music, even when so many people, including my friends, thought his work terrible."

"I admire your fortitude, madam," Freud said. "I rarely go to concerts, almost never. Every few years one Mozart opera. That's enough for me."

"Good heavens," she exclaimed. "How can one live in Vienna and not hear music?"

"It's quite easy, I assure you," Freud said. "I don't appreciate music. It's as simple as that."

"But it's the best way to study the human soul," Frau Königsrath persisted.

"But I'm not interested in the soul," Freud said gravely. "I'm interested in discovering the structure and processes of the mind. The *mind*, not the soul. Indeed, I'm not sure..."

"Doktor Freud has a big enough job, don't you think?" Fliess interrupted his friend's sentence that seemed all too frank.

The lady agreed. "My friends think your ideas are...well...rather strange," she said slowly.

"Very delicately put," Freud said and smiled. "What do they really think?"

"Well, frankly, that you exaggerate and overgeneralize. My sons-in-law...both of them...don't think there is half as much to sex as you seem to believe."

"And what do you think?" Freud asked kindly.

She smiled and blushed. "I haven't thought much about the matter," she said finally. "But I tend to agree with them."

"I consider the energy of sexual instincts—what I call the libido—much broader than what people think," Freud said in a low tone. "It includes much more than…than…"

There was a pause, and then Frau Königsrath said, "than the sexual act. Is that what you were about to say? Oh, Herr Doktor Freud, I have been a widow for more than twenty years, I have brought up two daughters, I have lived in Vienna all my life. I have admired Brahms's music for years, I know the Strauss family. Nothing shocks me. I live in reality."

Freud made a slight bow toward her, and Fliess said, "And in spite of everything, you haven't lost your charm!"

She smiled and urged Freud to go on.

"Yes," he said. "I include in 'sexual life' all expressions of tenderness which spring from primitive sexual feelings, even when those feelings have become inhibited or when the sexual aim has been exchanged for another. Our hysterical patients suffer from reminiscences. They have repressed so much."

"But how can you be so certain of repression? And why such an emphasis on long-forgotten sexual matters?" Frau Königsrath asked.

"I'm convinced that everyone hides the truth in matters of sex," Freud said with conviction. "The more I set about looking for disturbances of people's sexual lives, and the more skillful I become at pursuing my enquiries in the face of denial, the more regularly I am able to discover pathogenic factors in sexual life."

"But when my son-in-law says that a patient has a tumor in the left frontal lobe he always looks for independent evidence to support him. He never operates unless he has two other independent opinions," Frau Königsrath said.

"That's the difference between medicine and science," Freud replied. "The psychoanalyst may boldly demand confirmation of his suspicions from the patient. We must not be led astray by initial denials. If we keep firmly to what we have inferred, we shall in the end conquer every resistance by emphasizing the unshakable nature of our convictions."

The shocked Fliess stared unbelievingly at his friend's blazing eyes.

"But aren't you a physician, too, Herr Doktor Freud?" Frau Königsrath broke the awkward silence.

"Of course he is," Fliess answered. "And…"

But Frau Königsrath was not deterred. "How many patients have you cured?" she asked.

"Psychoanalysis doesn't always or necessarily lead to a cure," Freud replied. "Analysis places the patient in a position where he can get well;

before analysis this was not possible. But whether or not he really does get well depends on his wish to recover, on his will."

"You mean that if a patient gains some advantage from his neurosis, perhaps by tyrannizing his family, the patient might simply decide not to recover," Fliess suggested.

"All that weighing is unconscious, of course," Freud nodded. "But yes, that happens."

"So I should ask how many of your patients *have been* cured?" Frau Königsrath continued.

"A few," Freud replied. "But I haven't kept track of the numbers. We must remember that cure is always a matter of degree. And perspective. I'm basically not very interested in therapy. I usually find that I see in any particular case the theoretical problems that I happen to be interested in at the time."

"So you must be especially careful not to read your theoretical concerns into the patient's symptoms," Fliess suggested.

"Of course," Freud agreed. "But that never happens anyway."

Fliess raised his eyebrows and looked skeptically at Freud. "It seems to me," he continued after a moment, "that a series of successful cures would show the validity of your theory of neuroses and your conception of the unconscious. Then people would know that your work is not some harebrained piece of imagination."

Freud looked startled. "How can you say that?" he asked tersely.

"I'm not saying it," Fliess replied. "People in Berlin say it. Quite a few, in fact."

"And in Vienna, too," Frau Königsrath added. "So, Herr Doktor Freud, why don't you publish some successful case histories?"

"It's not as easy as you think," Freud answered after some thought. "Medical ethics force me to be very general and to hide much important personal material. That weakens the case as a demonstration of my psychology and methods. If I were to publish enough information, the identity of the patient would become known and I would be accused of violating the right of privacy."

Frau Königsrath nodded and pursed her lips. "I see your problem," she murmured.

"Besides," Freud continued, "case histories do not catch the essence of a life and its difficulties. The problem is that case histories have to be written down, on a few pages. Ah, how bungled our reproductions are, how wretchedly we dissect the great art works of psychic nature!"

His two listeners agreed. "Even so, I still think that half a case is better than none," Fliess said. "You have to convince people, and only facts will do that."

"I suppose people regard me as a monomaniac," Freud chuckled, and then he became serious again. "But I have the distinct feeling that I have touched on one of the great secrets of nature."

"Perhaps it has been a secret for so long that it seems outrageous to many people," Frau Königsrath mused. "And it seems outrageous to me, too," she added emphatically. "The music of Brahms never did."

"People need proof, Sigmund. Why would you deny them proof?" Fliess continued.

"I have no scientific proof," Freud answered with a tinge of sadness. "Only case histories. The parts of my theory are logically consistent. And I am careful in the inferences I make. That should be enough. I have faith in my data."

"Physicians should understand this," Frau Königsrath said. "And they may well convince the scientists. You have practiced for ten years now, you should have many, many cases. A few could no doubt be worked into a little book."

"I'll see what I can do," Freud said and rose. He excused himself and told his companions that he needed to be alone. They watched him go down the steps to the lake and walk along the shore.

During dinner Freud picked up the thread again. "A strange lady," he said. "And yet, intelligent and broad-minded. But I don't understand her."

"Frau von Königsrath was quite right in urging you to publish some supporting cases, Sigmund. If not now, at least in the near future."

Freud shook his head. "I just don't understand women. Minna does not ask for proof. And Martha doesn't either."

"Perhaps that's because they believe," Fliess suggested. "Our noble lady doesn't."

"I wish I understood women and their ways," Freud said wistfully. "It would make life so much easier."

"But you've been analyzing women for years, Sigmund," Fliess expressed surprise. "You should understand women quite well by now."

"I really don't," Freud replied. "I view them like all my patients—as sources of information about the workings of the mind." Then he added after a few moments, "As I told you before, I have my limitations as a therapist. In the first place, I get tired of people. Secondly, I am not basically interested in therapy. I have never had much craving to help suffering humanity. In fact, I don't like many of the human creatures on this earth. But as long as I can remember I have wanted to find out about the universe, how the human mind works."

"If the evidence for your discoveries is insufficient, or unclear, or ambiguous—and heaven help you, Sigmund, if all three together—people might follow you for a short time and then leave. You wouldn't have any way of convincing them. And they could easily make their own interpretations of the sketchy material you have provided so far." Fliess's tone was urgent.

"That's possible," Freud admitted. "If I ever *have* followers. Right now I have only you."

"And I'm not really a follower, Sigmund," Fliess reminded him. "After all, I have my own ideas—on bisexuality and the rhythms that pervade life."

"Yes, I know, Wilhelm," Freud said. "They are excellent ideas, too. Don't get me wrong, please. I simply meant that right now you are the only person who understands my work and appreciates it."

"I'm sure there are others," Fliess encouraged him. "You just don't know about them yet. Your dream book has been out for less than a year. For all you know, it might be read by some physician in London, Paris, or Zürich. Who can tell what will happen?"

Freud did not sleep well that night. The walking expedition had brought him close to nature and refreshed his spirit, but he was disturbed by the harsh questions Fliess had asked him. He thought that Fliess should have come to his defense on the terrace instead of supporting Frau Königsrath's concerns.

On the next day, the two friends rented a carriage to Buchau, a small village on the eastern shore. From there they climbed the "Weisse Wand" toward the Durra-alm. They spoke little, for Freud enjoyed the silent nature around them and the ever-changing views as they ascended the mountain. But Fliess was less enthusiastic than Freud, and after a picnic lunch from Freud's rucksack they decided to return by a different route. On the way down Fliess talked about bisexuality, and reminded Freud once again of his own priority in this exploration.

Ψ

The last morning of the "congress" did not start well. Freud was up early and had finished his breakfast when Frau Königsrath entered the dining room. He hoped she would not see him; but she did and made her way over.

"May I have breakfast with you?" she asked after the greeting. "My friends are still sleeping."

"Please join me," Freud answered politely. "I'm just having another cup of coffee, waiting for Doktor Fliess."

"I enjoy staying in a place where nobody knows me," she said enthusiastically. "In Vienna, everybody greets me, here I am ignored."

"I am ignored in my home town as well," Freud said with some regret.

"I must disagree with you, Herr Doktor Freud," Frau Königsrath said gently. "Even though it's early in the day, I must disagree. My sons-in-law tell me so often that you are quite well known. It's just that..." she hesitated, and a slight blush crossed her face.

"Yes?" Freud urged her on with some misgivings.

"Well..." she continued. "To be honest, my impression is that medical people dismiss you and your ideas. But they don't ignore you. How could they? Everyone is talking about your...your ideas about sex—and the unconscious."

"I'm only showing people what human nature looks like," Freud said. And then he added with a twinkle in his eye, "people may abuse my doctrines by day, they may object to them, but I am sure they dream of them by night."

"As far as I know—from what my sons-in-law tell me about their colleagues—there isn't all that much objection to your ideas," Königsrath said as the waiter filled her cup. "There are some prudes in Vienna, of course, but they don't really count. When medical people criticize your ideas it's not on the grounds of sexual prudery or hostility to new thoughts."

"What is it, then?" Freud asked in an unbelieving tone.

"Well..." she hesitated a moment. "Apparently it's your theory that neuroses have a sexual origin. Some psychiatrists think that's terribly old-fashioned...And then your methods..."

"Go on, please," Freud encouraged her. "I have few opportunities to listen to such charming critics."

"I only tell you what I hear," she smiled. "Free association seems so...so unscientific. And even I think that many of your interpretations are unconvincing. How can you be sure your interpretations are correct.?"

"My future work will demonstrate how correct my views are," Freud answered. "If people will only listen. But I doubt very much that the people of Vienna will do that. They are more likely to continue ignoring me and rejecting my ideas."

"But Herr Doktor Freud," Königsrath exclaimed. "As I said earlier, you're not ignored. Far from it. Just about everyone has heard of you and your ideas...But then, many intellectuals have trouble in Vienna—and the empire."

Freud raised his eyebrows.

"Yes," she continued. "I have many friends in the arts. From what I hear, many thinking people feel unhappy and unwanted in our lovely musical city...Karl Kraus and his magazine, for instance. Or Arthur Schnitzler, that sad little man with his plays. Or Viktor Adler, the socialist. I think they are all miserable, and they blame their misery on Vienna."

"You put me into good company," Freud said with a smile.

"I just want to point out that you are not the only one who feels alone. But while you may feel alone and abandoned, that doesn't mean we Viennese don't know you...And it doesn't mean we reject you."

After the waiter brought her rolls, Königsrath leaned forward and said in a low voice: "Herr Doktor Freud, just because you don't feel at home doesn't mean people don't accept you. You shouldn't read your feelings into other people..."

"It's a complicated matter," Freud replied. "You must allow me to see life as it exists for me. Mental life, the unconscious, dreams...we are just beginning to understand them. And I have the key."

"I'm not the only one who has trouble accepting the idea that the unconscious is involved in so many things...I believe that there is an unconscious in all of us, but..." her voice trailed off.

"Wait till next year," Freud continued. "I'm writing a new book, in which I demonstrate that unconscious motivation enters into most activities of daily life. I show that there is a continuity between the normal and the neurotic. There are only differences in degree."

She looked at him and raised her eyebrows. But before she could speak Fliess joined them and ordered breakfast. He mentioned that he had had an interesting dream that night, and Freud urged him to write it down so that it might be analyzed later.

"What about people who don't dream?" Königsrath asked. "And equally important, what about people who can afford only two therapeutic sessions a month? Can you help *them*?"

"Such infrequent sessions would be quite useless, I'm afraid," Freud answered. "But other people can do what I did: self-analysis. I analyzed my own dreams which led me back through all the events of my childhood. And I think that this kind of analysis may be enough for anyone who is a good dreamer and not too abnormal. Dreams, after all, are the royal road to the unconscious."

"But I'm not sure I could interpret my dreams," Königsrath said uneasily. "How do I know what the images and events in a dream mean?"

"I agree that's a problem," Freud nodded. "Normal people usually have relatively straightforward dreams, and thus interpretation is not so difficult. But a neurotic needs a professional, for only a psychoanalyst can decide whether a component of the dream is to be interpreted in one way or its opposite." After a few moments he added: "self-analysis takes courage. Courage to see and courage to accept."

Then Freud turned to Fliess and said: "For example, I have found love of the mother and jealousy of the father in my own case, as well as in my patients' dreams, and now I believe that it is a general phenomenon of early childhood."

"I haven't found anything like that in my childhood memories," Königsrath protested after some thought. "I can imagine that some children—boys—might feel that way. But *all* children? How can you be sure?"

"I *am* sure. Because my patients show this phenomenon, and I show it, too."

"Those events remind me of some ancient tragedy," Fliess remarked.

"Precisely," Freud said enthusiastically. "It's the old Oedipus legend re-lived today."

"How would you demonstrate its universal nature?" Fliess persisted. "I grant you, you may be right. But you need facts. From other cultures, too. People need to be convinced."

Freud leaned forward and said intensely: "If psychoanalysis can boast of no other achievement than the discovery of these repressed—and I do mean repressed—family interactions that remind us of King Oedipus, that alone would give psychoanalysis a claim to be included among the precious new acquisitions of mankind...After all, that...that Oedipal system may justly be regarded as the nucleus of most neuroses."

Königsrath still looked doubtful. "I find all this very interesting, Herr Doktor Freud, but I'm not sure I believe everything you say. It seems to me that you assume everybody has the same kind of psychological development you had. But is that really true?" She pushed back her chair.

"We are all human, aren't we?" Freud replied triumphantly. "Of course we follow the same pattern. After all, our physiological make-up is just about the same. I see only a few patients, most of them are quite wealthy. Yet I know that we all develop in the same way, we all go through this— what I might call Oedipus stage. I will continue to demonstrate the presence of such a stage in every child."

Königsrath rose and thanked them for the conversation.

"You are too harsh, I think," Fliess whispered when they were alone. "Do you really mean 'demonstrate' the Oedipus stage, Sigmund? Isn't the first step in science to see whether the phenomenon is indeed present or not?"

"But Wilhelm, I *know* it's present," Freud said. And after a moment he added quietly, "I possess the truth. I only need to demonstrate its existence. Just as it is my task to establish that neurotic behavior has sexual motives, for the most part."

"But wait, Sigmund," Fliess said sternly. "As a scientist, shouldn't you say: 'my task is to find out *whether* this neurosis has a sexual basis'? Remember your seduction fiasco."

"Don't talk to me about science, Wilhelm," Freud answered with some annoyance. "Your periods of 28 and 23 days, divided, added, or doubled as needed, aren't strictly scientific, either." Fliess stared at him, amazed. After a moment Freud said soothingly: "You are right, Wilhelm...I'm actually not a man of science or experiments. By temperament I am a con-quistador—an adventurer with all the inquisitiveness, daring, and tenac-ity characteristic of such a man."

Fliess did not answer for quite a while. Then he said slowly: "But Sig-mund, how often in all these years have you said to me that you are going to found the science of psychoanalysis?"

"It is...will be...a science, I assure you," Freud said with conviction. He looked out the window at the peaks across the lake. Fliess ate in silence.

Fliess had to be at the Jenbach train station by eleven o'clock. Freud would take an afternoon train but wanted to accompany Fliess to the vil-lage. In the carriage they again discussed Fliess's ideas about bisexuality and periodicity and their relation to psychoanalysis.

As they approached Jenbach, Fliess was saying, "Psychopathic phe-nomena—like so much else in life—are greatly influenced by periodic processes. So, when a patient deteriorates rapidly or improves within a few days, that is the result of physiological rhythms."

Freud shook his head: "I doubt that very much, Wilhelm. A patient im-proves because I infer certain psychological causes of neurotic behavior, on the basis of free associations. Then I discuss these causes that lie in childhood. The internal pressures are relieved, and the patient gets bet-ter."

There was a pause as the carriage approached the station and stopped. A porter unloaded the luggage while Fliess arranged his tickets to Berlin.

On the platform, Fliess said: "I rest my case on biology. It is the basis of all psychology. You admit as much when you accept my discovery of bi-sexuality and periodicity."

"But those ideas must be transformed before they can be included in my psychology," Freud reminded him.

"Perhaps that's where the problem lies, Sigmund. The problem of your psychological theory is that it isn't biological enough. It is not scientific enough."

"Good heavens, Wilhelm," Freud exclaimed. "You never criticized me like this before. What has happened?" And after a pause he whispered: "I used to depend on you so much."

"You still can," Fliess answered.

"Really, Wilhelm?" Freud asked without convictions.

"You know, Sigmund," Fliess said as the train approached. "After this congress of ours I really worry about your theory and your evidence. I see a great danger..." He raised his voice above the hissing steam: "...It seems to me that the thought-reader merely reads his own thoughts into other people."

Freud stared at him as the train came to a stop. Then he said hoarsely: "But Wilhelm! That would deprive my work of all its value..."

They shook hands and Fliess boarded the train. Freud remained as in a trance and watched the train disappear.

They never saw each other again.

Notes

For more than a decade, Wilhelm Fliess was Sigmund Freud's best friend, confidante, and sounding board. They met several times in various cities to discuss each other's ideas and provide emotional support for their continued work. The last "congress" (as Freud liked to call these meetings) was held in Achensee. It is not known what actually occurred there—but it must have been significant for both of them, since they never saw each other again.

The Achensee "congress," then, is a logical setting for our encounter with Freud. In the several conversations with Fliess, I have Freud express his ideas, hopes, and concerns. I also indicate the growing rift between the two men and their positions. The conversations with other characters (who are fictional) raise issues which were important at the time and continue to be significant.

In the course of their discussions, I have Fliess express his misgivings about Freud's methods and conclusions. Fliess's words on the station platform are taken from one of his letters; they must have been a great shock for Freud. The correspondence shows that the decline of the friendship was largely Fliess's doing, and I suppose that methodological questions were as significant here as more or less hidden scientific differences and perhaps rivalry.

Although Freud had not yet written his major books, the conversations foreshadow some later ideas. This is entirely fitting, since Freud developed his thoughts for years before publishing them. Indeed, it is said that *The Interpretation of Dreams*, which first appeared in 1899, contains the seeds of most later ideas.

Most of the information for this chapter is taken from several biographies, primarily *The Life and Work of Sigmund Freud* by Ernest Jones (New York: Basic Books, 1953); *Freud: the Man and the Cause* by Ronald Clark (New York: Random House, 1980); *Freud, Biologist of the Mind* by Frank Sulloway (New York: Basic Books, 1979); and *Freud: Living and Dying* by Max Schur, who was Freud's personal physician for several years (New York: International Universities Press, 1972).

I have also relied on Freud's voluminous correspondence with his best friend. A complete version has been edited recently by Jeffrey M. Masson: *The Complete Letters of Sigmund Freud to Wilhelm Fliess 1887–1904* (Cambridge: Harvard University Press, 1985). Unfortunately, practically all of the letters which Fliess wrote to Freud during these years have been lost.

A good introduction to Freud's basic ideas is found in his *Introductory Lectures on Psychoanalysis* (1917) and *New Introductory Lectures on Psychoanalysis* (1933). Both have appeared in numerous editions, e.g. New York: Penguin Books, 1973. I have consulted these, along with several other essays. I have also used two books that evaluate the empirical foundations of Freud's propositions and assess the validity of his ideas: *The Scientific Credibility of Freud's Theories and Therapy*, by Seymour Fisher & Roger P. Greenberg (New York: Basic Books, 1977); and *Freud and the Dilemmas of Psychology* by Marie Jahoda (New York: Basic Books, 1977).

5

ALFRED ADLER
A Meeting in Vienna, 1911

The great variety of individuals' symptoms and problems which the analysts encountered in their work raised questions about the adequacy of Freud's grand theory. Do all actions, dreams, and neuroses have the roots that Freud had described? Or might there be other causal factors that had been overlooked? While many of Freud's followers remained loyal supporters of his ideas, some broke away to found their own schools. The first defection, caused by fundamental differences in the conception of human nature, occurred in 1911. It transformed the normally friendly and congenial "Vienna Psychoanalytic Society" into a battleground of competing hypotheses that could not be tested at the time.

Alfred Adler was born on February 7, 1870, in Penzing, now a suburb of Vienna. He was the third of six children and the favorite of his father, a grain merchant. Meadows, fields, and forests were nearby, and all of his life Adler enjoyed flowers and appreciated nature. The family lived in comfortable circumstances, and his parents frequently took their children to concerts. Adler loved classical and light music, was a good singer, and throughout his life took advantage of Vienna's musical offerings.

During his early years he contracted not only the usual childhood diseases but also suffered from rickets and two accidents in the street. His delicate health and frequent visits to doctors probably contributed to his rather early decision to become a physician. During much of his school career he was clumsy in sports and mediocre in academic subjects, especially mathematics, but he graduated without difficulty.

In 1890 Adler entered the University of Vienna medical school, where he took courses in philosophy and psychology along with the usual medical curriculum. Five years later he received his medical degree and began to serve as an intern at the Vienna Hospital and Polyclinic.

In 1897 Adler married the daughter of liberal Russian emigrants and rented an office and apartment in a lower middle-class section of Vienna. Adler was a devoted father, and his wife Raissa applied many of his principles to the raising of their four children. He was convinced that men and women are equal in value and capacity and encouraged his daughters to prepare for professions.

Adler began his private practice a year after his marriage, first as an eye specialist and then as a general practitioner. His practice flourished, for he was not only a good diagnostician but also a kind and gentle man who impressed his patients with his concern for their welfare. While

Adler emphasized the treatment and cure of his patients as whole individuals—not just as "cases"—he also maintained scientific interests. From the beginning of his career he viewed sickness as part of an individual's personality, life, and social environment. For years he investigated the relationship between physiological and psychological processes, as these occur within a social context. This concern gradually led to a deeper interest in psychology and brought him into contact with Freud's work.

When Freud inaugurated the "Psychological Wednesday Society" he invited Adler as one of its charter members, even though Adler was not a student of Freud, had not attended his classes, and had not been psychoanalyzed. A few years later this group became the Vienna Psychoanalytic Society, and by 1911 Adler was its president.

Adler's first psychological paper appeared in 1904, and his first major book in 1907. The titles—"The physician as educator" and *Study of Organ Inferiority and Its Psychical Compensation*—illustrate Adler's two major interests: the broadly conceived education of children, and the close relationship between physical and psychological processes in normal and neurotic individuals.

These and other early works indicate that Adler's ideas were rather different from Freud's, and over the years these differences grew and were accentuated by events within the Viennese group of early analysts. In 1911 Adler left Freud's circle and brought several members of the society along to found his own school of "individual psychology." The two men never met again, although for years they lived in the same city. Adler respected much of Freud's work, but Freud rarely mentioned Adler's name again.

Adler's daily life was unpretentious. He was simple in speech, informal in manners, and nonchalant about clothes. Walking arm-in-arm with his friends was one of his great pleasures, as was the singing of songs, especially Franz Schubert's, at the piano with friends. From childhood on he was fond of people. He thought well of mankind and was optimistic about people in general and his patients in particular. Adler liked social gatherings and made friends easily. In later years, the Café Siller overlooking the Danube Canal became the unofficial gathering place of his colleagues and students. He joined them there whenever he could, and in the warm atmosphere of good will and fellowship the theoretical problems and practical applications of individual psychology were discussed far into the night.

Soon after the First World War Adler organized a number of child guidance clinics in Vienna. These were supervised by him, staffed by his students, and operated on the basis of his principles. His emphasis on the "whole person" led to the inclusion of all factors relevant to a child's problems and therefore involved the parents and teachers as well.

Adler believed that psychological principles should be widely disseminated so that everyone might use them, and he therefore went on frequent and extended lecture tours throughout Europe and North

America. During the 1920s he spent long hours in his private practice, various clinics, and lecture halls. He wrote when and where this was possible, in the hours around midnight and on trains, and took very few vacations.

His major interest always lay in therapy and in otherwise helping individuals, rather than in the logical and systematic exposition of a comprehensive theory. Thus he actually *wrote* only a small number of books—several of his larger works are actually lecture notes which were edited by other people.

Adler spent much of his time counselling children and devising appropriate therapeutic methods. Most of his adult patients came from the middle and lower class, and had life problems that were quite different from those of Freud's clientele. Yet Adler's general outlook on life was positive and he viewed the future of mankind with hope.

In many ways, Alfred Adler is Sigmund Freud's antithesis. Adler grew up in moderate but adequate circumstances, did poorly in school, and became a physician and therapist because he liked people and actually wanted to help them. As yet there is no large-scale biography and his writings have not been brought together in a *Collected Works*. But while he is not as well known as Freud and his ideas have not had a comparable impact, his contributions have been considerable—although they are not always acknowledged by psychologists or recognized by the public.

BASIC HUMAN CHARACTERISTICS

Adler's theoretical system is much less complicated than Freud's, and both the nature of neuroses and the causes of mental illness are viewed in simpler terms. There are relatively few major concepts and propositions, and hardly any about the unconscious, which to Adler is not nearly as significant as it is to Freud.

Adler calls his theory and perspective "individual psychology." There were two major reasons for using this label: Adler wanted to emphasize the importance of the whole individual, the indivisible person who always exists in a social context; and he wanted to separate his own psychology from that of Freud.

"Individual psychology" does not mean that we study the isolated person, but rather that we look at the whole individual with many close relationships to the social and physical environment. Family members, friends, co-workers, and other people we meet casually, all influence us as much as we affect them. The unique individual is the result of these interactions that impinge upon various inherited physiological and psychological characteristics.

Adler believed that one can understand a person, and especially the individual's physical and mental problems, only if one considers the total personality within the social setting. Help, and particularly the cure of a psychological problem, requires that we change all relevant aspects of a person, including relations to the context and, if necessary, the context itself.

Adler postulated that humans are conscious beings who are usually aware of their goals, the different possible ways of reaching them, and the major causes of most of their actions. This does not mean that we are aware of all our hopes, fears, and desires, or that we do not forget or repress events and ideas. But it does mean that unconscious factors play a relatively minor role in daily life. This emphasis on conscious factors in human affairs eliminated some thorny methodological problems.

Adler also postulated that future goals are the significant motivating factors of daily and other activities and thoughts. Instincts, drives, and sexual elements play relatively minor roles the importance of which varies from one person to the next and depends on the individual's circumstances.

Many of our ideas about the future and the goals that fit into it may be wrong, they may be fictions we make up or impossible ideals. Goals, then, are always subjective, and most are created by us on the basis of past experiences and present events. Over time, the normal person replaces fictional goals and an imaginary future with realistic expectations and reasonable possibilities that can be achieved.

To some extent, however, we continue to be affected by our subjective ideas of the future, which guide our thoughts, feelings, and actions today. If our vision is accurate, our actions will lead to success—we reach our goals and the future we anticipated comes about. To the extent that our vision is faulty or blurred, we will not behave appropriately and our actions will not be effective—we do not reach our goals and our future is not realized. In daily life, therefore, one should continuously reassess one's goals and visions of the future in the light of new information and present experiences.

Our goals, the circumstances in which we grow up (e.g., in a middle class, suburban family), together with various innate physiological and psychological factors (for example, a weak heart and high intelligence), and our unique early experiences, combine to produce a unique set of methods for reaching our goals, which Adler called our "style of life."

This concept is one of Adler's major contributions. The meaning is quite different from the term "life style" we use today, which refers mainly to a family's material consumption level. Adler postulated that the activities a person employs to achieve his goals combine with certain feelings, thoughts, attitudes, ideas, and views of the world to form a consistent system—the individual's style of life. This style is formed rather early in life and is quite difficult to change in later years.

Even while he was a member of Freud's group, Adler did not accept the notion that libido, or sexual, forces govern life. Rather, he believed that aggression was the dominant drive. Later he assumed that the "will to power" was the most significant factor. Eventually he came to the conclusion that "superiority" was every individual's major goal.

The most significant general task of any human being's life is "striving for superiority," by which Adler meant completeness and the development of one's potential. He also spoke of an "upward drive" and the "urge from below to above," but this does not imply a desire for social status, reputation, or leadership. Rather, it implies that people are not content to operate on a level below their ability, and that they strive to fulfill their capacities by working at the highest level they can.

The specific forms which this striving takes, however, vary from one person to another and depend on physiological, psychological, and social factors. We would expect, for example, that people with different physiques, intelligence, and musical aptitude would exhibit rather different means for reaching the goal of complete development (or superiority); the goal itself will vary, perhaps from the baseball Hall of Fame to Carnegie Hall. Furthermore, the subsidiary goals we try to achieve on our way to the major goal will also vary from one person to the next. Adler believed that for normal people both the goals and the means for attaining them are social, involving other people rather than oneself, and are socially beneficial rather than for one's own pleasure.

Adler's work is known for its emphasis on social phenomena. Unfortunately, the important concept here is difficult to translate. The German word "Gemeinschaftsgefühl" is usually rendered as "social interest," a poor substitute but the best short term there is. The original word refers to an individual's empathy, positive feelings for the community and its general welfare, the feeling that one is part of a warm close-knit group and should work for its benefit. Indeed, one might say that such a concern with the community's general welfare is a compensation for the individual's obvious weakness in facing life's problems.

Adler believed that this inborn feeling of social interest becomes manifest after careful guidance by parents and training in schools, and less often in the spontaneous games of children. His conviction that social interest, though innate, must be nurtured, led Adler to establish child guidance clinics and to advocate better schools and educational reforms.

From the very beginning of his practice, Adler had been impressed by the various compensations that many of his patients made for defective or problematic parts and functions of their bodies. Indeed, Adler became a psychiatrist partly because he observed that organ inferiority was not the only factor leading to compensation. Eventually he concluded that feelings of inferiority can develop from any real or imagined psychological, physical, or social shortcoming.

In general, inferiority feelings arise when individuals have the sense that some of their potentialities have not, or are not being, developed to the fullest. Adler postulated that inferiority feelings are normal and provide the major impetus for compensations—actions designed to help individuals reach their goals and develop to the limits of their capacities. Normal people discover their own appropriate compensating behaviors, while neurotics usually need therapeutic assistance to find effective solutions.

A Meeting of the Vienna Psychoanalytic Society

In the fall of 1902 one of Freud's students, the physician Wilhelm Stekel, suggested to Freud that it would be a good idea to bring together those few individuals who had shown some interest in psychoanalysis. In such a small group, theoretical and practical issues might be discussed more easily than in public.

Freud enthusiastically accepted the suggestion and invited three other physicians he thought might be interested: Max Kahane and Rudolf Reitler who had attended his lectures, and Alfred Adler who had commented favorably on Freud's books.

The group met on Wednesday evenings in Freud's waiting room at 19 Berggasse, and from the first engaged in lively discussions of theoretical issues and various applications of psychoanalysis. Guests were occasionally invited, but new members were accepted only upon unanimous invitation. At the typical meeting someone would present a paper, a discussion would follow, and the author would then have the last word. Originally, the meetings were very informal, no minutes were kept, and once a year a few seconds were devoted to administrative details. Many evenings Freud would accompany some members part of the way home and on his return stop at a cigar store.

The range of topics was immense. Sometimes Freud would present new ideas, for he often used the group as a sounding board. Or psychoanalytic methods would be used in discussions of smoking, chess, opera, novels, and whatever else caught the fancies of its members. While Freud encouraged such manifold uses, he was also careful to restrain the imaginative generalizations of overenthusiastic members.

The "Psychological Wednesday Society" grew rapidly and soon included some twenty persons of whom about a dozen attended regularly. Several of these later became famous as "followers" of, and "traitors" to, the cause of psychoanalysis. While most members were physicians, there also were journalists, educators, and other professionals. In 1906 the name of the group was changed to "Vienna Psychoanalytic Society," and when the group became too large for Freud's apartment the meetings were held in a room at the College of Physicians.

Ψ

Wednesday was Adler's busiest time of the week. During the morning he saw his patients at various city hospitals, and in the afternoon he met his students in one or another coffee shop. He frequently visited school officials and bureaucrats in the education ministry, for he was eager to try out his psychological principles on normal children in the real world. He would eat dinner at a restaurant, usually with some friends, before attending the meeting of the Vienna Psychoanalytic Society. It was rare indeed that he crossed the Danube before midnight on the way home to his apartment in the Praterstrasse.

February 22, 1911, had been filled with the usual appointments, hospital rounds, and house calls. In the late afternoon he met two of his students and discussed with them the teaching opportunities in a new school near Wiener Neustadt. He was excited and pleased—the school would employ some of his child guidance principles if two of his more experienced students would take positions there and make sure that the ideas were applied correctly.

He was in high spirits as he made his way to the Balalaika, a Hungarian restaurant just off the Schottenring near the university. His two friends were already waiting—the psychiatrist Wilhelm Stekel, who was a charter member of the Psychological Wednesday Society and who supported Adler's ideas, and Carl Furtmüller, a high school teacher in his early thirties who had joined the Society in 1909 and was one of Adler's closest friends. Both respected Freud and his work, but both were more impressed by Adler's down-to-earth ideas and friendly manner.

Adler liked the Balalaika because its dim chandeliers endowed the murals of scenes around Lake Balaton with the misty effect of sitting near the shore on a half-moon night. The men had just ordered wine when the strolling violinists came to their table. "You choose—it's your evening," Stekel whispered, and Adler requested melodies from the Gypsy Baron. The musicians played well, and Adler was happy and pleased. He asked them to play again and joined them in the refrain *"Ja, das alles auf Ehr."* At the end, several of the guests at other tables applauded, and the older violinist refused the money Adler offered.

"Give it to Saffi," Adler smiled and pressed the money into the man's hand. "She deserves it."

The musicians bowed and left to play at other tables, and several times that evening Adler would hum the melodies that danced and sighed across the rooms. Stekel had some editorial matters to discuss with Adler, for they were co-editors of Freud's journal *Zentralblatt für Psychoanalyse*. Furtmüller listened patiently, amazed that Adler could be so cool and professional in light of what might confront him later that evening. The journal questions were finally settled by the time dessert arrived, and Furtmüller commented on Adler's equanimity.

Adler leaned back and smiled. "Freud and I have always had our differences," he said and brushed some crumbs from his lapels. "Our patients have come from different social classes—and so their problems are different. Freud wants to discover—I want to help others..."

"He has a one-track mind—and you don't," Stekel interjected. "And—well, I could go on for another five minutes."

"Please don't," Adler chuckled. "That serves no purpose. Only the future matters."

"I knew after your presentation in early January that there would be a fight," Stekel continued. "And indeed those two recent meetings have been...rather unpleasant."

Furtmüller nodded. "I have the feeling that Freud set it all up—set you up," he murmured to Adler.

"Of course," Adler nodded. "But remember that I grasped the opportunity. I have never hidden my ideas, but I haven't presented them well, either." He hesitated and poured himself another cup of coffee. "So, when Freud asked me whether I wanted to outline my position, I said to him 'Sure, I'll take a couple of evenings to present my ideas in clear and concise form.'"

"And you did," Stekel said enthusiastically.

"Freud was impassive, as always," Furtmüller sighed. "But did you see the others? I thought a couple of them would have a stroke when you said that sexuality was not all that important and could not be a major factor in most neuroses. Their facial expressions were priceless."

"They did not show much of a scientific attitude," Adler remarked. "But I think that my data will convince them eventually."

Stekel shook his head. "I doubt it," he said slowly. "Too many members of the Society are today in the position that I was in some years ago."

"Oh?" Furtmüller asked. "What position was that?"

Stekel hesitated. "Well," he answered after a few moments, "I'm really embarrassed."

"Go ahead," Adler urged him on. "You're among friends."

"I know," Stekel said, "but I'm still embarrassed..." After a while he added: "I once said at a meeting—it was several years ago and we were still the Psychological Wednesday Society. We were all sitting in Freud's waiting room...I said, one night before Freud came in, that I was the apostle of Freud who was my Christ."

They laughed, and Stekel blushed slightly. "I'm still a good Jew, so you can imagine what a *faux pas*..."

"And now it looks like an even bigger one," Adler said and patted his friend's arm. "Especially after people see my next article in the *Zentralblatt.*"

"What's it going to be about?" Furtmüller asked.

"I think I mentioned it to you last week," Adler replied. "The theme is that people's actions are largely determined by their ideas of goals in the future. I haven't worked out all the details, but I am certain that the general notion is correct. In spite of philosophical problems one might have with teleology. But people do think and behave that way. All of my patients do, and everybody else I know does. Anyway, it's the present idea of a future goal that drives us on, not some sexual trauma that pushes us...to put it bluntly."

"Oh, brother," Furtmüller whistled softly. "That's the end."

"The end might come earlier," Adler said calmly. "I'll see how it goes tonight. If people continue to be narrow-minded and unscientific, if they attack without regard for data, then I'll leave. Just like that." He snapped his fingers.

"Really?" Furtmüller asked, astonished.

Adler nodded. "Just like that. It's a matter of free scientific inquiry. I have already discussed it with Raissa."

There was a long silence. Stekel seemed to count the lights on a nearby chandelier. "If there is a break, then what?" he asked calmly.

"We form our own group," Adler said easily, with a gleam in his eye. "I mean, I'll form a new group where people can discuss their ideas. In freedom. Where I can talk about inferiority, compensation, and the desire for superiority and not relate everything to libido. Some people will join me, others will stay with Freud. It's not all that complicated."

"I suppose so," Stekel said after a while. "Actually, the idea has already occurred to me. I thought about it right after that meeting in early January, when people were so blind and nasty and unscientific...I may come along and join you."

"But why can't we simply recognize that there are different viewpoints?" Furtmüller asked. "Eventually, empirical data will show which one is correct. That's what science is all about, isn't it?"

Adler nodded. "Many people in the Society are not scientists. And Freud defends his dogma."

"Let's hope for the best," Stekel said and folded his napkin. "It seems to me so logical...some neuroses have a sexual basis; other neuroses are, as you say, compensations for inferiorities. And some neuroses come from a still different root. Isn't that possible?"

"It's possible," Adler said. "Especially when people with neuroses come from very different backgrounds. After all, the social context is extremely significant." He looked at his watch. "It's past eight-thirty," he exclaimed. "We better start."

They paid and hurriedly put on their overcoats. Then they walked arm-in-arm along the Währinger Gasse toward the medical school. They crossed the street in front of the building that housed the College of Physicians.

"Good luck," Furtmüller said to Adler on the steps leading to the main entrance, and Stekel added, "To all of us."

In the foyer they met Paul Federn who nodded without a smile. On the way to the second floor they heard the clock strike nine. The meeting room was large, with a heavy wooden table in the center and comfortable chairs around it. Already at this early hour the air was thick with smoke, for some men had lit cigars. Adler shook hands with the two Grüner brothers and took the president's chair, while Stekel and Furtmüller sat near the other Adler supporters. Freud sat at the other end of the table, surrounded by Gaston Rosenstein and others who agreed with him rather than Adler. Paul Federn sat next to Freud, readying a sheaf of papers to take notes of the proceedings. Margarete Hilferding, a physician and the first woman member of the Society, took the last chair, next to Adler.

When everyone was settled, Adler said that he counted twenty persons, more than a quorum, and that the meeting would start. "Tonight we continue the discussion we suspended two weeks ago," he said amiably. "Who will begin?"

Victor Tausk was the first to speak. He had been a lawyer and journalist and was now studying medicine in preparation for becoming a psychoanalyst.

"What you call the desire to be superior is just a manifestation of the libido," he began. "So I ask: why not call it that? As Professor Freud has shown many times, the motor of a neurosis—if you want to put it that way—is the inhibited psychic energy that doesn't find its proper way for some reason. I don't think we need to add anything to this accepted role of the libido. Certainly not some drive for superiority."

"I fully agree," said Ludwig Jekels, a psychiatrist from Poland who was one of Freud's few personal friends among the Society's members. "The substitution of such relatively simple concepts as inferiority and superiority for the complex workings of the libido is just one aspect of Doktor Adler's deplorable tendency to simplify neuroses and their causes. In fact, I think Doktor Adler *over*simplifies. He and his students don't pay enough attention to the great complexity of neuroses and the even greater complexity of the unconscious."

"That's a good point," agreed Eduard Hitschmann. "In my own experience and on the basis of the many papers I have heard at these meetings over the last five years, it is evident—almost self evident—that neuroses are more diverse than Doktor Adler implies. And their causes are more diverse, too, for problems of sexuality and repression take many forms."

"But must all people be as complicated as Doktor Freud asserts?" Stekel asked. "I grant you that some neuroses are exceedingly complex, but I think many are quite simple. We find the same variations among causal factors. The simplicity of a theory is not a scientific argument against it. Just the opposite, it seems to me. A simple theory, simple concepts, and so forth, are quite adequate—if they are valid. Just think of Isaac Newton."

"It seems to me, however, that Doktor Adler oversimplifies in order to be understood by uneducated people," Hitschmann replied. "One form this oversimplification takes is the removal of sexuality from neuroses and from the psychopathology of everyday life."

"Please wait," Adler said and turned to Hitschmann. "I am convinced that psychological knowledge should be widely disseminated, so that it can help people arrange—or rearrange—their lives. What is important to me is the widespread use of psychology, not whether a theory is simple or complex. That dimension is irrelevant. Don't you want psychological insights known to everyone, used by everyone?"

"Of course," Hitschmann agreed. "But not at the cost of oversimplification."

"I'm not a physician, just a lawyer," Franz Grüner said. "So I speak as an intelligent layman without an axe to grind. I see something else behind this debate about simplicity and the general use of psychoanalytic knowledge. By keeping theories very complex—overly complex, I might say—and by introducing new concepts and hypotheses all the time, psychoanalysis becomes such a complicated edifice that one can't understand it without specialists. I think that psychoanalytic knowledge is in danger of becoming so esoteric that its use and application remain hidden from the public. Such a state of affairs also justifies high fees..." his voice trailed off, and there was a silence. Several members rearranged the papers in front of them.

"I don't want to read too much into the complexity issue," Adler said after a few awkward moments. "But I can assure all of you that I have not deliberately simplified anything—the nature of neuroses, the causes of neuroses, or my general theory about mental life. Everything I have written and said is a reflection of how human beings think, how they view the world, how they behave in daily life and when they are troubled. I stand by my data, the facts I have gathered in more than ten years of practice."

"Perhaps the difficulty lies in the fact that Doktor Adler has not really practiced psychoanalysis," Jekels said slowly.

"Or better, perhaps Doktor Adler *has* practiced some form of psycho-analysis but used his own labels for our concepts," Hitschman added.

"That's a good point," Freud agreed. "Actually, I would go a bit farther. After listening to Doktor Adler's two papers some days ago I must say that I resent the fact that the author talks about the same things I do, but doesn't call them by the name they already have. And I don't appreciate the fact that Doktor Adler fails to establish any relationship between his new terms and the old terms we all know. Just to give you one example, and a flagrant one: Doktor Adler talks about 'psychic hermaphroditism' as if it were something fundamentally different from bisexuality. Doktor Adler hasn't discovered anything new—he just uses new labels."

Freud stopped and seemed to contemplate a spot about two feet in front and slightly above him. Hardly anyone dared move, for these were the strongest words the Society's members had ever heard Freud use on a public occasion.

"Worse, I see Doktor Adler's antisexual tendency as a step backward," Freud continued. "Such a reduction of sexual factors will make his views more popular, because there will be less resistance to them. But these views are no longer part of psychoanalysis. I have spent years analyzing the unconscious in great detail, and now Doktor Adler just about throws it out. He presents us with an ego psychology, a surface psychology, if you will, not a depth psychology."

Everyone looked at Adler, who hesitated for a few moments before re-plying. "What worries me," Adler began, "is that Professor Freud and his students find the same thing over and over again: repressed sexual trau-mas, sexual fantasies, the libido everywhere. It seems to me that some kind of stereotype has been created. And that stereotype has replaced true analysis. There is a danger that dogma will replace science."

"But the same thing is true in Doktor Adler's theory," Rosenstein said. "How often in these last few weeks have we heard about superiority, 'wanting to be on top,' 'up from below,' and so on?"

"The problem is..." Freud took the floor again. "The problem is that Doktor Adler's case materials consist of individuals with untidy conflicts, distorted and deformed personalities, but no real and genuine hysterias and big neuroses. In the latter kind of patient I have never found any deli-rium about 'underneath' and 'on top.'"

Adler was calm when he spoke. "Surely I'm not responsible for the kinds of neuroses my patients have! Don't we all recognize that mental illness takes many forms? That neuroses have many roots? Some are sex-ual, but not all, by any means. I'm not responsible for the character of my patients! I have nothing to do with the conflicts of patients whom other analysts treat! And I admit that I'm very interested in the welfare of children. But I *am* responsible for coming up with correct explanations of my patients' problems! How else can I—or anyone—come up with an effective cure? To put it bluntly, I don't think I find a correct explanation for all neuroses on the Procrustean beds of the unconscious and of libido theory. Some factors might *appear* to be sexual, but when we look behind them we discover something else, for example the drive for superiority."

There was an uncomfortable pause until Stekel said: "I have gradually become convinced that much of what Doktor Adler says is new and valuable. Yet we all must be careful not to overgeneralize. The one thing that worries me is that Doktor Adler wants to abandon the concept of repression. At least, that's what it seems like to me. To my mind, repression cannot be replaced by anything else at all."

Freud nodded. "I have always recognized the quality of Doktor Adler's descriptions of personalities, and I appreciate his case studies. I fault them only because they do not emphasize the psychology of the unconscious. And I wonder..." He hesitated and lit another cigar. "I wonder whether the ego develops a desire for importance because of some libidinal problem. After all, we know what is in the foreground, what is primary: some aspect of the libido."

"I would add this," Rosenstein said. "We can see, concealed behind so many of Doktor Adler's concepts, such as superiority, many of Professor Freud's concepts. Such new terms simply confuse everyone. We should stick with one set of concepts that we have found effective in scientific analysis and therapy."

Furtmüller was about to answer, but Rosenstein motioned him to wait. Then he continued, "Because of Doktor Adler's personal relations with academic psychology, education, socialism, and the feminist movement, he has come to interpret everything as a desire for superiority—even things that are obviously sexual. By denying the power of the sexual, by saying that sexuality no longer plays a prominent role in civilized people, Adler overlooks the fact that it is precisely this so-called civilized condition that must lead to neurosis." He nodded to Furtmüller.

But Stekel quickly interjected, "I am quite willing to dethrone sexuality if that is required by the facts our patients bring to us."

Now it was Furtmüller's turn. "Some people said tonight and two weeks ago that Doktor Adler is simply recasting Professor Freud's ideas in his own words, and others indicate that there are fundamental differences. Evidently we do not all see the same thing in Doktor Adler's work—or in the Professor's. Perhaps we should simply recognize that Professor Freud and Doktor Adler analyze different patients and pay unequal attention to social factors. Eventually, empirical data should—will—help us resolve this debate. But it may take some time, perhaps more than a year, of careful comparative study."

Gustav Grüner, who had joined the Society only a few months earlier, agreed: "I for one can see more similarities than differences between Doktor Adler's and Professor Freud's theories."

Adler nodded. "It is not my aim to devalue Professor Freud's conception of neurosis and its mechanisms. I only want to obey the practical and theoretical necessity of placing Professor Freud's work on a broader basis."

But Freud shook his head. "It's not as simple as that," he said sternly. "There are great differences, and we should admit them. I consider Doktor Adler's doctrines to be wrong and, as far as the development of psychoanalysis is concerned, dangerous. These are scientific errors, brought on by the use of wrong methods and by drawing too much on social and biological factors. But these errors do great credit to their creator. Even though I reject the content of Doktor Adler's views, I appreciate their consistency and logic."

Stekel made an effort to be calm and said hoarsely: "What I find unscientific is the position that everything can already be found in Doktor Freud's works. As I gradually familiarize myself with Doktor Adler's views, I find that they are in no way abstractions or errors. They involve great progress in our understanding of human characteristics—and neuroses."

"I don't think anyone says that the things Doktor Adler describes are not to be found," Freud said after a pause. "But those things are not where Doktor Adler says they are. I repeat: those things are not found in the conscious ego, but rather in the unconscious. Doktor Adler overlooks unconscious motives. And he overlooks sexual motives. Those are errors, in my view. And they are dangerous."

"I consider much of Doktor Adler's work of unusual value," said Paul Federn, one of Freud's earliest students. "It's just that he has been guilty of a few mistakes in thinking. Thereby he has succeeded in turning all our psychoanalytic material to his own use."

"Can you give us an example of such an error in thinking?" Franz Grüner asked coldly.

"Of course," Federn replied eagerly. "Doktor Adler's great error in thinking is that he does not see libidinal wishes behind neuroses. I think it would be advisable, and would serve to the advantage of Doktor Adler's valuable views, if he were to be somewhat more skeptical with regard to his own findings and look for the repressed libidinal factors behind whatever he does see."

"Good heavens," Stekel exclaimed. "Shouldn't you and others here"—he looked around the table—"be somewhat more skeptical about your own findings?"

There were some mutterings around the table, and Federn blushed. But before he could reply, Otto Steiner said: "Our strong emotions this evening cry out for a psychological explanation. I think our discussions these last few meetings have touched on our most secret complexes. I think Doktor Adler's work is misconceived and dangerous. Perhaps that's why his supporters have done such a poor job pleading their case. On the other hand, it's too bad that Herr Professor has allowed these emotions to be bottled up for so long. For more than four years now Doktor Adler has deviated more and more from Professor Freud's doctrine. His turning away from sexuality, which is reminiscent of the early Christians, seems downright anachronistic today, when we, in a kind of renaissance, are trying to link up with the sensual joys of the ancients."

"I don't believe my ears," Furtmüller whispered to Stekel, who nodded and wrinkled his nose.

"We have come together to examine the libido and the unconscious," Steiner continued. "And now Doktor Adler brings us back to the surface..."

"To reality, away from imagination," Hilferding said softly, but loud enough for all to hear.

"...So close to the surface, in fact, that we would have to rename our association. Doktor Adler's ideas do not fit into our association at all." Steiner's face was pale when he finished.

Everyone looked at Adler, who carefully arranged some papers in front of him. Freud stared at the same point in space that had held his attention before. Then Adler said slowly, choosing his words carefully: "I simply reject Herr Steiner's objection. But I must say that, if I were in his place, I would not have found the courage to make such a speech. When I consider all the comments made tonight, and two weeks ago, I can only say that I stand by my data and my interpretations of the facts in my patients' lives."

Several members nodded while others did not move.

"Tonight my ideas were attacked," Adler continued. "All of the speakers have expressed some respect for me as a person. But you can spare me those expressions. I expect all that will change—and quickly. Tonight I mourn. What died tonight, in my opinion, is the spirit of free scientific inquiry. What we need is a society for free psychoanalysis. Free from preconceptions. Free from dogmatism."

The room was silent, and the cluster of lamps hanging from the ceiling shone blue through the thick cigar smoke.

"The speaker has had the last word, as is our custom," Freud said at last. He seemed tired and his voice was heavy.

"I move we adjourn this meeting," Federn said softly.

"I remind the committee members that there is a business meeting right after this scientific meeting," Adler said in a matter-of-fact tone.

Everyone rose and most people left the room. No one spoke. Adler walked out with Furtmüller. In the hallway he said: "Wait for me. Let's have melange and tortes at the Café Siller."

"But you have that committee meeting," Furtmüller replied. "That might last quite a while."

Adler smiled at him. "Not this one," he said. "I am going to resign the presidency of the Society." Furtmüller looked crestfallen. "Don't worry," Adler said cheerfully. "We'll have our own group in a few weeks. It'll be more interesting, and more useful, too. Not to mention...more scientific."

Adler left him and went back into the meeting room. Furtmüller paced the hallway until Adler joined him a few minutes later.

"It's done," Adler said almost joyously. "Now we can live."

"I'm sorry it came to this," Furtmüller said quietly as they put on their overcoats.

Adler shook his head. "Don't feel sad. I agree with the Fledermaus. Remember?" On the way down the stairs Adler sang the aria from Strauss' famous operetta:

> Glücklich ist
> Wer vergisst
> Was doch nicht zu ändern ist.
> ("Happy are
> Those who forget
> Whatever can't be changed.")

Outside it was snowing. They hailed a cab and drove to the Café Siller.

Notes

This meeting of the Vienna Psychoanalytic Society actually occurred. In fact, there were four climactic meetings in January and February of 1911 during which Adler presented his position. The circumstances of those meetings were those I have sketched. At the end of the meeting on February 22nd Adler resigned from the Society's presidency. The individuals mentioned in this encounter attended at least one of the four meetings. Furtmüller and Stekel were especially close to Adler, and I imagine that they probably went out to dinner before the meeting.

Since Adler liked to sing and was fond of Viennese operettas, the encounter's ending is quite in his character.

I have relied primarily on three books: *The Individual Psychology of Alfred Adler,* edited by Heinz L. Ansbacher and Rowena R. Ansbacher (New York: Harper & Row, 1964); *Alfred Adler: the Man and His Work,* by Hertha Orgler (London: Sidgwick & Jackson, 1973); and Adler's own *Social Interest: A Challenge to Mankind* (New York: G. P. Putnam's sons, 1964).

A fascinating glimpse into the workings of the Society is provided by the book *Minutes of the Vienna Psychoanalytic Society,* edited by Herman Nunberg and Ernst Federn (New York: International Universities Press, 1974). Volume 3 contains the reports of meetings during 1910 and 1911, including those of January 4th, February 1st, 8th, and 22nd, 1911. I have combined the discussions of the last three meetings into one. The statements I ascribe to the participants in the meeting of February 22nd reflect their general positions, although these were not necessarily expressed on that evening. The less than polite exchanges illustrate the heated debates that shine through the Minutes.

6

CARL GUSTAV JUNG
Eranos in Ascona, 1934

The second defection from Freud's grand theory occurred barely a year after the first. Again there were irreconcilable positions based largely on differences in data, their interpretation, and practical implications. Freud, Adler, and Jung considered themselves scientists, objective investigators who relied on empirical data. But many of their concepts were amorphous and could not be measured, and many of their hypotheses were too vague to be tested. Hence it was very difficult and almost impossible to tell whose ideas reflected reality.

Carl Gustav Jung was born on July 26, 1875 in a Swiss village on the shores of Lake Constance. He grew up in Laufen, and later in Klein-Huningen near Basel, small villages in which his father served as pastor. His childhood was solitary until a sister was born when he was nine. Even during his school years, which were not altogether happy, he preferred to be alone and was much given to brooding. During his late teens he had many disheartening talks about religion with his father; they did not understand each other.

In 1895 he entered the University of Basel as a medical student. In spite of the poverty that followed his father's death, he enjoyed his university years and made quite a few friends. Jung received his medical degree in the summer of 1900 and in the Fall became assistant staff physician at the Burghölzli Mental Hospital near Zürich.

There he worked hard and spent many hours reading books and journals in the new field of psychiatry, for he wanted to *understand* mental illness (especially schizophrenia) and not simply cure patients. Soon after his arrival he began a long series of experiments on verbal associations, using the latest laboratory equipment. Patients (as well as suspected criminals) were given words to which they had to respond. Jung noted the words a person associated with the stimulus word, the time required for the response, and the intervening behaviors. From the individual's reactions Jung deduced the nature and sources of neurotic symptoms (later called complexes) and, in the case of criminals, some aspects of their transgressions. These empirical studies brought Jung considerable attention, especially in the United States.

At the same time, however, Jung was greatly impressed by Freud's seminal book, *The Interpretation of Dreams*. In 1906 he sent Freud a copy of his own book *The Psychology of Dementia Praecox* (an illness now called schizophrenia). Within a short time their correspondence grew into a friendship that lasted half a decade. Jung was greatly impressed by psychoanalysis and Freud's contributions to knowledge about human nature; both their visits to each other and their letters were filled with discussions of theoretical and procedural aspects of psychoanalysis. Freud, in turn, saw Jung as the first major non-Viennese and non-Jewish follower and indeed as his successor. Freud thought more highly of Jung than of his Viennese colleagues, arranged his election as president of the International Psychoanalytic Association, and appointed him editor of its journal. But by the Fall of 1909, when Jung and Freud travelled together to the United States to give lectures at Clark University and receive honorary degrees there, some mutual disenchantment had occurred. Eventually their different conceptions and approaches became obvious even to them, and by the Fall of 1912 their estrangement was complete.

Jung, for example, defined psychic energy (libido) quite broadly and included creative and other positive forces within it, while Freud held a much narrower sexual conception. Freud took the Oedipus situation, incestuous wishes, and sexual images quite literally, while Jung considered these as rather symbolic and believed that they often mean something very different.

By November 1912 Jung and Freud were openly writing about their contrasting views; a month later their correspondence was quite acrimonious, and in January 1913 their letters and personal relations ceased. The complex intellectual and emotional roots of the break—and of the friendship itself—have been discussed many times and need not concern us here. Suffice it to say that afterwards Freud hardly ever mentioned Jung again, while Jung retained a general respect for Freud and continued to acknowledge his contributions.

During the ten years following his break with Freud, Jung wrote two major books; one on changes of the libido (which defined his major differences with Freud), and one on personality (*Psychological Types*). He also wrote many essays and articles, gave lectures in several countries including the United States, and gradually established his own school—which he called analytical psychology. He lived with his wife and children in a spacious house in Küsnacht, now a suburb of Zürich, where he saw a large number of patients and students. Over the decades he gave several courses at the University of Zürich, at the Federal Polytechnic Institute, and especially at the Psychological Club (which became the center of Jungian psychology). Many of his seminars were given in English, for a growing number of foreigners came to study with him.

Over a period of more than sixty years, Jung wrote—and frequently revised—almost a dozen major books. He also contributed a large number of essays and articles to magazines and newspapers directed to an audience of educated general readers. Altogether, his writings fill eighteen volumes of *Collected Works*. His conception of human nature developed over many years, but he never set down a comprehensive and clearly stated system. Thus it is much more difficult to gain an understanding of his ideas than it is to comprehend Freud's theory. Further difficulties arise because his views matured over time and were expressed differently and in various places. Jung saw no serious problem here because he viewed himself as on a journey of discovery, where precise statements and a complete theory are not possible until the end— which is not yet in sight.

The metaphorical nature of his basic conceptions and his amorphous hypotheses have made it difficult to assess his contributions to our knowledge of human nature. This is especially true of his major books, which are always erudite and sometimes unclear. His essays and articles, on the other hand, are well written and provide fascinating insights into contemporary social and psychological topics. When one reads Jung's short pieces one cannot help but be impressed by his learning and grand conception of human nature. It is only when one goes deeper and discovers inconsistencies in concepts and propositions that one begins to wonder. Yet it is quite possible that these problems of coherence and composition reflect the multivariate character and great complexity of human nature and its expressions in daily life.

BASIC HUMAN CHARACTERISTICS

Jung was careful to distinguish overt actions from internal processes and devoted many years to the analysis of their relationship. The first steps on this inward journey today are commonly recognized as part of basic social psychology—although the modern labels differ, of course.

The individuals we meet in daily life play various roles in particular settings. People behave differently in various situations, they say different things and may even appear to be different persons altogether. Jung called the outward appearance, the public image we try so hard to establish and maintain, our *persona*, after the Greek word for the mask that actors wore on the stage to indicate the character they portrayed.

In order to know the "real" person, one has to go behind the persona. This may be difficult if individuals have come to identify so closely with their persona that they live their lives through it—as does the sales manager who sees everyone as a consumer. A balanced life, however, requires that we have an effective persona, recognize it as such, and can "take it off" to be ourselves. To some extent we all try to impress others, of course, and we often do what is expected rather than what we want to do. Most of us can differentiate between the public and the real self and know the limitations of each; but if we do not—then we must labor to change our ways or seek help. Sooner or later we must live with our real self.

Behind the persona there exists what we now would call the individual's basic personality. Jung explained many behaviors and feelings by postulating two major personality types based on a person's fundamental orientation (sometimes called attitudes). The two labels have become part of everyday language: *extraverts* prefer to interact with others and like to manipulate the external world: their basic orientation is toward people, events, and things in the outer world. *Introverts* prefer to be on their own and are interested in the inner world: their basic orientation is toward their own inner life. We must be careful not to conclude anything about egoism and altruism: the extravert can be either an egoist or an altruist, as can the introvert. The differences Jung delineated have some implications for behavior, general life-style, and the ease (and difficulty) with which one learns various skills and ideas.

Less accepted today is Jung's division of major psychological processes into two sets of opposites: sensation—intuition, and thought—feeling. Sensation tells us that something exists, while intuition tells us where it comes from and where it is going. Thinking tells us just what exists, while feeling tells us how valuable or agreeable it is.

In most people, one of these processes dominates while its opposite is neglected or poorly developed. When the four major functions are combined with the two major orientations, we have eight basic personality types. The orientations tell us what a person is most interested in, while the dominant function indicates what the major problems are likely to be, (which reflect the less developed or inferior function).

For example, introverted-intuitive persons (typically artists) are often unusually creative but they are frequently out of touch with external reality and have difficulty getting along with others because the opposite pole of intuition, namely sensation, is frequently neglected. Scientists are typically extraverted-thinking types of people who emphasize reality but often seem rather cold and impersonal because feeling, at the opposite pole of thinking, is often neglected. For psychological well-being—which Jung saw as balance and the harmonious working of opposites—one should work hard to develop one's neglected functions.

To Jung, however, personality is not as important as *psyche*, the human being's dynamic inner structure. In the original German he frequently used the word "Seele," which is usually translated as "soul." When Jung spoke of "Seele," however, he meant primarily the complex system of internal elements and processes. The most significant component of these is the unconscious, which consists of two parts. One is the *personal unconscious*, which contains forgotten and repressed thoughts, feelings, and experiences much as described by Freud. It also contains *complexes*—emotionally charged perceptions, thoughts, and feelings centering on various experiences, which crop up periodically and affect many of our actions.

For example, if my childhood relations with my father have been normal, all is well. But if we have disagreed and fought since my earliest memories, I am likely to develop a "father complex" which will attract to it—and color—all kinds of other thoughts and experiences. In an extreme form, I may not be able to stand older men, or may resent any suggestions from older people, or rebel against any form of authority.

Jung postulated that underneath the personal unconscious there lies the *collective unconscious*, by far the larger and more powerful component. This controversial idea developed when he noticed that some of his patients and other people he met had dreams which contained elements found in primitive cultures, ancient myths, and the esoteric writings of medieval philosophers. He explained the similarity of images and symbols in different cultures and historical epochs as manifestations of the unconscious which humans share by virtue of their human character and common genetic structure. The collective unconscious contains not only the animal features of humans but also the sources of creative energies, all that is good, bad, and unique to the human race and any one member of it.

The collective unconscious consists primarily of archetypes, the primordial images of common events, experiences, and beings which reflect the essence of human existence. There are hundreds of archetypes, including the "wise old man," the "mother" and the "eternal youth," and each affects our behaviour in some way.

Throughout his work, Jung paid much attention to symbols as they appear in myths, paintings, dreams, religions and daily life. Symbols are important because they represent attempts to satisfy instinctual needs. He postulated that symbols transform instinctual energy into various objective forms ranging from artistic endeavors to the mundane activities of daily life. Indeed, symbols are the objective manifestations of archetypes, which can express themselves only through symbols. While these are intriguing ideas, there are as yet few empirical data to support them.

The collective unconscious also contains our notions—of which we may be only dimly aware—regarding members of the opposite sex. The idea of what women are like (in the view of a man) is his *anima*, and a woman's notion of what men are like is her *animus*. These notions (sometimes called archetypes) exist at birth, and when we meet individuals of the opposite sex we behave toward them not only according to what we know about them as persons but also in terms of our animus or anima.

For example, the kind of spouse we seek often is influenced by our animus or anima; but since these ideas do not reflect living creatures, no actual person can possibly measure up to our expectations. Men project their anima onto women and see things that are not there. Women do the same thing. In the extreme case we may spend our lives looking for the "right" mate, and in the tragic case we may marry the person who seems to come close to our animus or anima and then discover that the individual does not correspond to our notion at all.

Jung believed that men and women have elements of both sexes within them and must come to terms with that fact. Men often have difficulty recognizing their feminine aspects and women their masculine aspects. Jung always considered women and men equal: they have different characteristics, but each totality of elements is equal to the other in value, worthiness, potential, and significance of expression. This is probably the major reason why in the early years most of Jung's important students and followers were women, while most of Freud's were men.

Jung described two important processes which have been employed by others since—usually without acknowledging the source. The first process is *individuation*, by which the amorphous totality of the infant breaks into several major parts that grow and develop over the years. As individuals begin to think and feel, become aware of sensations and intuition, and gradually learn what their good and bad qualities are, they come to understand the contradictions and conflicts among opposites within them. One becomes aware of previously unconscious elements and begins to "work things out" by accepting and modifying these elements so that one can live with them.

For example, we should strive to bring the basic mental processes— thinking and feeling, sensation and intuition—into harmony so that none will be neglected or overemphasized. If we are very good in thinking but have trouble feeling, for instance, we should make special efforts to develop our capacity to feel. We must learn "to let go" so that we can express ourselves—yet we must be tied to our context well enough to lead a normal life (by keeping negative or anti-social impulses in check so that they won't become destructive).

This working-out of internal conflicts and this development of previously neglected functions requires years of hard work. Many people gradually accomplish this labor on their own, while others need assistance—from friends or relatives, spouse or therapist, philosophy or religion.

The second process Jung postulated is the need for wholeness, for the development of self and all of one's potentialities. He differs from some later writers in that he recognized that such a goal is not reached naturally and easily. Hard work is required to develop one's neglected functions, and it is by no means easy to bring conflicting feelings into harmony or to see people as they really are rather than as projections of one's anima (or animus). Indeed, very few people reach the goal of perfect wholeness, and Jung was aware throughout his life that he himself had a long way to go.

An Eranos Conference

On the idyllic Ticino shore of Lake Maggiore in southern Switzerland, the hamlet of Moscia climbs the hills above the winding road from Ascona to Puerto Ronco. There, Mrs. Olga Fröbe-Kapteyn had constructed a lecture hall in the gardens of her modest villa, Casa Gabriella. The buildings with their red tile roofs and whitewashed walls shimmer through the luscious vegetation of the steep hill side, halfway between the narrow beach and the road. Their verandas afford magnificent views of the lake and the wooded hills on the farther shore. Beginning in 1928, Mrs. Fröbe organized theosophical lectures there which attracted visitors during the summer months.

In early 1933, Mrs. Fröbe persuaded Jung to invite several of his students and friends to a series of lectures she was planning that summer on various topics of Eastern philosophy and analytical psychology. The name given to these new annual conferences has become famous: Eranos, signifying in ancient Greece a banquet to which each participant is expected to bring some intellectual gift worthy of the invitation.

The first Eranos conference was held in late August and consisted of fifteen lectures on yoga and meditation. Half a dozen distinguished experts on Eastern religion and philosophy made the conference a great success. Jung spoke on the individuation process and was so pleased with the intellectual atmosphere that he agreed to return the following summer—and indeed he participated every year until 1951. Throughout the decades, Jung's students, friends, and other visitors provided an appreciative audience for scholars from all over Europe whose talks soon ranged beyond the communion of East and West.

After the morning lecture, the speaker and a few other guests assembled on the terrace overlooking Lake Maggiore to lunch at a large round table. In the afternoon, there would be another lecture, swimming and sailing, or excursions through the countryside. The major participants usually stayed at the Monte Verità Hotel on the hill above Ascona, made available through the generosity of its owner, the Baron von der Heydt, a Dutch banker who was also an art collector.

The success of the first conference led to the planning of another for the following August. A dozen scholars were invited to discuss symbolism and the spiritual life in East and West, while Jung spoke about archetypes and the collective unconscious. In the following years, the annual themes varied; they came to focus more on subjects related to analytical psychology and less on the encounter of East and West. Jung enjoyed the company of scholars from diverse fields; in conversations at midday on the terrace or in the evening in the candle-lit rooms of Casa Gabriella, he learned from them and clarified his own ideas.

The lectures were given in German, English, or French, and were published in annual "Eranos Yearbooks" edited by Mrs. Fröbe. Some of the more significant contributions have appeared in several volumes of "Papers from the Eranos Yearbooks."

Ψ

On a bright morning in late August 1934 Jung spoke to a large audience of visitors and friends on "archetypes of the collective unconscious." After the lecture, about a dozen Eranos participants and guests walked slowly from the hall to the terrace of Casa Gabriella. A gentle breeze rustled through the leaves, and birds sang in the trees that veiled the sun-drenched hillside and embraced the verandas.

Barbara Hannah, who had been studying with Jung for several years, paused repeatedly to marvel at the view. "The perfect setting for a psychological conference," she exulted to her companion, an older lady who had helped Jung with his work for many years and now was president of the Psychological Club in Zürich. "The wisdom of professor Jung—it almost makes me forget the theosophical paintings in the hallway."

Toni Wolff smiled. "Those will be gone in a couple of years. Remember, this is only the second year of Eranos. How lucky that Jung and Mrs. Fröbe arranged these conferences. Where would we be without her generosity and help?"

Hannah nodded. "Luck indeed—or perhaps it was fate. One never knows about such things. Just as I simply *had* to leave England and visit Zürich."

"It has been a long visit—and it'll become longer, won't it?" Wolff smiled. "And speaking of visits, how do you like the hotel? Isn't it marvelous? We are being spoiled."

Hannah agreed. "I've never seen so many paintings and excellent ones at that—in one place outside a museum. And they are hung in guest rooms! These nights have been like sleeping in a picture gallery."

"Too bad so few people see the paintings," said Sigrid Strauss-Kloebe, an analyst from Munich who had come up behind them. "Just the guests during the season, and no one when the hotel is locked up the other months."

Wolff shrugged her delicate shoulders. "Most museums have more paintings than they can exhibit. And when the baron gives his paintings to a museum some day—I'd guess in Holland—I bet most of them will be stored in some attic."

"You are too realistic for me," Hannah laughed.

"Just the wisdom of middle age," Wolff said with a smile. "And that wisdom tells me we should hurry and not let the others wait."

"Right you are," Strauss agreed. "Professor Jung must be starved. He doesn't like the meals at the hotel."

"The food they buy is good," Hannah said, "but the cooking is mediocre—or so people say. As for me, food isn't all that important."

"A good attitude," Strauss nodded. "It saves one from a lot of grief—especially when one travels." The women walked quickly.

"Here we are," said Wolff and stepped onto the terrace shaded by great cedar trees. She greeted the nearby guests and continued: "We just couldn't tear ourselves away from the view."

"It *is* a beautiful spot," Jung agreed and smiled. He rose from the low wall surrounding the terrace, where he had been in amiable discussion with several guests. "But you can see the lake from here, too," and he pointed through the lattice of branches.

"Lunch is ready," Mrs. Fröbe called out in her gentle voice. "Please, sit wherever you wish."

Her guests took seats around a large round wooden table set for fifteen and loaded with bread, cold meats, and salad. Two maids brought bowls of soup.

Ernesto Buonaiuti, professor of history at the University of Rome, stood up and began to serve wine to the guests. He saw a look of consternation cross Mrs. Fröbe's face, and joked: "I'm the perfect wine steward. I've always loved to give pleasure to people. And since Mussolini fired me, I *have* been looking for a job." Everyone joined in his laughter, and several guests praised the wine when Buonaiuti mentioned the year.

"A present from the baron," said Mrs. Fröbe. "He sent over a couple of cases a few days ago. With a note 'a minor gift for a major conference.'"

"How nice of him," said Emma Jung. "Thoughtful as always." When the glasses were filled, Carl Jung proposed a toast: "To our generous hostess." Mrs. Fröbe blushed, for she was a very private person who did not like attention.

The guests ate in silence and enjoyed the rustle of leaves and the song of birds in the trees around the terrace. Sunlight and swaying branches formed dancing silhouettes on the table, plates, and food. After a few minutes, Jung said: "A good meal as always, Mrs. Fröbe. I don't mind talking for two hours or more, but afterwards the speaker does deserve a reward—such as this. Thank you so much for your hospitality."

Mrs. Fröbe smiled and lowered her eyes. She still was not quite used to the Zürich psychologists and their friends from all parts of Europe.

"I don't mind listening for a couple of hours, either," said Heinrich Zimmer, the famous expert on India from the University of Heidelberg. "As long as the speaker has something to say. Like you." He nodded toward Jung, who raised his glass and smiled across the table.

"When I hear you talk about archetypes they make such good sense," the physician Gustav Heyer said. "And I can't imagine why anyone would doubt the existence of the collective unconscious—or its influence on the individual. Yet, many of my friends in Munich think I'm a bit crazy when I talk about such things."

Jung laughed heartily. "As long as they don't think that you are completely crazy, you need not worry. What do you think is the problem?"

"Some people find the hypothesis of a collective unconscious quite outrageous," Heyer replied. "It doesn't seem possible that there can be something underneath the personal unconscious. They find it hard to believe. Of course, even today some people consider Freud's theory of the unconscious equally outrageous."

"For some people, the implications are not very comforting, either," added Carl von Cammerloher, an analyst from Vienna. "The idea that there is something ancient and universal in us—that modern individuals have archaic-elements in their souls—is perhaps a bit frightening."

"Yes, that's a good point," Heyer agreed. "It is difficult enough to accept the fact that a fetus repeats the stages of human evolution. But at least as an adult you are far beyond those stages..."

"And need not worry about looking and behaving like a fish," Buonaiuti chuckled.

Heyer smiled and nodded. "But now you are confronted by the possibility that an ancient heritage is still within you and might surface at any moment."

Jung sighed. "Yes, even after all these years there are problems—and they will remain." He shook his head: "I know what you mean. Here in Switzerland many people don't understand what I'm up to, either. And yet, as I said this morning, it is an empirical fact that the same psychological material exists in the myths of all cultures and in the dreams of modern people, and in the delusions of some patients. The best way to account for these identical images is to postulate a collective unconscious. There's no other good explanation."

"As far as I can tell, the problem is not so much the facts you mentioned," interjected Rudolf Bernoulli, "but the explanation that ties them all together."

"But would people rather say—'well, I don't know why the images and events of myths appear in modern people'? I doubt it," said Buonaiuti.

"I agree," Mrs. Strauss nodded. "Modern people don't like mysteries..."

"Well now," Jung loudly interrupted her. "I doubt *that!*"

Mrs. Strauss blushed slightly and continued: "I meant that modern people don't like to be left groping for answers. Today, people like to have questions and answers wrapped up in tidy little packages. Archetypes don't fit the bill."

Jung nodded. "The problem is that...simply talking about an archetype, say the 'wise old man,' is a pale substitute for experiencing it. Archetypes, after all, come to life only when we patiently try to discover why and in what fashion they are meaningful to us."

"But it seems to me..." Buonaiuti began and hesitated. Jung turned to him and smiled encouragement.

"It seems to me," Buonaiuti repeated, "that the notion of 'collective unconscious' does provide a tidy explanation for the fact that widely different people experience similar images."

"Except that the hypothesis is so difficult to test," Bernoulli cautioned. "My colleagues at the Federal Polytechnic always want proof. Statistical proof. Experimental proof. And I think people outside the universities want the same thing—though to a lesser degree, perhaps."

"But university people and scientists with their materialistic orientation use working hypotheses, don't they?" asked Cammerloher. "And this particular working hypothesis—if you want to call it that—is reasonable. It makes a lot of sense, and it works."

"That's precisely the point," Heyer said. "I talk about archetype and the collective unconscious in my practice all the time. My patients understand quite readily, and they benefit."

"Proof exists in the eyes of the believer," Jung continued. "I have discovered certain empirical facts...among them the existence of archetypes and the collective unconscious...but I cannot afford the time to convince others. I talk about these facts and their human significance, but I can't spend years looking for the kind of proof everyone will accept."

After a pause, Jung continued: "All those personal things like incestuous tendencies and other childish tunes are mere surface phenomena. What the unconscious really contains are the great collective events of all time. In the collective unconscious of the individual we see past history—and tomorrow's events are prepared. When the archetypes are activated in a large number of individuals and come to the surface, as we see in Europe today, we are in the midst of history—the making of great events. I saw this in 1914 and I see it again today..."

After a while Wolff said: "All one can do is talk about these facts of the human psyche and hope the words will sink in. Professor Jung will do just that in his lectures at the Polytechnic this coming semester."

Jung nodded and smiled at her. "And then there are some people in England who want me to come next year. If I go, I'll use the lectures at the Tavistok Institute to present the same materials. I think the British are more open-minded than many people on the continent."

"Just as Freud's ideas were at least discussed by people in England long before they were accepted in Austria," interjected Friedrich Heller, a professor from the University of Marburg.

"But there's no comparison," cried Erwin Rouselle, director of the China Institute at the University of Frankfurt. "Freud's ideas are nothing compared to Professor Jung's contributions."

"We must give Freud his due," Jung said and raised his hand as if to quiet an audience. "He is a great man who taught us much. And what is more, a man in the grip of his daimon. His ideas are revolutionary, and he has made significant contributions. We would still be in the jungle without him." He hesitated and then said with an impish smile: "Freudians, of course, are a different matter."

"To get back to the main point," Zimmer said, "as you were talking this morning I thought back to my experiences in India and other places. The postulate of primordial images that are common to all people and to members of a race and culture, and the idea that these archetypes of events and situations make up an individual's collective unconscious—all that appeals to me. Because it shows that there is a common humanity in all of us." And after a few seconds he continued, "I like the idea that there is a bond among human beings—a spiritual identity, if you will, besides the obvious physiological similarities."

"But surely it's not simply a matter of your 'liking' an idea or proposition?" Jung asked with some concern. "What does one's 'liking' have to do with empirical facts?"

"Well," Zimmer answered after a few moments. "Facts and theories are greatly influenced by our emotional reactions to them, don't you think? If I like a fact—let's say I have experienced it myself, or it appeals to me for some reason—then I'm going to approach an explanation, or hypothesis about it, quite positively."

"True enough," Jung nodded.

"But if I don't like a fact, let's say because it conflicts with some of my pet ideas, then I'll be negative, and perhaps even antagonistic toward a hypothesis about it. Unless, of course, the explanation eliminates the fact."

"And so...?" Wilhelm Hauer asked eagerly. "Don't stop there."

"Well, my conclusion is that you can't separate the fact of archetype from people's feelings about that fact and people's theories about that fact—or even its existence."

Several members of the roundtable nodded in agreement, and Rouselle said: "I haven't heard anyone make disparaging remarks about psychological types. Indeed, it seems to me that Professor Jung's two major character types have entered everyday language—the introvert and the extravert are walking around Europe. If you are right, Professor Zimmer, one would conclude that these ideas have been accepted because they are emotionally neutral—or at least are considered much less outrageous than the proposition of archetype and collective unconscious."

Zimmer nodded and was about to speak when Jung said: "You may be right, Professor Zimmer. But there is another factor, the symbol. So much of the content of the collective unconscious is expressed in symbolic form, as in dreams, myths, paintings, and so on. One of modern man's problems is his rationalism, which leads to a separation of life and symbol. When one doesn't understand symbols, when one can't even recognize them, one can't get a clear idea of where they come from, what they are, what they mean. And then one is at the mercy of the psychological underworld, isolated from the cosmos…" He paused a moment and turned to Rouselle. "On the other hand, psychological types, and especially introvert and extravert, have no symbolic contents. They don't have much to do with symbols."

"Modern man, and I think especially Europeans and Americans, are too steeped in the sensory world to appreciate symbols," Heyer suggested.

"You're probably correct," Jung said. "But what a sad comment on our civilization. Symbols and images are the means by which sense impressions are transformed into spiritual experience; they are the language of the unconscious through which we can catch a glimpse of the universe and of the powers within us. So you see that we need both: sensory impressions and symbols."

"Yes, one can see the disintegration of symbols everywhere," Heller agreed. "Even the madonna is losing some of her symbolic power…As I will show you all tomorrow morning, the madonna isn't what she used to be…"

Jung politely interrupted; "Here we have another problem, though, which won't be solved until the pope proclaims the dogma of the Ascension of the Blessed Virgin. The feminine element in all of us must be recognized." He paused and continued after a few moments, "The feminine principle—nature or matter—must be equal to the masculine principle—spirit. And this equality must be metaphysically anchored in the figure of a 'divine woman.'"

"But, who is not a goddess in the Greek sense," Heller added.

"You're right," Jung nodded. "Such a dogma would bring a modern tone to the symbol, a new relevance for the modern individual."

"Astrological symbols are in the same difficulty," Strauss suggested. "As I said a couple of days ago, people take to astrology without knowledge about the basic symbols. They have no feeling for them. It's just an intellectual interest and a desire for certainty in an uncertain world."

"Which means, basically, no commitment at all, don't you think?" Cammerloher asked.

Strauss nodded, and Jung emphatically agreed.

"That's why I am looking at symbols in other places and times," Jung continued. "If my ideas about archetypes, are correct, then I should find primordial images—of typical human events, and expressing typical human needs—just about anywhere. And now I think I have discovered a fertile new area, an area full of symbols, where archetypes and their symbolic representations are beautifully evident."

"How interesting," Zimmer exclaimed, "What's the area?"

"Alchemy," Jung said enthusiastically. "In the work of alchemists I've seen the same phenomena I observed in myths and in modern people. It's quite extraordinary...Or perhaps not. Anyway, I'm just starting my investigations. So far I've read only two or three books, but they are fascinating. When I have some definite ideas, and when I have some interesting facts, I'll present them to you. Perhaps here at the Casa Eranos...If Mrs. Fröbe invites us."

Mrs. Fröbe smiled. "Of course, Professor Jung," she said happily. "The meeting of East and West, the discovery of symbols, all this work requires years. And to live well, in terms of our psychic needs—that's the task of a lifetime... For that we need analytical psychology. So we'll need many more meetings here."

"Well said," Jung cried. "A toast to the future. May the next Eranos meeting be as stimulating and fascinating as this one."

"As a student and lover of India I'm all in favor of these conferences about my pet subject," Zimmer said and filled his glass. "But I do think we might expand the agenda in the future."

"I agree," said Rouselle. "China is my specialty, but I have to admit that there are other continents—just a few."

Mrs. Fröbe joined in the general mirth and looked at Jung: "We've already discussed some possibilities. We'll just see what comes along."

"I quite agree with you," Jung said. "There are many other interesting topics and some other pressing issues. For example, I do believe..." he hesitated for a moment and leaned toward Zimmer and Rouselle. "I do believe that westerners cannot solve their own psychological problems by going East. The East is too different. When we try to find solutions to our personal problems, or look for answers to personal questions, Eastern religion and Eastern philosophy are nothing more than a form of avoiding responsibility. A fruitless attempt that's bound to fail. I have the greatest respect for the wisdom of India and China, but I don't think a European can live by it. Their wisdom helps us understand that the opposites within us are equal and must be accepted to achieve equilibrium and harmony—as we see, for example, in mandalas. When we in the West suppress one pole and reject the opposite pole, or do not even recognize it, then our psyche is in danger. It sickens—as it has in Europe today. But it makes no sense, at least not to me, to avoid the creative tensions that arise from opposites within us—by sailing to China or flying off into nirvana."

"Well said," Zimmer agreed. "One can learn from Indian philosophy and religion, but there is little sense in westerners accepting all or even most of those precepts." Rouselle nodded, although he seemed reluctant.

"And the East can't benefit all that much from our philosophy and religion?" Buonaiuti asked.

Zimmer nodded, and Jung agreed: "Just think of our missionaries and their failures."

"Do you mean that we have enough symbols and energy in our culture?" Heyer asked and turned to Jung.

"Of course," Jung replied. "It's just that we have forgotten how to work with them, to understand them. For many years now I have thought about the relationship between the symbolism of the unconscious and Christianity, for instance. I am convinced that we must leave the door open for the Christian message...and indeed I consider it of central importance for us. However, that message needs to be seen in a new light, in accordance with the changed conditions of life today. Otherwise it stands apart from the times and has no effect on the individual's wholeness."

"Which would be tragic," Hauer said. "After all, when a person does not keep going on the path toward individuation, toward wholeness, the psyche sickens."

Jung nodded, and Heyer added, "Indeed, as you mentioned last year, neuroses are often the results of losing one's way."

"Yes, unfortunately," Jung said. "But then we can use therapy to help individuals bring their opposites into harmony, help them back on the road toward developing their potentialities. The actual work of growth, however, must be done by the individual. People must use the tools that are most appropriate for them and for their culture and time. For us, that means, for the most part, western symbols and western ideas, along with universal symbols such as the mandala. I don't mean to downgrade the East, by any means, but I think—indeed, I am sure—that for western people western tools are most appropriate. Only they can be really effective."

After a few seconds, Rouselle added: "when we know something about the Eastern way, if I may use that phrase, we'll have a better understanding of our own, western way."

"After all, there are innumerable variations of the road to psychological well-being," Fröbe interjected.

Jung nodded. "We all know that individuation is a personal journey. But while it is an internal and subjective process of integration, it also has social aspects." He paused a few seconds and lit his pipe. Then he continued, "The unrelated human being lacks wholeness, for one can achieve wholeness only through the soul—and that cannot live without some relationships with other people."

"What about the hermit or the holy man in a cave?" Hauer asked.

"Well," Jung replied slowly. "I would want to find out from him how far he has progressed on the path to individuation. I would be surprised if he has gone far."

"Some don't talk to anyone, and haven't for years," Hannah interjected.

"True enough," Jung replied. "An excellent way to avoid facing others—and perhaps even oneself. But we see a similar kind of avoidance—of responsibility to ourselves, I would say—in some modern people. Individuals who wander from one philosophy to another, from culture to culture, always looking for external answers to their questions, for external solutions to their problems. They strike me as rather pathetic creatures. Like lost children who believe in miracles for which they do not have to work. But they don't know why they are lost..."

"...And often don't know they are still children," Zimmer added.

"There are no miracles when it comes to the human psyche," Jung concluded. "Only hard work. For years. We therapists can guide and help. But the work must be done by the individual. Hard work."

"I wonder why people continue to look for miraculous answers and solutions," Heyer mused. "Some of my patients have spent years looking for miracles."

"People who ask me for horoscopes also seek miracles," Strauss added. "They still believe that stars are guides."

"I think it's a form of laziness," Bernoulli suggested after some hesitation. "Spending a year looking for miracles is just an excuse for being spiritually lazy—for twelve long months."

Jung joined the others in laughter. "A capital idea," he shouted happily. After several moments of general joviality, he continued, "Actually, there may be quite some truth to your point...But I think that fear is another factor. The fear to look inside oneself and at one's life. It's easier to look when one has ties to other people and to the real world—as I did after the War, thanks to my wife." He smiled at her, a few chairs away.

"I've been thinking, Professor Jung," Zimmer broke the silence. "Your study of alchemy makes sense to me. But most people will not see that alchemy is only a source of data for you. They may well accuse you of being a modern-day alchemist. And your enemies will encourage that view. I see a danger here. Some people already call you a mystic—just because you study myths and symbols."

Jung laughed. "Yes, I have been accused of being a mystic because I study myths—again, simply as a source of data."

"Perhaps my husband will soon be accused of being an architect," Emma Jung added. "Just because he is building a tower at Bollingen."

"Or a captain because he likes to sail on Lake Zürich," Toni Wolff said and joined in the laughter.

"You must admit that alchemy and myths are rather—shall we say, unconventional—sources of information about human beings," Bernoulli said.

"But today there are so few others," Toni Wolff replied defensively. "Perhaps in the future..." her voice trailed off.

"Yes, who knows what methods might be used in the future," Jung reflected. "The study of the psyche is still in its infancy."

"And we don't know to what extent physiological factors operate," Heyer interjected.

"Right," Jung nodded emphatically. "Schizophrenia, for instance. I've always suspected a physiological, perhaps even a biochemical basis for that disease. Since I studied it first some thirty years ago, I've been amazed at its resistance to psychological treatment. So, I accept the fact of schizophrenia and let other people discover the causes. There are enough neuroses to keep us busy for centuries."

"Just as you accept the fact of religion and of dreams," Heller added.

"I have always thought that Freud was rather pathetic in his view that religion is an illusion without a future and that dreams are mainly repressed wishes," Heyer said.

"Well, at least very narrow," Jung replied. "The dream is a normal and natural phenomenon. A dream does not mean something it doesn't contain. Confusion arises largely because a dream's content is symbolic and may have several meanings. Freud never realized that." He shook his head. "Freud is too much of a 19th century scientist, he is too rational."

"Do you think you might be accused of being too religious?" Heller asked, and then he added, laughing, "along with being a mystic, alchemist, and so on?"

Jung shrugged his shoulders and smiled. "It doesn't matter what others think. I *know* that God exists—it's not just a matter of belief with me. And religion? Today, as always, people need the general ideas and convictions that give meaning to their lives and enable them to find a place for themselves in the universe."

Jung leaned back in his chair and looked out over the lake. Then he relit his pipe and continued, "Human beings can stand the most incredible hardships when they are convinced that they make sense. But people are crushed when they have to admit that on top of all their misfortunes—

they are taking part only in a 'tale told by an idiot.' Religious symbols give individuals and their lives sense and meaning."

"And so one would expect fewer Catholics among neurotic patients?" Hauer asked.

"That's precisely what I find," Jung answered. "Most of my patients over the years have been Protestants and Jews. I've seen very few practicing Catholics."

"When patients want to go back to their religion, even when it's early in the therapy, what do you do?" Zimmer asked.

"When I am certain that their religious convictions are returning—and when I'm sure that they aren't looking for an excuse to escape from analysis—I encourage them to return to their religion. Afterwards, they are usually much better off. Let's face it, most religions are good therapies, and Jesus was a great healer." After a moment, Jung added with a twinkle in his eye, "Perhaps the greatest therapist—we are just amateurs by comparison."

"Such facts—like the need for roots and for religion—by themselves are mysterious and uncomfortable. They cry out for explanations, for ways of dealing with these problems," Cammerloher said.

"Or at least people imagine that they hear those cries," Hauer suggested lightly.

Cammerloher nodded. "Yes, and the more important the facts, the stronger the desire to explain them."

"But first we must be certain—absolutely certain what the facts are," Bernoulli said.

"That's why I'm interested in facts and not so much in theories," Jung added. "I'm fascinated by the empirical facts of archetypes, and by the empirical manifestations of the collective unconscious...And therefore," he continued after a pause, "I may never set down a systematic and detailed theory...I'll be proud of that incomplete work because it isn't really a matter of neglect."

"Is that why you have used different therapeutic procedures besides your own?" Zimmer asked.

Jung nodded. "People are always amazed when I tell them that I have treated some patients in the Freudian fashion, and I have worked with others using Adler's way, depending on the character of their neuroses. Freud's way and Adler's way are as useful as mine—the nature of the illness determines which method I use. Sometimes I just tell a patient to go out into the real world and try to make a go of it."

"But isn't that rather cold-hearted?" Zimmer asked.

"I only do it in certain cases, after I come to the conclusion that nothing else would be as effective," replied Jung.

"Could you give us an example?" Hauer asked.

"Well, let's see," Jung answered after a moment. "Yes...An American lady came to see me—oh, more than ten years ago. She complained of agoraphobia; one of her symptoms was that she could not travel by train. I could not see any connection with other problems, so I told her to take a train ride each day, for as long as she could stand the journey. Her chauffeur followed the train in her car, ready to pick her up at any station. Each day her trip was a bit longer, and after a month she travelled to the end of Lake Zürich. Her agoraphobia had just about disappeared."

"Amazing," Hannah interjected.

"Theories are fine," Jung observed with a twinkle in his eye. "But only if they work. We mustn't forget our good friend William James."

"But some of your writings seem rather theoretical, at least to some people," Bernoulli persisted. "Not your articles, perhaps, but your books. The one on psychological types, for instance."

"I've noticed that, too," said Emma Jung with a smile.

"I suppose it's because I have more of a feeling for the audience in lectures and articles than in books," Jung replied. "At least, it's more fun to write essays. And then, of course, I have to be more careful with books. I think I'll have to revise them again and again as I discover new facts—and mature."

"That will make the publishers happy." Strauss interjected.

"And confuse the enemies," Toni Wolff added.

Jung leaned back and smiled: "The point is, I'm not trying to build theories, I'm not trying to construct one over-all grand theory à la Freud. After all, any psychological system is a personal, a subjective confession. Indeed, I don't think there will ever be an Einstein of the human soul... I'm just being empirical."

"But what does 'empirical' mean—in this context?" Bernoulli asked.

"Quite simply, it means that I describe the facts that I discover in my patients, in ordinary people, in fairy tales, in art, and in myself—not to mention myths and alchemy. Just facts...And even today," Jung chuckled, "...even today I can't make head or tail of all these materials, as the English say," and he nodded toward Barbara Hannah. "The really complex and unfamiliar parts of the mind, from which symbols are produced and our creativity arises, are still virtually unexplored."

There was a pause until Toni Wolff said: "And that's why Professor Jung keeps revising his books, his articles, his lectures,...and his ideas."

"Precisely," Jung said amiably. "Today I don't have all the facts about the human psyche, about the life of the soul. No one does, as yet. And so, when new facts come to light, we have to change our ideas and hypotheses. Unlike the Freudians who never change."

"All of this means that it's rather difficult to be a Jungian," Heller said with some gravity. "It's much easier to be a Freudian."

"And much more depressing, I think," said Buonaiuti.

"Ah," Jung cried. "Freudians are always certain of the revealed truth...there are so few changes in the system...and lately, none."

"In spite of all the obvious shortcomings," Strauss interjected.

"Well," Jung shrugged his shoulders, "Let's not get into that. I don't have a system in the usual sense, and I hope I never will. In that sense you might say that I am not a Jungian. ...Yes, I would say: 'I'm glad I'm not a Jungian.'"

The dismay of the assembled guests was evident in the long silence that followed. After several seconds that seemed like hours, Buonaiuti spoke up:

"I like that attitude...It enables us to make new discoveries and use new ideas. Eight years ago I was excommunicated, and three years ago I lost my professorship—just because my ideas did not fit the pope's beliefs or Mussolini's system...Yes, I'm all in favor of freedom—to discover, to accept, and..." his eyes twinkled as he said slowly, "to reject or modify."

"Bravo," Jung shouted and clapped his hands, and the others around the table applauded as well. Jung stood up with a glass in his hand...

"A toast to archetypes, to the collective unconscious—and to Eranos."

His companions sipped their wine and slowly placed their glasses on the round table. The wind rustled through the great cedar above.

"Shall we go for a swim?" Jung asked. "I can hear the lake waters calling to us."

Notes

The Eranos meetings, held annually since 1933, exemplify Jung's work and life. Here he gathered with colleagues, friends, and students to discuss his own and others' ideas. He frequently used these occasions to present first drafts of later articles and books. The individuals we meet in this encounter either presented papers at Eranos that year or were present as listeners. I imagine what the participants are likely to have said, based either on their profession or the papers they presented.

In her article "C. G. Jung and the Eranos Conferences," (*Spring* 1977), Aniela Jaffé describes the Eranos meetings and atmosphere in considerable detail. I have also relied on the conference's proceedings, *Eranos Jahrbuch 1934*, edited by Olga Fröbe-Kapteyn and published (as were the succeeding volumes) by Rhein-Verlag, Zürich (1935). English translations of several Eranos lectures have been published in *Papers from the Eranos Yearbooks*, 3 vols. (New York: Pantheon Books, 1954).

There are many books about Jung and his work. I have relied primarily on his own *Memories, Dreams, Reflections* (New York: Random House, 1963); and on Barbara Hannah's personal memoir *Jung: His Life and Work* (New York: G. P. Putnam's Sons, 1976). In addition, I have consulted several of his essays, published in *The Collected Works of C. G. Jung* (Princeton: Princeton University Press, 1953–1979). Good introductions to Jung's ideas are contained in *C.G. Jung: Word and Image*, edited by Aniela Jaffé (Princeton: Princeton University Press, 1979); and in *Man and His Symbols*, edited by Jung (Garden City: Doubleday, 1964).

7
LUDWIG BINSWANGER
A Stroll in Kreuzlingen, 1954

Not all of the analysts who disagreed with Freud became outcasts and even enemies. One of the few who contributed to our understanding of human beings and yet remained on friendly terms with Freud was a Swiss physician. On the basis of his experiences he introduced some philosophical dimensions which seem quite plausible. The resulting conception of human nature appears to be more complete, yet the additions are extremely difficult to test. His work exemplifies what may be psychology's greatest dilemma: the more complex a model of human nature is, the more difficult the validation of that model seems to be.

Ludwig Binswanger was born on April 13, 1881, in Kreuzlingen, a picturesque town on the shores of Lake Constance in northern Switzerland. The family was well established in the area and had produced a number of physicians. His father was director of a private clinic for the mentally ill which had been founded by his grandfather. One of his uncles, Otto Binswanger, was a professor at the University of Jena medical school who became known as one of the major early opponents of Freud's theory of hysteria.

The boy attended local schools and studied at the universities of Lausanne, Heidelberg, and Zürich. He pursued a normal medical curriculum but added several extra philosophy and psychology courses. In 1906, Binswanger received his medical degree from the University of Zürich and spent the following year as a volunteer physician at the Burghölzli Mental Hospital. There he worked under Eugen Bleuler and did research for his dissertation under Carl Jung. He became greatly interested in the subject of his doctoral thesis, galvanic reflexes during association tests, but he was even more fascinated by the new ideas and therapeutic methods which emanated from the work of Sigmund Freud.

In February 1907, when Carl Jung and his wife visited Freud for the first time, Binswanger accompanied them to Vienna. He was greatly impressed by Freud's personality and captivated by the new psychoanalytical ideas. Soon he was an ardent supporter of psychoanalysis and joined the Zürich group of the International Psychoanalytic Association. More important, he and Freud soon established a friendship that persisted for more than thirty years.

Binswanger married in 1908 and returned to the family clinic. His father died in late 1910, and soon thereafter Binswanger became the chief medical director of the "Private Clinic for Nervous and Mental Patients," also known as the Bellevue Sanatorium. From then on he and his family of six children lived in Kreuzlingen.

The sanatorium usually had about eighty patients, served by at least four physicians and a large support staff. There Binswanger tried out Freud's new methods, long before the First World War and in spite of attacks and economic implications for his institution (such as an attempted boycott). He treated not only neurotics but also tried to help psychotics (who could not be successfully analyzed, according to Freud). During the 1920s, as Binswanger saw an increasing variety of patients in his sanatorium, he became aware of the limitations of psychoanalytic theory and methods. Yet even while he developed the outlines of what eventually became existential analysis, he remained on good terms with Freud.

His cordial relations with Freud lasted for more than three decades, in spite of growing theoretical and therapeutic differences. During these years they saw each other about a dozen times and exchanged numerous letters. On three traumatic occasions in Binswanger's life—in 1912, when a malignant tumor threatened him with only a one-to-three-year life span, in 1926 when his youngest son died, and in 1929 when his eldest son died—Freud showed himself to be a wise and supportive friend. By the early 1930s their correspondence had waned to one or two postcards a year, but Binswanger always held Freud in high esteem.

Binswanger's professional life did not revolve around psychoanalysis, for his outlook was too open for any orthodoxy. In his 1922 textbook *Introduction to the Problems of General Psychology*, for example, he did not even mention psychoanalysis. That topic was to be treated in a second volume devoted to applications of psychology, but that book was never finished. By the mid-1920s his interest had shifted to the relationship between phenomenology and psychology, which eventually developed into what is now known as existential psychology. His seminal work, *The Basis and Understanding of Human Existence*, was published in 1943. This was followed by numerous essays, articles, and case histories describing his theory and methods.

After the First World War Binswanger became increasingly unhappy with psychoanalysts' dissection of individuals into separate components and began to look for new approaches to mental illness. Eventually he came to reject not only the theories of Freud, Adler, and Jung, but theories as such, for he believed that they impose an artificial structure on the patients and their lives. He also began to doubt the effectiveness of methods employed by psychiatrists. In his own work he could see that individuals are whole human beings who face certain problems in the world—the world *they* see and understand. Eventually, Binswanger became convinced that the usual scientific procedures which had proven so successful in physics, chemistry, and biology, could not elucidate the problems his patients faced or even come to grips with the patients as whole human beings.

In casting about for a more suitable approach, one which would allow him to consider the whole person living in the world, he was attracted by the phenomenology of Edmund Husserl, the German philosopher. But it was not until the publication of Martin Heidegger's classic *Being and Time* in 1926 that Binswanger found an adequate intellectual basis for his new approach to the study of individuals and their problems.

BASIC HUMAN CHARACTERISTICS

At first glance, Binswanger's view of human nature seems to be a straightforward reflection of daily life. But this simplicity hides great complexity and a number of significant implications. His basic postulate is that individuals are integral wholes that are essentially indivisible. A human being cannot be understood as long as we see only a collection of elements, be they organs or theoretical constructs.

The second postulate states that human actions are motivated, in the sense that people have goals which they try to achieve. Binswanger holds that people are not things, and that the determinants of physical and natural events are quite different from the roots of human behavior. To explain the falling of darkness, for example, we consider the earth's rotation and its position vis-a-vis the sun. To explain human actions, however, we cannot talk about causes but must consider motives. When darkness falls, we may be motivated to turn on the light—or we might enjoy the dusk and wait for the evening star. Causality reigns in the world of things, but motivation rules the human world.

These postulates led Binswanger to reject all those conceptions of human nature which dissect human beings and analyze the components. Thus, he does not talk about the mind as opposed to the body, or about the unconscious or the ego as causes of behavior, and he rejects the assumptions of instinct and drive. Actions occur because individuals are motivated to accomplish certain ends (leaving aside, of course, physiological reflexes).

Furthermore, Binswanger postulates that people are free to choose among courses of action and that they are responsible for selecting one or another activity of the several open to them. At first glance, Binswanger's emphasis on freedom and responsibility—shared by most existentialists—seems to be an overstatement. Is a ten-year-old child really free to choose between going to school and not attending? We must remember that Binswanger is talking about normal adults who live in a particular society and historical period.

This leads to Binswanger's fourth postulate: the individual is an inextricable part of the world. By being born into a certain family, class, city, and culture, a person learns only a few of the many activities, ideas, norms, and values that exist on earth. Thus a child's contact with languages—and how much else!—is rather limited. The specific world in which any particular individual lives is always a reflection of a society's culture and history. The normal individual comes to terms with these limitations and adjusts to "the facts of life" that make up the world into which he or she is born. So far there is little that is new or startling.

But now Binswanger describes another limitation. He postulates that people live not only in the objective world studied by the geographer, biologist, and sociologist, but also in a world they design. Individuals construct "their world" from the things and events they perceive, leaving out whatever they do not perceive and modifying much of what is objectively there. A person's subjective world-design imposes further limitations on his choices—or might suggest a choice when there really is none. The design of my world might be reasonably accurate, or it might be much broader or narrower than reality, and it might include a host of distortions.

Many high school students with above-average intelligence, for example, plan to study at a university. We would conclude that the life and future they envision—or their "world designs," as Binswanger would say—are quite reasonable, and we would predict success (if the economy holds out). But some intelligent youngsters may believe that they are not bright enough to go to college and therefore might not even sign up for the appropriate high school subjects. The world such students design and live in—full of people who are much more intelligent, and with few openings for dunces like them—does not reflect reality. We might well predict an unhappy life, especially in later years. Or a teenager might construct a world in which such positions as nuclear physicist or astronaut require only average intelligence, drive, and mathematical insight. This world design is again faulty, and again we would predict unhappiness, with failure guaranteed.

Binswanger's postulates—about the significance of motivation and free choice, and about individuals who design their world and then live within it—reflect some common-sense aspects of human existence. For most of us, however, these postulates remain unspoken and we do not worry about them or their significance and implications. Binswanger examined these postulates in great detail and used them to describe the events of daily life and the difficulties we face.

A major problem arises when the human need to live an authentic life is not met. Our life is authentic to the extent that it corresponds to our nature and capacities—as we see them and as they really are. The girl who is interested in machines should have the opportunity to become an engineer or auto mechanic, and the boy who likes to cook should be able to major in home economics. A person's interests, rather than the ones our culture prescribes, are the important factors in an individual's authentic life. The need to develop one's potential is a closely related aspect of human nature. Indeed, such a development is often at the center of an authentic existence.

There is no guarantee, of course, that people know their potential or understand what occupation and life-style would lead to an authentic existence. Hence one can easily make wrong choices—and not only in one's education and job. Fortunately, life presents us with a long and complex series of choices which allow us to rectify earlier mistakes; unfortunately, we often do not see the mistakes until it is too late. Both these aspects of life contribute to our fate.

Binswanger's psychiatric training led him to consider the implications of wrong choices, ignorance about one's potentials, and the tragedy of inauthentic lives. Eventually he concluded that the primary task of any therapy is the discovery of a patient's potentialities and the several aspects that together define his authentic life. Only then can a therapist help—by showing the patient the road to both.

Binswanger also postulated that human beings face several ontological problems—inescapable problems that arise simply from the fact that we are human beings with feelings and desires, who think and project, who are aware of might-have-beens and death. The normal individual gradually learns to come to terms with uncertainty, the struggle for meaning, and death. We all ask questions: who am I? what is the meaning of my life? why must I die? Over the years we develop and discard answers, or perhaps we fill our days with activities and our nights with noise so as to avoid both the questions and the answers. A normal individual who leads an authentic life faces these human problems and comes to terms with them, all the while realizing that there is no one best solution.

Binswanger's conception of human nature at first glance seems to be both simplistic and rather forbidding. But when we consider the implications of his postulates and look beyond the technical terms we easily recognize ourselves—or at least our friends. What we recognize is not so much what we can see in a mirror, but rather what we perceive in the quiet of the night.

On the Shore of Lake Constance

The Second International Congress for Psychotherapy was held in Kreuzlingen during the summer of 1954, and on July 25th many of the participants visited the Bellevue Sanatorium. In spite of his age Binswanger had prepared an address for his visitors; the title, "Existential Analysis and Psychotherapy," reflected his major concerns for the past three decades. That evening he opened his home to the many friends who had come from all over Europe and enjoyed their conversations until past midnight.

The next morning he rose late and decided to take a stroll along the shore of Lake Constance. He walked rather slowly and stopped repeatedly to contemplate the ancient trees along the promenade; after more than seventy years he still marvelled at the many hues of the lake and the old games that seemed so new to the children playing in the sand.

He quickly noticed that a young couple, barely into their twenties, were apparently following him; they kept their distance and stopped whenever he did. Their clothing and manner showed that they were not Swiss, he thought, and he began to wonder what they were up to. So he sat down on one of the many benches facing the lake and decided to wait for them. They stopped some distance away, talked with each other for quite a while, and then directed their steps to the bench.

"Excuse me," the young woman asked timidly in German. "Are you Professor Binswanger?" The old psychiatrist nodded. "Yes," he said in English, for he had recognized the American accent.

"My name is Susanna Stevenson...I just graduated from college...and I wonder whether...we might talk with you."

Binswanger rose and smiled. "Of course," he said as they shook hands. "Would you like to walk with me? Or we could sit down here."

Stevenson looked greatly relieved. "This is my friend Miguel Arenas," she introduced her companion. "He is a student from Spain. We are both interested in psychology."

"How do you do," Arenas said in rather broken German. "I am so pleased to meet you." He bowed and they shook hands.

"My Spanish is very poor," Binswanger sighed. "Shall we speak English? I've had many patients from England and the United States, but only one from Spain."

"I understand German better than I speak it," Arenas said. "I also know English." After a glance at his friend he continued, "We'll walk with you if you wish or sit here if you prefer."

"Well, then, let's go on for awhile," Binswanger suggested. "It's too early to rest."

The three walked in silence along the promenade until Binswanger asked: "What brings you to Switzerland? And Kreuzlingen? It's such a little place!"

Stevenson laughed shyly. "My father brought me along. He is a psychotherapist in Los Angeles and attends the congress here. And my friend..."

"I'm reading philosophy," Arenas interjected. "But I want to relate philosophy to actual people, to real life. That's why your ideas appeal to me."

"I studied psychology at Pomona College...that's a small college in southern California...and a professor there talked about your work," Stevenson continued. "Actually, I'm looking for an antidote for all the academic psychology I've had to swallow these last four years."

"Yes, I suppose I'm a good antidote for that," Binswanger chuckled. "I'm always glad to hear that my ideas are alive and well in faraway places. And I always welcome pilgrims to Switzerland."

"A friend of mine from Uruguay says that Switzerland has contributed nothing to civilization—except cuckoo clocks," Arenas said with a smile. "But he doesn't know much about you, or Carl Jung, or Hermann Hesse."

Binswanger laughed. "Perhaps our mere existence shows Europe and the world that people can live in peace—with their neighbors and with themselves."

"I thought I would never hear you speak of 'mere existence,'" Stevenson chuckled. Her voice now had more confidence.

"That's the problem with language," Binswanger said and shook his head. "So many important words have several meanings, and others have lost the sense they once had. Freud, you know, had a hard time with the word 'unconscious.' Especially when the German—with two words and meanings, as you know—was first translated into English."

"Not to mention Martin Heidegger," Arenas added. "I began to study German just so I might understand '*dasein*' and '*sosein*'..." He paused and then said dejectedly, "but it's a hopeless task."

Stevenson agreed. "I'm almost reconciled to hyphenated English words half-a-foot long."

"Even the Germans aren't all that happy, sometimes," Binswanger chuckled. "Some philosophers, professors of literature, and others have said that Heidegger is using big new words to clothe small, old ideas. They are wrong, of course. I think Heidegger has made a major contribution to the intellectual life of this century. But in any case, one must be very careful with words and their meanings."

"Do you consider yourself a psychologist or a philosopher?" Arenas asked.

"I'm a psychiatrist, of course. Don't confuse me with a philosopher. I don't think or write like one, even if I look like one." Binswanger wagged his finger in mock anger: "And for heaven's sake, don't confuse the psychology I practice with academic psychology. There is a world of difference. After all, I deal with real people, with real lives, with real problems, and with actual despair and joy, genuine tears and laughter. When I look at a patient, I see a human being. A complete, complex, whole individual. I don't care about abstractions...not at all."

"One of the things I admire about you," Stevenson said and blushed slightly, "is your broad-minded open attitude. Existential psychology is so different from Freud's, yet you two remained friends."

"It takes two people to form a friendship," Binswanger said softly. After a few moments he continued, "Those were great years, full of youthful excitement. I had admired him before we met, and from that first day on we liked each other. Even though he was fifty and I twenty-five. Ah, those evenings, when we talked in his dimly-lit study, surrounded by books and antiquities..."

"What was he like?" Arenas broke the silence.

"I had lots of questions, of course," Binswanger continued. "He answered them fully, and in a very kindly fashion. I don't think he ever raised his voice with me. He smoked his cigar while we talked, made very few gestures. Once in a while he would pick up one of the little statues on his desk. In those early days Freud struck me as keen and benevolent, never superior..."

After a few moments the old psychiatrist continued: "In the decades that followed he retained his kindness, at least toward me. When my little boy died at eight, and later my eldest son at twenty, Freud wrote to me. Very good—lovely—letters. I treasure them to this day."

"He was a different person with Adler and Jung, wasn't he?" Stevenson asked. "So he must have had several sides to his personality."

"Just like everybody else," Arenas said. "Why is it, Professor Binswanger, that you and he never had a falling-out?"

"It's a rather complex matter," the old man answered. "One of the most important aspects of our friendship was the fact that I was never a threat to him or his theory, as Adler and Jung were. I was never his disciple in the sense the others were, and so there was no need for me to rebel, to exert my independence or show off my originality. I just applied philosophical ideas and Heidegger's concepts when I discovered that Freud's were rather limited...Too limited for me and the work I was doing in my sanatorium."

"Did you work with Jung, too?" Arenas asked.

"For about a year," Binswanger answered. "When I was a young man— just out of medical school, in fact—I worked at the Burghölzli. There I studied under him, collecting data for my thesis. But that was long before he had worked out his system. In later years...well, we have seen each other occasionally. But I don't hold much with his theory—or any other theory, for that matter."

"But don't we need theories to help us explain things?" Stevenson asked.

Binswanger shrugged his shoulders. "I don't think so. Consider. Theories either give us pigeonholes into which we put symptoms and people—as when we say that someone suffers from an unresolved Oedipus complex—or they give us Procrustean beds that distort reality." There was conviction in his voice as he continued, "I was glad to leave the theories of Freud and Jung behind me. Just as the individual is free to choose and is responsible for his choice, so I—as a therapist—must be free to assess a client's symptoms and be responsible for what I do with him. A theory reduces my freedom and diminishes my responsibility."

"But how, then, do you explain..." Stevenson began.

"My dear young friend," Binswanger said and stopped to look at her. "Why in the world do you always want to explain everything? Why don't you want to understand? Simply—understand? Explanations always reflect theories and are no better than they. I want to describe a person, his problems and predicaments, so that I can understand the whole, complex marvelous human being. From that understanding I can discover the best methods to use in a therapy. Theories always dissect the human being. But I am interested in the totality of a person. The individual who is part and parcel of the world. The world he designs and lives in, and the world beyond—the world of potential."

"Your words remind me of my favorite author," Arenas said. "The Spaniard Miguel de Unamuno. In his book *Del Sentimento Tragico de la Vida*— how do you say it in English, Susanna?"

"The Tragic Sense of Life," his friend answered.

"Yes," Arenas continued. "In that book Unamuno talks about the total human being, not the one studied by psychologists or biologists. The individual of flesh and bone; who is born, suffers, and dies; the real person."

Binswanger nodded. "I remember those words. Unamuno also speaks of death and immortality. I like that book very much, even though I don't agree with everything he says. We existentialists also take death into account, for it is part of everyone's being. When scientists study reflexes or memory they come up with trivial results, it seems to me. Trivial because the real individual is lost. The individual cannot survive—exist—in the laboratory. There we find only the organism. Real individuals act in the world, they use their memories. The memory a psychologist studies is something rather different from the memories of individuals who live in the worlds they design, who contemplate their own deaths because they are aware that other people have died."

Stevenson shook her head. "One of my brothers is a physicist, the other an astronomer. Both use theories to explain and predict events in the universe. Very small and very large events. And their discoveries are not trivial, it seems to me."

"Theories are fine in the natural sciences," Binswanger agreed. "Without the theories and discoveries of physicists, our engineers could not build bridges and railways. And how much do farmers—and we all—owe to botanists! But human beings are different. And that very different subject requires a very different method for gaining any understanding at all."

"When a person is dissected and the parts are studied in isolation, we still don't understand that person when we add the parts or otherwise put them back together," Arenas said.

"I don't follow you, Miguel," Stevenson said. "What do you mean?"

"Many parts of people are similar to those of animals," Arenas answered. "Many of our organs work much as do the organs of dogs, horses, and whales. But the whole human being, the totality of parts, is very different indeed. Do you remember what Unamuno writes in the first chapter of *Tragic Sense*? What he says there about the human being could not be said about anything else, no other animal, nothing."

"That's true," Stevenson agreed. "But I can't just dismiss science and the scientific method. Another brother, the eldest, is a physician. When I listen to him I realize how much science has done for mankind. Biochemists, neurologists—you name the fields—have worked with people, and helped them, by using scientific methods. What else is responsible for our medicines, operations, and all kinds of cures? Medicine has become successful precisely because scientific methods have been used."

"You have rather convenient brothers," Binswanger chuckled. "How many more are there?" He smiled and placed his hand on Stevenson's shoulder.

"A sister, who is a psychologist," Stevenson said. "And that's it. Perhaps it's my training and family background, but I can't help thinking that science is more effective and significant than you think."

"You have been in college too long, Susanna," Arenas turned to her. "And you haven't been around me long enough. We Spaniards aren't much for science—but we are for the full life. The same thing goes for Latin Americans."

"I think you're talking about stereotypes, Miguel," Stevenson suggested. "A Spaniard or Brazilian with an IQ of 130 could easily be a great scientist."

"Of course," Arenas said slowly. "And there are as many people with such intelligence in Spain as there are in England or Germany. But...not as many of my countrymen are *interested* in science, I think. Perhaps..."

"Wait, a moment, wait," Binswanger said and raised his arms in a soothing gesture. "We are getting off the track." He turned to Stevenson and continued, "I never said that science is useless or that the scientific method cannot tell us about human beings. But I do think—indeed, I know from many years of experience—that we must use other methods as well, along with science, to understand the individual as a total being who lives in the world." He paused for a moment in the shade of a tree and looked out over the lake. Then he said, "We observe people carefully, and we try to discover their past and present. We must be sure that our data are accurate. So, we have to be scientific."

Stevenson nodded.

"I've found that mere observation isn't enough, however," the old psychiatrist continued. "But instead of using theories to explain my observations, I use empathy—that's always important, empathy—to *understand* the human being I observe. To understand a person's motivation. To understand the client's problems. To understand what I might do to help. Have you read my case history of Ellen West?"

Stevenson shook her head. "One of my professors gave a lecture on the case, but the situation wasn't very clear to me."

"Well," Binswanger said, "I don't want to burden you with a long story. The point of the case history is that her problem—originally centering on eating—can be understood very well in terms of the philosophical concepts Heidegger uses to describe the human condition. If I had limited myself to the methods used by other psychologists I wouldn't have gotten half as far."

"How would Freud or Jung have handled her case?" Arenas asked.

"I don't know," Binswanger replied. "And please don't say 'her case.' Just say, 'her.' Because therapists don't handle cases—we try to help human beings. That's all. A Freudian analyst probably would have seen some sexual aspects in Ellen West's inability to eat. Perhaps a fear of impregnation. There you see the problem with so many therapies: the human being is taken apart and only some of the parts are analyzed. From one limited viewpoint. Then the pieces are put back together. But the reconstruction is false, for it reflects a particular theory and does violence to the indivisible nature of the individual, her integrity."

"But what if only one part of a person is sick, or has a problem?" Stevenson asked. "When I have a headache, I do not need a complete physical examination and a wide-spectrum antibiotic. I just take aspirin."

"For an occasional headache, of course," Binswanger replied. "And for an occasional moment of 'feeling blue,' as you Americans say, no existential analysis is needed. But when you have persistent headaches the doctor looks you over completely, doesn't he? An ongoing depression requires that we look at you and your life in the world. *Your* world. Isn't that so?"

"But without a deep causal analysis, what can you accomplish?" Stevenson persisted. "If I remember correctly, Ellen West committed suicide a few weeks after she left your sanatorium."

Binswanger nodded. "As I wrote in the case history, her death was part of her existence and therefore could not be prevented. Her life had been robbed of its meaning, of its existential ripening you might say, which is always and only determined by the future…And she saw no future."

Binswanger looked at Arenas who seemed doubtful.

"Existential analysis," the doctor continued, "approaches human existence with no other consideration than the uncontestable observation that the individual is in the world, has the world, and at the same time longs to get beyond the world. That kind of perspective leads to a wider and deeper understanding of individuals—their lives and problems, if you will—than psychoanalysts can achieve."

"But how can you be sure that Ellen West saw no future, or that an early and self-imposed death was part of her existence?" Stevenson asked. "You are certain, and your colleagues are—but doctors make mistakes…That's why I don't want to give up well-founded theories, and especially scientific methods whereby researchers can check on each other's inferences and conclusions. Those methods have been so effective, they have told us so much about the world and mankind. Today we know so much more about people than we did a hundred years ago. Aren't we better off than Wundt?"

"Have experimenters and psychoanalysts told us about individuals or have they described certain parts of people—and sometimes, no doubt, imaginary parts?" Binswanger asked with a twinkle in his eyes. "Remember Freud's incorrect theory about infantile seduction as a cause of neuroses. By the way, he wrestled with that problem for several years…"

"Well, I must admit that experiments usually tell us about rather small aspects of human beings," Stevenson replied.

"And don't forget, Susanna, that experimental results don't always fit together or make sense," Arenas added. "What happens when you eliminate experiments with animals? How much of psychology is left? How many studies are there about human beings?"

"A great number, of course," Stevenson replied. "But your other point is well taken. No comprehensive picture of 'the human being' has yet come from the laboratory."

"The most important question here is about... significance," Binswanger said slowly. "Existential analysis is a way of gathering significant information about relevant aspects of human beings. I recently read an article by one of your well-known experimentalists—I think his name was Skinner or something like that. He showed beautiful learning curves of pigeons and pointed out how similar these are to the human curves. But what is the significance of this, I ask you. What is the significance? In my approach there are no numbers or graphs. I talk about the human being's need to live an authentic life and to develop the potentials with which one is born. I talk about coming to terms with one's future in general and one's death in particular. I talk about the choices we face throughout life and our responsibility for the choices we make..."

"It seems to me that such an approach puts a tremendous burden on the individual," Stevenson said. "One no longer has the excuse of 'bad luck' or 'fate.'" After a pause she continued: "And there is another thing that bothers me...People who aren't well educated, or have never learned to think things through, or simply aren't of a reflective turn of mind—what about them?"

"My dear young friend," Binswanger answered. "Education and learning don't guarantee anything. You must have faith in the God-given mental equipment people have when they are born. Average intelligence and average insight are all one needs. The question is: can you recognize the possibilities before you, or do you consider everything as a necessity that cannot be changed...just because it is there? Education does not guarantee that one sees possibilities. The possibility of changing one's job, one's apartment or house, the city one lives in at the moment or one's life style. And of course, if one sees only given necessities, and no possibilities, then one has no choices and need not make any decisions. Consequently one is relieved of all responsibilities...At least in one sense...But such a person, it seems to me, gives up what is most distinctly human. When one gives up imagining possible futures, when one refuses to notice or evaluate possibilities, then one ceases to be free."

"Do you think that perhaps people refuse to see possibilities just because they don't want to shoulder the responsibility of making choices?" Arenas asked.

"I've met quite a few people like that," Binswanger answered. "They always strike me like the 'hollow men, heads stuffed with straw' that T. S. Eliot describes in his poem. Actually, it doesn't matter whether one begins by not seeing possibilities or by being afraid or responsibility. The end result is the same: an inauthentic person. So the job of the therapist is to help people recognize possibilities and accept responsibility for the choices they must make."

"But without scientific procedures, how do we know that what you say is correct while somebody else's ideas are not?" Stevenson asked anxiously. "How can you be sure that *your* answers are better than someone else's...say, Jung's?"

"My dear young friend," Binswanger smiled, "I have no answers, and I don't give any to my patients. One person's authentic life is different from another's, one individual's potential is not the same as someone else's. My task is to help people discover what is the authentic life for them, what their potential is. Then I—like any other therapist—try to help people achieve their future. After all, the discovery of the meaning of one's life—sometimes I think of it as existential ripening—is always and only determined by the future. I mean, our actions tomorrow as well as our actions today are so greatly affected by what we hope for and prepare for. When the past weighs down our life, we are deprived of a reasonable look into the future. That was true of Ellen West and it is true of many other people...the healthy as well as the sick."

"These are all matters of degree, I suppose?" Stevenson asked.

"Of course," Binswanger replied.

"I've always been fascinated by the many different ways in which people approach the same thing—death," Stevenson said after a pause. "To me, for example, Unamuno makes too much of death in general, he dwells too much on his own end. I find Socrates' view much more congenial..."

"For some people it is a rather simple event, I think," Binswanger said. "After Ellen West had decided to commit suicide, she seemed much happier, more composed, one might almost say 'more normal.' She was ready to die; it was part of her future."

"That sounds a bit callous to me," Stevenson whispered.

Binswanger shrugged his shoulders. "People approach death very differently because it fits into their different world designs. When I talked to her just before she left the sanatorium, Ellen West had a rather nonchalant attitude toward death."

"A matter of perspective, perhaps?" Arenas suggested.

Binswanger nodded. "Many years ago, my little eight-year-old boy died suddenly amidst great suffering. My heart almost broke. And then, in 1929, my eldest son died at twenty under tragic circumstances...I was devastated..." He paused and adjusted his glasses. "Of course, I myself am quite prepared to die—as anyone should be at 73."

"Is it important to know *why* people have different views of death?" Arenas asked. "Just as long as we recognize different views and don't impose ours on others?"

Binswanger nodded. "Our approaches to death are closely related to the world we have constructed, and understanding that design is more important than knowing the causes. Everyone designs his own world, which may differ more or less from the real and objective world. It is the subjective world, the world design, that counts, and part of every world design is death."

"Even if one denies that there is such a thing?" Stevenson asked.

"Of course, Susanna," Arenas answered. "A world without death is rather common. Especially among some young people I know."

"Don't leave out the middle-aged materialists driving their fast cars to gourmet restaurants, Miguel," Stevenson added with a chuckle. "Some people my parents know in Los Angeles..."

"But the main point," Binswanger interrupted, "is that we must understand a person's world if we are to understand that person's life and problems. After all, the arbitrary division of object and subject, of individual and environment, has prevented us from truly understanding the complex human being. Human existence involves both. Always. In fact, I have known some people—and not only patients—who had designed several worlds that were in conflict with each other. An individual can move from one world to another, so to speak, usually with little difficulty. At any one moment, though, the individual and the world he designed form one whole unit."

"How do you find out what kind of world a person has designed?" Stevenson asked. "Can patients, for example, really describe the world they have constructed for themselves? I don't think I'm aware of every aspect of my world design."

"Most people can describe their world—or *worlds*—quite well," Binswanger answered. "Although perhaps not perfectly, I agree. I usually ask many questions over a long time. I also use word-association tests and Rorschach tests. As you see, I'm open to all kinds of methods...even scientific ones," he smiled at Stevenson.

"Where do you draw the line between normal and neurotic people?" Arenas asked. "In terms of the world they design? It seems to me that might vary from one time of life to another."

"A difficult problem indeed," Binswanger replied. "Generally speaking, the major characteristic of normal people is that they and their worlds form a unity that is open and flexible. Open to new experiences, new facts, new ideas that might require a modification of their worlds and new ways of living in those worlds. Normal people recognize the possibilities before them and take responsibility for their choices—even if only reluctantly. The main point is, they do not confuse possibilities with necessities."

"I don't quite follow," Stevenson interrupted.

"I think that the world today is full of people who believe that they have no choices," Binswanger continued. "Many people believe that their life necessarily takes a certain course. They believe that they are stuck in a certain town or job, for instance, and that there are no other possibilities. But that is true only rarely, if ever. It takes great courage to say—especially to oneself: 'no, this job or life-style is not the only one I can have. There are other possibilities for me.' Cowards see no possibilities and therefore need not make choices and be responsible for those choices."

"But there *are* limits; and some people see crazy, outrageous possibilities that don't really exist, or make no sense," Stevenson said.

Binswanger nodded. "Yes indeed. But normal human beings use their imagination and judgment to recognize and evaluate possibilities. Then they choose the course of action that balances the external limits, the possibilities of their world and future, and their own authentic existence. That is the essence of human freedom."

"What about the actual world we live in today?" Arenas asked.

"Of course we must earn money and get along with our fellow citizens," Binswanger replied. "Adjusting to the objective world is part of normal life, as long as one is also able to live an authentic life within those limits."

"Do you think that it is more difficult to live an authentic life now than it was for people a hundred years ago?" Stevenson asked. "There are so many limitations today—laws, conventions, technology..." her voice trailed off.

"And what about the freedom in primitive tribes?" Arenas added.

Binswanger thought for a moment. "It's difficult to make historical comparisons, because all we have are partial descriptions. We can't talk to people who lived a hundred years ago, and it is difficult to talk to members of primitive tribes today...But I think...that there were as many limitations in the past as there are today. You know, historical descriptions rarely show us what the real limitations were. It's only when we place ourselves *into* the life of a person of the eighteenth century, or of Central Brazil today, that we can understand the limits they saw, the motives that possessed them. Such an understanding requires more than just historical or anthropological descriptions. No, until I am proven wrong I'll assume that limitations have been rather similar over the centuries. We're simply more aware of today's limitations and see the past through rose-colored glasses."

"I wish I could believe that," Arenas sighed.

"It's fashionable these days to be negative," Binswanger said. "And perhaps my life has made me something of an optimist—at least in that respect."

"I hope I can be as serene and wise as you are—when I'm your age," Stevenson said.

"Become interested in psychoanalysis—and then go beyond it," Binswanger laughed. "But be careful. Once psychoanalysis gets hold of you, it will never let you go. It will continue to influence you practically and theoretically, and no one will be able to say that it has not become part of your life."

"But I thought you were no longer a psychoanalyst," Arenas said quietly.

"I let other people put labels on me," Binswanger replied with a laugh. "My own life task was determined not only by my interest in psychoanalysis, but also by my effort to expound and judge it critically. In a very real sense, psychoanalysis spurred me on to plunge ever deeper into the problem of human existence...and to attempt to master life philosophically and scientifically."

"Perhaps your ideas will be a catalyst for others," Stevenson suggested. "I probably won't hear about your work in graduate school; but in later life...who knows?"

"Good luck in that adventure...your life and your future," Binswanger said and smiled.

"May I come by your house tomorrow and have you sign a book?" Arenas asked with some hesitation. "I would like to have a memento of today."

"Of course," Binswanger answered. "I'll be happy to do that. Here is my address." He gave each of them his card and then they shook hands.

Notes

I have included this chapter on Binswanger to illustrate psychology's wide range of topics. While "existential psychology" may be of little interest to North American psychologists, the melding of psychology and philosophical perspectives is of significance in Europe.

This encounter is set in Kreuzlingen, a city on Lake Konstanz where Binswanger spent all of his life. I have chosen the date (July 1954) because it was an occasion when psychologists from all over Europe came together to honor Binswanger's work. The two students and what they say are imagined. I have directed the conversation to those issues which are problematic for young scientists who are more at home in the world than in the philosopher's study.

For biographical material I have relied primarily on Binswanger's own *Sigmund Freud: Reminiscences of a Friendship* (New York: Grune and Stratton, 1957). Binswanger's ideas are presented in *Existential Psychology*, 2nd ed., edited by

Rollo May (New York: Random House, 1969); and in *Existence*, edited by Rollo May, Ernst Angel, and Henri Ellenberger (New York: Basic Books, 1958). Two of Binswanger's case histories are contained in that book. It is probably more useful to read Binswanger's articles than his books; some of the former are collected in *Being in the World: Selected Papers*, edited by Jacob Needleman (New York: Basic Books, 1963). The work of Viktor E. Frankl is more accessible and covers much of the same area: *Man's Search for Meaning* (Boston: Beacon Press, 1959); *The Unheard Cry for Meaning* (New York: Simon and Schuster, 1978).

PART THREE
THE EXPERIMENTERS

8

JOHN B. WATSON
A Dinner on Long Island, 1923

The psychologists we met in the last four chapters constructed grand theories of human nature. They wanted to understand the activities and thoughts of individuals, and tried to reduce individuals' difficulties. As we saw, however, the analysts' theories contained many vague concepts and untestable hypotheses, especially about the human being's internal state. The major procedures these psychologists employed required that inferences be made from a person's action or words—but there could be little assurance that such inferences led to valid conclusions about the person's internal state. These significant problems led many psychologists to question the usefulness of inferences as a method and the internal state as an explanation of human behavior.

John Broadus Watson was born on January 9, 1878 near Greenville, South Carolina. His parents, who were poor and not well educated, exerted a powerful influence through the examples they set. His mother was deeply religious, a rigid and fervent member of the fundamentalist Baptist community. His father, a farmer, taught him various manual skills, and together they roamed the countryside and went hunting. In 1891, when the boy was thirteen, his father abandoned the family; the son never forgave him.

Young Watson did not like school or its discipline and did poorly. The boy's frequent wildness and defiant attitude got him into numerous difficulties; he had many fights, was arrested twice, and is said to have liked animals more than people.

But in 1894 his life-style changed completely; perhaps he could see what lay ahead if he continued in his old ways. At the age of sixteen he entered Furman University, doing odd jobs and helping in the chemistry laboratory to pay his expenses. He worked hard and did well in his studies (philosophy and psychology), but he was still quite shy and did not have much of a social life. There was a problem with one course in his fourth year; so he stayed an extra year and graduated in 1899 with a master's degree.

After a year of teaching in a one-room rural school he enrolled at the University of Chicago to study philosophy under John Dewey. But he was greatly disappointed in the philosophy courses he took, and especially in Dewey himself. With the encouragement of a young psychologist, James R. Angell (who later became president of Yale), Watson switched fields and began to study the behavior of animals. He was especially intrigued by questions about the ways in which animals learn, the age at which learning becomes possible, and the limits of learning. He did very well in his studies in spite of earning a poor living as a janitor, busboy, and animal keeper.

Watson now established what was to be the hallmark of his later studies: he investigated what animals (usually rats) actually did, how they reacted in various situations such as simple and complex mazes, how they learned to manipulate simple levers and complex pulley arrangements. He rewarded the rats by giving them bread soaked in milk (bought with his own money). In all of this work he differed from other psychologists who usually tried to introspect for the animal by presuming what the animal saw and thought—as if the rat were human.

In the course of his meticulous experiments Watson studied what are now known as learning curves, the gradual improvement of performance with practice. In all of his work, he was careful not to ascribe human feelings to rats or to endow them with internal processes analogous to human experiences. Internal mental processes might well exist, he admitted, but he argued that at the moment there was no way of studying them in an objective fashion. The psychologist Angell and the philosopher George Herbert Mead were interested in his work, which he published with borrowed funds under the title *Animal Education*.

In 1903 Watson became the youngest Ph.D. at Chicago and stayed on as instructor. He continued his studies of animal learning and taught courses in that area as well as conventional psychology which emphasized introspection. Although he was still poor, he married Mary Ickes (whose brother Harold later became Franklin Roosevelt's Secretary of the Interior). He reported his work in prestigious journals and soon was recognized as an authority on the behavior of animals.

Watson's articles on animal learning impressed many scientists, and his well-designed and carefully-executed experiments contributed greatly to psychology's becoming a recognized "hard science." Gradually he developed his own ideas about learning and behavior, but for several years he kept these to himself until his "system" was reasonably complete. By 1908 he had such a reputation that Johns Hopkins University offered him a full professorship.

When Watson moved to Baltimore he was one of the youngest professors in the United States, and by 1909, when he became editor of the *Psychological Review*, he was one of the most respected men in the field. By now he was also experimenting with other animals, notably monkeys and birds, and suggested that human psychology would benefit greatly from his and others' laboratory studies of animals. Most important, his many behavioristic ideas were merging into a theory.

The result was a series of lectures which he gave in early 1913 in New York city. A large audience was fascinated by his ideas on psychology as seen by a behaviorist, and by his view that the prediction and control of behavior form the major purpose of psychology.

These lectures are now considered to herald the beginning of modern behaviorism with its emphasis on experiments, overt actions, and other aspects of human life that can be observed (rather than having to be inferred). Watson's views came to be generally appreciated and widely accepted among psychologists as well as the general public. This occurred not only because he was an effective and persuasive speaker, but also because psychologists and others were ready for new ideas and willing to try them out. Watson's ideas were fascinating in their own right and held promise that they might be used to better understand human beings and solve human problems.

In 1914, Watson was elected president of the American Psychological Association and published his ideas in a book entitled *Behavior*. Now he turned to the study of human beings, especially children, and two years later had established a comprehensive research program at Johns Hopkins' Phipps Psychiatric Clinic. He began by studying the characteristics of newborn babies and the early development of infants.

After a rather unhappy experience in the army—as a research psychologist—he returned to the Phipps Clinic to concentrate on research about child development. He studied maturation, the growth of motor skills and muscular coordination, the operation of reflexes, and the origin of fears. He also began to present his major ideas, their empirical basis and their implications for practical concerns such as child-raising, to a wider audience.

Nineteen hundred twenty was a momentous year for Watson. It started out well enough with the publication of his major book, *Psychology from the Standpoint of a Behaviorist*. Here he advocated both laboratory experiments and the careful, systematic observations of behavior in real-life situations. Watson admonished everyone to be careful in drawing conclusions for human beings from animal experiments, and he argued vigorously that psychology should be useful to the average person in dealing with the problems of daily life.

Later that year Watson was part of a messy divorce which brought his extra-marital affairs to the front pages of newspapers all over the country. In January 1921 Watson married his former graduate student and laboratory assistant, Rosalie Rayner. Johns Hopkins University had asked for his resignation even before the divorce, and Watson now went to live in New York city. There he quickly became a successful executive with the J. Walter Thompson advertising agency.

For the next twenty years Watson received no academic offers, and few psychologists wanted to have anything to do with him. After some half-hearted attempts to continue academic work and experimental studies of children, he devoted most of his attention to the advertising business. He also wrote articles for popular magazines on all kinds of psychological topics, giving advice to readers and making suggestions regarding the solutions of personal difficulties. The public soon came to regard him as an authority on psychology in general and child raising in particular. After 1928 his book *The Psychological Care of the Infant and Child* became an influential and controversial manual in many families.

Watson raised his children—a boy and a girl in his first marriage, and two boys in the second family—much as he advised other parents to do. He was convinced that psychological research pointed to the need for a rather distant and objective relationship between parents and children. He taught that parents should be kind and firm, talk with their children as much as necessary but hug and kiss them as little as possible. Watson believed that too much affection would spoil children and harm their emotional development and independence. True to his teachings, he showed little affection to his children; he never kissed his sons during the 1920s and in the evenings sent them to bed with a handshake.

During all these years, academic psychologists considered Watson an outcast. Some were worried that the scandal of his divorce would reflect on the respectability of psychology itself, others were appalled by his extreme ideas and his popularization of them, and a few, perhaps, were jealous of his financial success. Watson still gave public lectures, but his style became less scholarly and his ideas more rigid. He and his wife led an active social life, even after they moved from New York city to a small farm in Westport, Connecticut. By the early 1930s, however, Watson gave fewer lectures and did less writing. In 1936 his beloved Rosalie died, and Watson withdrew from public events to a silent life on his farm.

BASIC HUMAN CHARACTERISTICS

Whenever we look over the work of Watson we must remember that his research career was cut short after barely fifteen years. At the age of forty-two he found himself academically and scientifically "out in the cold." He no longer had the intellectual stimulation and critical reactions from respected colleagues, and new research data no longer set limits to his imagination. In a very real sense, his youthful exuberance had no chance to mature; and instead of the mellowing that comes from continuing debates, the following twenty years of professional isolation exaggerated his early position and hardened its lines. No one can say what his ultimate views would have been had he remained an active researcher. But it is likely that the books which made him infamous in the eyes of many—*Behaviorism* in 1925 and *The Psychological Care of the Infant and Child* published in 1928—would have been quite different. In his autobiographical note he regretted their hasty composition and expressed sorrow that he did not know enough at the time to write the books he really wanted to write.

Watson has contributed to our understanding of human nature in two related areas: the methods one might use to study human beings, and information about some specific human characteristics. His ideas were not always original, but they constituted a significant elaboration, extension, and novel application of existing notions (especially the experiments of Ivan Pavlov).

Watson's major aim was to establish psychology as the objective science of behavior that would remain in touch with the major concerns of daily life. He wanted to get away from the introspection of Wundt and his followers as well as from the vague empathy employed by William James. In their place he advocated the use of laboratory experiments, systematic observations of real-life situations, what we now call "psychological testing," and verbal reports. He preferred laboratory experiments because the researcher can structure the environment and change various factors when necessary. Furthermore, in animal studies the history of the organism is known, so that one need not make guesses about previous conditioning. Together, these four methods enabled Watson to study behavior while making few inferences. Now he could rely almost completely on observable events that can be checked by other observers.

Since in his day not much was known about the physiology and operation of the brain and central nervous system, Watson included little of these in his system. Indeed, he called the human brain a "mystery box" and attempted to explain behavior with minimal references to it.

Watson considered behavior as an extremely interesting aspect of human beings, worthy of careful study in its own right. In fact, he proposed that the aim of psychology is to describe and explain the "stream of activity" that constitutes daily life. Here he differed from most of his early colleagues who were more interested in the mental processes and the internal determinants of human action. He did not deny the existence of consciousness in animals or human beings, but he questioned its usefulness in explaining behavior—as long as we have no measures of consciousness that can be replicated by independent observers.

Watson's emphasis on observable behavior and his reluctance to infer causal factors that others sought within the organism—be it rat, monkey, or human being—naturally led him to analyze the circumstances in which the action occurs. Thus he came to study the context as an important—and eventually to consider it the *major*—determinant of behavior.

It is relatively easy to design significant laboratory experiments involving animals. Factors in the context can be manipulated at will and the animal itself can be influenced with little difficulty—for example by depriving it of food or water. But the behavioral principles that are discovered by these methods cannot be applied directly to human beings. In his early years, at least, Watson argued that the results of animal studies are interesting in themselves but cannot be simply extended—they only provide us with hints about human characteristics. Some principles of human behavior might be implied by laboratory experiments with animals, but before they can be applied to humans—before we can say just what people do, or why or how—the behavioral principles have to be tested in the human situation. In later years, Watson held this view with much less rigor and vigor.

Finally, Watson was disturbed by the partial nature of many psychological investigations. Some researchers had studied perception, others memory, some learning and other judgment. Watson believed that the human being should be studied as a whole organism, as an entity that reacts to environmental conditions. It is true that he often studied limited aspects of the human being—emotions, thought, habits, the creation of fear, and the development of motor skills—but his major concern was always with the whole being.

Watson's psychology centered on the relationship between external stimulus and behavior, summarized in the famous S → R paradigm. Especially one variation, the conditioned reflex, held his attention for many years. According to this principle, when an established stimulus-response link is paired with a neutral stimulus, eventually the neutral stimulus is followed by the earlier response. Thus Watson conditioned Little Albert to fear a white rat by producing a loud noise whenever the child reached for the animal, whereas the boy originally had been attracted to small white furry animals. Initially, Watson considered the reflex as a "convenient hypothesis," but in later years he came to view it as the basic unit of behavior.

From his laboratory studies, Watson drew the conclusion that the determinants of behavior are to be found in a persons' social and physical context. Eventually he came to deny the existence of human instincts and inherited capacities. But this position of extreme environmentalism has not stood the test of time. Psychologists and biologists have demonstrated that inherited capacities play a role in human behavior. And even though we do not know yet what the limits are, it is quite certain that physiological, neurological, and in the last analysis genetic factors are significant factors in human behavior.

Watson believed that humans, like animals, learn through conditioning. His data showed that conditioning is significant in animal life, and he simply extended those learning principles to the human world. Later it was discovered that conditioning—as Watson viewed it—plays only a relatively minor role in human behavior. As we will see in the following two chapters, people learn in other ways that are much more complex and efficient.

When we look at Watson's work in these three areas—the conditioned reflex, the role of environment, and conditioning—we cannot help but regret that his scientific career was cut short. Had he been able to continue his careful investigations, he probably would have discovered the limitations of his earlier positions. Without the discipline imposed by new data and debates with colleagues, Watson over-extended his ideas instead of qualifying them, and his positions became rigid rather than retaining the flexibility of live thought. The truly scientific "wait and see" attitude of his early years was replaced by doctrine and certainty—to everyone's loss. The specter of John B. Watson that arises before us when we think of the darker aspects of "behaviorism" is the older man with rigid beliefs, not the young scientist with fascinating ideas and new methods.

At least the kernels of Watson's ideas in these three areas are still with us (even though one cannot really say that Watson actually discovered them). But the implications for child-raising that Watson saw in laboratory studies are—and were—not really there. When Watson began to study children at the Phipps Clinic he was a pioneer. There were few if any reliable studies of child development, and his own work was not extensive enough to yield any definite conclusions. Certainly there were no empirically-founded principles from which such implications could be derived. As at least one biographer has suggested, Watson may have derived his ideas about child-raising largely from his own unhappy childhood. Perhaps he advocated a distant and formal relation between parent and child because he himself had felt such traumatic pain when his beloved father abandoned the family and walked out of his life.

A Dinner on Long Island

Stanley Resor, president of the J. Walter Thompson advertising agency, hired John B. Watson in early 1921 at a salary of $10,000—a great amount of money when new college graduates were lucky to earn $2,500. The first assignments were menial indeed, for Watson was to learn the advertising business from the bottom up. He observed the selling of rubber boots in the South and of Yuban coffee in the Midwest, and that summer he clerked at Macy's for two months. In this way he became acquainted with marketing procedures and problems which later helped him develop very effective advertising campaigns. During the first few years, his major job consisted of doing research for the agency and consulting on various advertising projects. In 1924, Watson became a vice president, and within five years he was the highest paid employee of the company and the director of several national campaigns.

After 1921 the Watsons lived in a comfortable home on Long Island. A son, William, born in November 1921, and a maid completed the household. John Watson spent long days in his office in Manhattan and went on frequent business trips, while Rosalie led an active social life with her numerous friends in the artistic and theatrical circles of New York. They went to many parties and gave frequent dinners, and John had little time for academic psychology.

His interests in child development persisted, however, and he sought ways of combining his job with research in this area. In 1922 the Laura Spellman Rockefeller Foundation began to sponsor a project at the Manhattan Day Nursery, initiated by Watson and carried out by Louise Phillips, a graduate student in psychology at Columbia University. Every Saturday Watson spent a few hours with Mrs. Phillips at the laboratory, discussing new data and research problems. In spite of major difficulties—such as lack of adequate control over children and ignorance of the children's history and home life—significant results were achieved.

On a Saturday evening in the Fall of 1923, the Watsons invited Louise Phillips and her husband Steven to dinner. Rosalie had invited several other guests from her large circle of friends: the well-known Broadway actor Sidney Hendricks, Irene Colbert who had sung a major role in the musical *Golden Nuggets*, and Geraldine Arroz the concert pianist. James

Firham had written many articles about classical music and the modern theater and was now assistant editor of the magazine *Long Island Night Life*.

John Watson was fond of spirits and, like so many others, considered Prohibition an intellectual challenge. He had many connections in Canada, and the Watson parties were famous for the high quality of imported liquors. During the meal, the conversation centred on Arroz's just completed concert tour of South America and Hendrick's recent success in *Cozy Rooms*. Louise and Steven Phillips said little, for they were younger than the others and led more prosaic lives.

After dessert John Watson suggested that the terrace would be an ideal place on such a pleasant evening for some wine served in coffee cups. As the guests followed their host, Louise Phillips stayed with Rosalie to chat. They had been friends at Vassar College but had seen little of each other since Rosalie's marriage. When they were about to join the others on the terrace some time later, the guests were discussing psychological matters.

"By now our friends know quite a bit about psychology," Rosalie whispered. "But we often get into arguments. John has a way of bringing up his pet subject."

Phillips chuckled. "A man so full of grand conceptions has a right to do that. And shouldn't we all know psychology to understand ourselves?"

"Of course," Rosalie smiled. "And I support John a hundred percent in spreading the word."

When they appeared on the terrace, John Watson pointed to an empty chair next to him. "I know it's impolite to keep a hostess from her guests," he laughed, "but we are still in love and so we must sit together."

"Good heavens," Irene Colbert cried in mock surprise. "And you've been married for almost three years!"

"I'm not sure about the future of marriage in general," Watson replied, "but I *am* sure about this one. It was made in heaven—even if we said our vows here on earth."

Rosalie sat down beside her husband, while Louise Phillips took a chair next to Sidney Hendricks.

"Speaking of earth," Arroz said to John Watson, "what you just said about emphasizing behavior makes a lot of sense to me. But I can't help thinking that you're leaving out a great deal of what is human. Truly human."

"Emotions," Hendricks suggested. "And feelings, thoughts. Aren't those the things that make us different from dogs?"

"Psychology as the behaviorist views it is a purely objective experimental branch of natural science," Watson said firmly. "Its theoretical goal is the prediction and control of behavior."

"That sounds a bit frightening," Arroz said with a worried look at Rosalie.

"I'll go along with you for the sake of argument, John," Hendricks said slowly. "But consider this. When I'm on the stage there is a certain chemistry with all the other actors and we all have a good feeling for the author's words and message. And as any good actor will tell you, there often is—actually there always should be—a sense of communion with the audience. I always get a warm feeling from the audience when they are with me and like the play."

"I agree," said Colbert. "When I sing, and especially when I sing a great number, I can feel the audience's reaction—even when I don't see any one person."

"A behaviorist can talk about those things quite intelligently," Watson said amiably. "In my lectures at the New School for Social Research last year, for instance, I persuaded quite a few students of that."

"Young people don't have as many emotional experiences as we've had," Colbert said and pointed to everyone in turn. "And they haven't lived with feelings for as long as we have."

"And they don't *know* as much as we," Firham suggested. "So they are easier to convince."

Rosalie Watson looked at her husband, but before he could answer she said: "How much do we know about what goes on inside us? We can't study feelings directly. Feelings and emotions—we only know about them from what we hear people say and observe what people do."

"But I *know* what I *feel* when I play a Chopin nocturne, or the Tchaikovsky piano concerto," Arroz said with conviction.

"I'm sure you do, Geraldine," John Watson said amiably. "But I would have great difficulty studying your feelings, not to mention understanding them. We know so little about the human brain—that mystery box."

"What psychologists do, therefore,..." Louise Phillips halted and looked at Watson. He smiled, and she continued: "we look for explanations that don't involve inferences about what goes on inside a person."

Watson nodded. "We recognize that there is this mystery box, that something goes on there. But we try to explain human actions without focusing on that mystery box."

"And yet—I know what goes on inside my mystery box," Colbert persisted. "And I *know* yours is working too, John."

Watson laughed. "Of course, Irene. But I'd have a tough time telling you just what goes on inside me. And you would have difficulty describing your feelings—to anyone."

Before Colbert could answer, Phillips said, "Introspection is of limited use. Psychology won't go anywhere until we use different methods."

"That's right," Watson nodded emphatically. "Introspection forms no essential part of psychology's methods." After a pause he continued, "The scientific value of psychological data does not depend on the readiness with which those data lend themselves to introspection—or consciousness."

"I can see that in the case of animals," Firham said. "But humans have an inner life, don't they?—At least, I do. What about that aspect of life?"

"I'll give you an example," Arroz said. "When I play Schubert, and especially the Impromptus of Opus 142, I'm overcome. Last year, when I played them in Carnegie Hall, I played them for myself, really. I wasn't aware of the audience. I played the Impromptus for me, for Schubert—I simply felt, how can I say it?...A part of the universe, and..." she stopped, at a loss for words.

After a few moments, Watson said softly: "There you see the problem, Geraldine. You try to describe what goes on inside you—you use introspection—and you have trouble expressing yourself..."

"We all do," Colbert interrupted. "I have similar feelings when I sing and I can't describe them either."

"But darling," Rosalie Watson broke in, "How can you say you have similar feelings when Geraldine hasn't told us about hers? Aren't you just guessing?"

"I don't think so," Firham answered. "When I heard Weingartner conduct Beethoven's Seventh last year... I too had feelings that were similar to those Geraldine tried to describe. And that also happens at a good performance of Hamlet."

"But it's clear to me that Rosalie is right," Watson began.

"Of course," Hendricks laughed. "You have indoctrinated her."

"No, conditioned her, poor child," Colbert said in mock sorrow.

Watson joined in the laughter. Then he said: "To be serious for a moment, what you just tried to tell us about your inner life—or what you feel when you hear great music or a great play—shows how correct I am in getting away from introspection."

"You mean to say that I don't have such...such...such oceanic feelings when I play Schubert?" Arroz asked impatiently.

"No, Geraldine, I'm not saying that at all," Watson replied.

"That 'oceanic feeling' sounds like something Sigmund Freud would appreciate," Firham suggested.

"No, I don't think Freud would like that either," Watson said simply. "It's not factual enough. Too fuzzy. But look, Geraldine, you no doubt have such feelings. Or at least, feelings you describe that way. But words—in any language—are so limited that you can't describe your feelings to me. I don't know what you mean by 'oceanic,' really...I'm sorry."

"Perhaps that's because you like Tchaikovsky more than Schubert," Colbert suggested. "If you loved that Impromptu, the first one of Opus 142, the way Geraldine does, you would know what she means."

"That's just it, Irene," Watson said. "I would perhaps understand her feelings—because I experience them myself, not because she describes them to me. But actually I could never be sure that my feelings are similar to hers... You know, as a behaviorist I don't deny feelings, passions, dreams, and hopes... I have some of those myself. I just say that psychology can't deal with them until we have objective ways of describing and measuring them."

"But aren't there outward manifestations of inner feelings?" Firham asked.

"Of course," Rosalie Watson replied. "But we often have a hard time finding out just what that manifestation refers to, what it means. Even a simple behavior could have all kinds of roots."

"I don't quite follow you, Rosalie," Arroz said.

"Let's say I come to your house next Saturday afternoon, Geraldine. You are listening to a recording of Caruso while you are in the kitchen preparing a meat loaf."

"Good heavens, Rosalie, what an imagination!" Firham cried.

"Let me continue, Jim...After I greet you, Geraldine, I notice tears in your eyes...Now I wonder, why the tears? Are you moved by Caruso's aria or reacting to the onions you are cutting for the meat loaf?"

"Capital, my dear," Watson shouted. "What a splendid example of the problem."

"Well, Rosalie, how would you decide?" Hendricks asked.

"She'd simply ask her, Sidney, what else?" Firham suggested.

"Or she would observe how many onions have been cut," Watson added. "If Geraldine has just started on her first onion, she's reacting to Caruso."

"But if there is a pile of cut onions, Geraldine is reacting to Caruso or the onions or to the opera of which the aria reminds her," his wife continued. "It would be impossible to say which."

"You can still ask," Firham persisted.

"But would she know, and would you believe her?" Louise Phillips replied. "One would want some kind of objective measure."

"Good old Louise," Rosalie Watson said. "The true scientist, doubting everything."

"Of course you can believe me," Arroz said pointedly.

John Watson smiled. "We don't doubt your word, Geraldine," he said gently. "But Mrs. Phillips has a good point. When it comes to inner feelings, we may believe what someone says, and that person may well be honest and sincere, but even then the words may not reflect what is really going on...That's why it's better to rely on behavior and not introspection."

"But if you consider only behavior, what's the difference between humans and animals?" Firham asked.

Watson thought for a moment. Then he said: "the behaviorist recognizes no dividing line between man and brute."

"But remember Mozart," Arroz protested. "No rat ever wrote a sonata."

"At least none that we know about," Firham said facetiously. "And yet, in some little hole..."

"Wait just a minute," Watson continued sternly. "The human actions we study today are limited by our methods. When new measuring tools are discovered and improved instruments are developed, we can open new areas to observation and objective analysis. For the moment, however, psychology must do without consciousness."

"That puts a great limitation on psychology," Firham said. "It seems to me that much of what we are—so much that makes us human—lies precisely in those mental states. When you cut those out of psychology there doesn't seem to be much left."

"Right now I feel like another cup of wine," Colbert said and fingered the saucer.

"I observe your hand, I hear what you say, and John is getting the bottle from behind his chair," Rosalie Watson said. "You may feel like a sip of wine, but what really counts is what you do about getting it."

"But Irene wouldn't say anything if she didn't feel like a cup of wine," Arroz observed. "If you just consider behavior, you leave out a lot."

"True enough," Rosalie Watson replied. "But behaviorism still includes many significant areas of life."

"I hate to always sound like a skeptic," Firham said, "But I'd like to hear some specifics."

"Well, Jim, let me try," John Watson began. "In my opinion, behaviorism is a science that allows us to understand the marvelous range of human actions we see all around us. Such an understanding can—should—be the basis of everyone's daily life. Imagine what the world would be like if we raised children properly! What if we made it possible for children to learn all the skills they need to develop their capacities and to get along with each other? And what if we then provided youngsters with a new world—a world unshackled by folklore, foolish customs, and insignificant conventions! You know how much all of those things restrict a person!"

"But, John..." Arroz interrupted.

"Hear me out, please," Watson persisted. "Look, I'm not saying that people should go to some God-forsaken place and form a colony, or go naked and live a communal life. I'm not asking that we eat roots or have 'free love.' What I do ask is—that we give behavioral principles a chance to work. Because only they can give people real opportunities to lead decent, happy lives."

"What you say sounds good, I must admit," Firham said. "But again I ask you, John, what about actual, concrete examples?"

"Take Albert, the little boy of eleven months who liked animals. As part of an experiment I hit a steel bar with a hammer whenever he stretched his hand to pet a white rat near him. After a few trials he became afraid of the white rat, and that fear soon extended to a white rabbit and even a seal-skin coat. You see, we conditioned fear of white furry things where no fear had existed before. Doesn't that show the effectiveness and power of conditioning?"

Hendricks nodded and was about to speak when Colbert exclaimed: "But John, what a nasty thing to do! The child was barely a year old! What about poor little Albert now? Does he still fear rabbits?"

"Is that the kind of experiment you do?" Arroz asked and turned to Louise Phillips.

"Oh no," Mrs. Phillips shook her head vigorously. "I could never work on such a project. I very much prefer benign experiments, where we try to help children. The work with Peter, for instance."

"Before we get to Peter, what about little Albert, poor thing?" Colbert asked.

"We lost contact with him soon after the experiment," Rosalie Watson replied unhappily. "The last time I saw him he was still afraid of the white rat..."

"I think he'd be much better off if he hadn't been conditioned to fear white furry animals," Hendricks said. "Who knows what else he has learned to fear by now?"

"But if you can condition fear into a person, so to speak, can't you condition fear out of a child?" Firham asked. "I mean, why couldn't you try that?"

"That's just what Louise Phillips is doing now," Watson replied. "Since we discovered that emotional responses could be put into an organism we are quite eager now to see whether they can be eliminated; and if so, by what methods."

"Oh, good," Hendricks exclaimed with relief. "What are you doing? Does it work?"

Watson smiled; "The experiment isn't finished yet, Sidney. But so far the results look very good."

"What *are* the results...so far?" Arroz asked eagerly.

"Go ahead, Louise, tell us," Rosalie Watson prompted.

Mrs. Phillips looked at Watson and hesitated. He smiled and nodded, and she described the situation and routine at the Manhattan Day Nursery. "First, Dr. Watson and I tried to reduce fears that the children already had by removing the object from the child's life. One girl, for instance, was afraid of rabbits. We talked to her parents and made sure that she would not see a rabbit for a while. But at the end of two weeks she was still afraid. We repeated the same method on about thirty other children with various fears, but the method simply did not work."

"So we are inclined to believe that the method of disuse in the case of emotional disturbance is not as effective as is commonly supposed," Watson said.

"How about talking with the children?" Hendricks suggested. "If they are old enough and can discuss their fears."

"We tried that, too," Louise Phillips said. "But it didn't work either. Then we tried social pressure. Little Arthur was afraid of frogs. But even after the other children made fun of him and called him names, Arthur still yelled in fright when he saw a frog—even when the frog was in an aquarium."

"So we came to the conclusion that we should *do* something," Watson continued. "It would be best, of course, to create a fear in a child so that we would know the history, and then try to remove it. But that wasn't possible..." he glanced at Louise Phillips, "and so we decided to work with children who were already afraid of something that we could manage."

"Yes, my good friend Louise is very sensitive," Rosalie Watson interrupted.

"Admirable ethics, I would say," Steven Phillips murmured.

"I just couldn't produce a fear in a child," his wife said firmly. "In most lives there are too many fears already. Why add one? Especially since we are not perfectly sure of how to eliminate fears—new *or* old..."

"Louise's problem is that she likes children too much," her husband added.

"Actually, it doesn't matter," John Watson said with a benign smile. "We've worked on this project for only a few months, and already we have a pretty good idea of what works."

"Well, come on, tell us," Colbert urged.

"We have just about finished working with a little boy, Peter," Louise Phillips began. "He is three years old and was afraid of many things: white rats, rabbits, fur coats, cotton balls, fish, and even some toys."

"Good heavens," Arroz interrupted. "What a poor little thing! One can just imagine what his life will be like when he grows up."

"Unless he outgrows his fears," Firham said.

"But that's not likely, is it, John?" Colbert asked.

Watson shook his head. "Very unlikely…Possible, but not likely. And then it wouldn't be a simple 'growing up' but something else that we don't know about."

"Tell us what you did," Rosalie Watson pressed.

"We showed Peter in many ways that other children played with the things he feared, and we noticed some improvement," Louise Phillips said.

"Only very little, actually," Watson interjected.

"Then Peter was in the hospital with scarlet fever," she continued. "On his way home he had a terrible experience with a large dog, and when we saw him again in the nursery he was as fearful as ever."

"I hope you didn't give up on him," Hendricks said anxiously. "It's a challenging case, isn't it?"

"Then we decided to do the opposite of what happened to little Albert," Louise Phillips replied.

"What do you mean?" Arroz asked.

"Well," Phillips said, "with Albert, Dr. Watson associated some aversive thing, a loud noise, with a nice white thing, a rat. The two became connected, and eventually the frightful noise led to fear of the rat—and some other white furry things, even a Santa Claus mask. So we thought, why not associate a feared thing, a rabbit, with something nice? And that's exactly what we did—but very gradually. We asked Peter's parents to allow us to give him an afternoon snack, just a glass of milk and some cookies. He ate in a high chair at one end of a room that was…oh, some forty feet long. Then we put a rabbit in its cage far enough away so Peter's snack was not disturbed."

"Actually, it was close to the other end of the room, if I remember correctly?" Rosalie Watson asked.

Steven Phillips nodded. "Yes. I was surprised at the distance needed to keep Peter calm. That may well be a good empirical measure of fear."

"But one would have to know all the other factors, including what the fearful child is doing," John Watson cautioned. "If the child is bored, or upset from something else, the necessary distance might be greater."

"That's enough, John, please," his wife said impatiently. "Let's hear what Louise has to say."

Louise Phillips smiled and continued: "We marked the spot where the cage was on the first day, and each day after that we put the cage with the rabbit a little closer to Peter in his high chair. After several days…actually, more than three weeks…we were able to place the rabbit on the table next to Peter. And then, one fine day, Peter was able to eat with one hand and pet the rabbit with the other."

"What about the other things he was afraid of?" Arroz asked.

"Peter then was no longer afraid of fur coats and feathers either. And he doesn't mind a white rat, though he doesn't play with it yet," Phillips replied.

"What a marvelous experiment!" Colbert exclaimed. "Does this method also work with other children, other fears?"

"We don't know that yet," John Watson answered. "We are studying other children now, but the experiment isn't over yet."

"The results are very promising," Louise Phillips said happily. "This method of gradually approaching a feared object in the presence of pleasant things seems to work. Perhaps others can benefit from our discovery."

"So far our conclusions are tentative," Watson cautioned. "In Peter's case we didn't know the origin of his fears."

"And it didn't matter," Steven Phillips added. "They were reduced anyway."

"Yes," Watson agreed. "But to really understand what's going on we need to know more about the origin of fears. We need to study how fears are transferred from one object to another, from a rat to a rabbit to a beard. Only when we have more experience with building up some primary fears, and reducing them, can we be sure of what's going on."

"But then we run into ethical problems," Steven Phillips reminded him, and Watson nodded.

"Even now, though, I think that there is more to the origins of fear than just the simple pairing of stimuli," Louise Phillips said. "From watching my own little daughter, it seems to me that children tend to fear the unexpected and unusual. Fear probably develops when the individual knows enough to recognize his inadequacy to cope with a strange or sudden experience."

"I agree with that," said her husband. "Of course, we need to perform some more experiments. One gets all kinds of good ideas from watching a child all day. It pays to have one's own children."

"We are raising Billy according to my principles," John Watson said happily.

"You know, John," Rosalie reminded him, "Billy seems to be afraid of goldfish. I'm not sure yet, but I've noticed that he's staying away from the aquarium. Perhaps you can try out the new method on Billy."

"I'd wait until the method is perfected," Colbert said. "You don't want to hurt Billy."

"It won't hurt Billy," John Watson assured her. "The method helped Peter, and it's helping other children, too, as Mrs. Phillips said. So it's safe enough for me to try out on Billy."

"You're more courageous than I would be," Arroz said. "I wouldn't expose my children to such methods."

"I'm not courageous, dear Geraldine," John Watson said. "I know I'm right, that's all. I've been studying child development for years now, and I know what my experiments and observations show. I also know what conclusions one must draw from them."

"Conclusions for what?" Hendricks asked.

"For child raising," Watson answered enthusiastically. "Soon parents will be able to raise their children correctly, in the scientific way. On the basis of behavioristic principles."

"I always thought parents have done a reasonably good job," Hendricks chuckled. "For thousands of years. Why this concern all of a sudden?"

"Because what is crucial—really crucial in one's life—is what one learns," Watson replied. "I don't believe there are inherited capacities or talents."

"Everybody knows how to talk, and many people can act in some way," Hendricks said emphatically. "But a *great* actor builds on a base—a capacity—he is born with. Absolutely."

"Or consider pianists," Arroz added. "Lots of kids take piano lessons, but only some have talent. And a very few end up in Carnegie Hall. The difference between the many and the few is talent."

Watson shook his head. "You see what I mean when you observe children from birth. So much depends on the training that goes on in the cradle and afterwards. The behaviorist would not say: 'this boy inherits his father's capacity or talent for being a fine swordsman.' He would say: 'This child certainly has his father's slender build of body, the same type of eyes...' And he would go on to say: '...and his father is very fond of him. He put a tiny sword into his hand when he was a year old, and in all their walks he talks sword play, attack and defense, the code of duelling and so on!' A certain type of physiological structure, plus early training, account for adult performance."

"What you say sounds reasonable—in that case," Firham said slowly. "But can we say the same about every occupation, every complex task? What about mathematics?"

"Or ballet," Colbert added.

"Or consider Michelangelo," Hendricks joined in.

"The specific task doesn't matter," Watson replied. "If you teach a child early enough to handle a brush or a chisel..."

"Or a piano," Arroz interrupted with some passion.

"A chisel, or a *piano*," Watson continued, "you'll eventually have a painter or a sculptor—or a pianist."

"That sounds more like a belief than a fact," Firham groused. "What about children who don't care about a brush or a chisel or a piano? What about children who prefer to run, or watch animals, or do math problems?

Aren't these early likes and dislikes reflections of different talents, of different capacities?"

Again Watson shook his head. "Not nearly as much as people think. You know, I would really like to set up a grand experiment—one that would last for several years. I would start with a dozen healthy, normal infants, and set up an environment in which to raise them. Then, you pick one or another baby at random, and tell me what you want the baby to become. Doctor, lawyer, artist, chief, merchant, even beggar and thief, as they saying goes. A few years later the youngsters will be well on their way to those occupations. What's important is training in the right kind of environment. Abilities, talents, race, ancestors, what have you, don't matter much if at all."

"I won't believe that till I see it," Arroz shook her head.

"Even if you don't do that experiment, you should write a book about child raising, John," Firham suggested. "You would help a lot of parents— and become a millionaire to boot. You know, sometimes I think Elsie and I made quite a few mistakes in raising our children."

"Old Stanley Resor pays me well enough," Watson laughed. "I'd write the book not for money but to get people to raise their children correctly. Many adults would be so much better off and so much happier if their parents hadn't...well...how shall I put it...raised them so poorly."

"Well, John, you've whetted my appetite," Hendricks said eagerly. "How should one raise a child?"

"I haven't worked out all the details," Watson replied. "But eventually I'll write that book."

"Oh, come on, give us some idea of your approach," Colbert urged. "I need to know, in case I get pregnant soon." She laughed, and the others joined in.

"My method of child raising is based on psychological research and is designed to prevent the problems so many children—and parents—have today," Watson began.

"What are those problems, John?" Arroz asked sweetly. "I mean, besides disobedience and disrespect."

"Those aren't the major problems, Geraldine," Rosalie Watson replied. "John is concerned with the more serious problems that stay with children into adulthood."

"Oh ho," Firham said with mock anxiety. "Such as the problems you see in me?"

During the general hilarity, Watson filled the cups of his guests and called for the maid to bring another bottle. Then he said: "The problem is that children don't learn to be independent, they remain emotionally immature because they remain attached to their parents."

"But isn't that natural, John?" Arroz asked. "Aren't all children born dependent and emotionally tied to their parents?"

"To some extent, of course," Watson nodded. "But parents should help them to stand on their own two feet—emotionally, I mean—as soon as possible."

"What would you suggest, then, Dr. Watson?" Steven Phillips asked.

Watson thought for a moment and then he said: "I would advise, never hug or kiss your children, never let them sit on your lap. If you must, kiss them once on the forehead when they say good night. Shake hands with them in the morning."

There was a long silence, and some of the guests looked shocked.

"Rosalie, dear," Arroz said finally, "Is that how you are raising Billy? He's barely two years old!"

Rosalie Watson nodded. "I try to follow John's system, but once in a while I sneak in a hug and a kiss—or two."

"I always thought children that age need a lot of affection," Colbert said firmly. "I hope you don't ruin Billy."

"My methods are based on solid research," John Watson said loudly. "Fact is, children don't need hugs and kisses. *Parents* want to hug and kiss, and too much of that is detrimental to a child's proper emotional and psychological development."

"Spoken like a true professor..." Hendricks began.

"Ex-professor, and well-to-do because of it," Watson interrupted him with a sad smile.

"Yes," Hendricks continued. "And I agree, John, that too much affection—like too much of anything—is probably bad. But why go from too much to nothing? Isn't there a happy and effective median?"

"It's better not to hug and kiss, because parents do it mostly for themselves," Watson assured him. "Talk with your children as much as you want to, discuss any topic they like. But be careful with affection."

"What do *you* do, John, with little Billy?" Arroz asked with concern in her voice.

"I've never kissed him," Watson replied, "and I don't intend to start any time soon. I talk to him as much as he wants to. I tell him that I love him. And I shake his hand in the evening."

"I sneak in a kiss and a hug once in a while," Rosalie whispered into Colbert's ear.

"But Billy is only two years old," Arroz persisted. "Words don't mean as much now as they will later. Right now he needs love—and the *experience* of parental love."

"I don't think that love can be transmitted in a hand shake," Firham added.

Watson shrugged his shoulders. "I look at the results of psychological research and draw the logical conclusions, Jim. That's all I can do."

Firham shook his head and chuckled. "When your book is published, John, parents will come and string you up in your garden."

"Perhaps," Watson smiled. "But I have faith in people. They will accept the results of research. Psychology will set them free."

"I don't know why I'm always disagreeing with you today," Colbert said. "But I don't see how psychology can set us free. It seems to me that Freud has burdened us with all kinds of unconscious monsters, and he tells us that we are slaves to the id..."

"Oh, good heavens, Irene," Rosalie Watson interrupted. "Don't get John started on Freud, please."

"Actually, I used to think well of Freud," John Watson said and wagged a finger at his wife. "That was in 1905, when I first became acquainted with his work. Later on, of course, I changed my mind." He chuckled, and Rosalie stroked his arm.

"Rosalie mentioned to me the other day that you had actually studied philosophy," Hendricks said. "Why did you leave that field—I mean, I'm very glad you did."

"Yes indeed," Watson reminisced with a smile. "At the University of Chicago I studied philosophy...during my first year there. God knows I took enough philosophy to know something about it. But it wouldn't take hold. I passed my exams but the spark was not there. I got something out of the British school of philosophers, but nothing out of Kant, and, strange to say, least of all out of John Dewey. I never knew what he was talking about then, and, unfortunately for me, I still don't know."

"And then you began to study animals?" Louise Phillips asked.

Watson nodded. "At Chicago, and later on, I never wanted to use human subjects. I hated to serve as a subject. I didn't like the stuffy, artificial instructions given to subjects. I always was uncomfortable and acted unnaturally. With animals I was at home and I felt close to biology—my feet on the ground. And then I began to think: Can't I watch animals and discover everything that other students are finding out by watching humans?"

"When you were in Chicago, John, did you attend many concerts?" Arroz asked. "To get in touch with the truly human?"

Watson shook his head. "No, Geraldine, those were frightfully busy years. I did so much more than simply study for many, many hours a week. I also had to earn a living. For two years I used to dust professor Angell's desk and straighten his office and clean the apparatus. I delivered books for an instructors' circulating library for $1.00 per Saturday. Life was hard, and I had no time for music—or much of anything but study."

"I couldn't live without the Emperor Concerto," Arroz said.

"Nor I without song," Colbert added.

"And what would life be without theater?" Hendricks asked. "After all, that's where we learn to understand ourselves and mankind."

John Watson looked surprised. He was about to speak when the others began to illustrate their views with events from their lives and the careers of friends. He listened to his guests and looked out over the garden, an empty cup in his hand.

$$\boxed{\Psi}$$

Notes

I have chosen the encounter's date and setting to reflect the watershed of Watson's life: the end of his academic years and the beginning of a new career in the advertising business. He lived with his new wife on Long Island, and their active social life included, I imagine, conversations on psychological topics. All subsidiary characters are fictional, as are their words and those of Rosalie Watson.

I have relied primarily on David Cohen's *John Broadus Watson: the Founder of Behaviorism* (London: Routledge & Kegan Paul, 1979), which describes both his life and major ideas, and on his own chapter "John Broadus Watson," in *A History of Psychology in Autobiography*, vol. 3, edited by Carl Murchison (New York: Russell and Russell, 1961).

The classic *Behaviorism* (New York: W. W. Norton & Co., 1930) outlines Watson's major ideas. A fascinating account of the experiment with Little Albert, and of the myths and errors that have accumulated over the years, is given by Ben Harris in "Whatever Happened to Little Albert?" *American Psychologist* vol. 34 pp. 151–160, (February 1979).

9

B.F. SKINNER
An Evening in Houston, 1962

B.F. Skinner is probably the best known American psychologist today. His views have aroused lively controversies, and the philosophical debates on his ideas are not likely to be resolved in the near future. It is sometimes difficult to look at his basic work as such, because so many people are emotionally involved in the various implications they see. Yet an understanding of the basic work and an objective assessment of it are essential if we want to appreciate his contributions to our knowledge of human nature.

Burrhus Frederic Skinner was born on March 20, 1904 in Susquehanna, Pennsylvania. His father was a lawyer who worked for the Erie Railroad and later opened a private practice. Many relatives had lived in the town for several years, and the family was warm and close knit. A younger brother died at sixteen.

The boy roamed the countryside with his friends and spent many hours constructing all kinds of mechanical gadgets. He attended the same school his parents had, but broadened his education by reading as many books as he could and by performing various experiments at home. During these years he developed literary interests, wrote poems and stories, and played the piano and saxophone.

At Hamilton College Skinner majored in English literature, and after his graduation in 1926 decided to prepare for a writing career. But after two years—which he spent at home trying to write, in Greenwich Village working in a book store, and in Europe—he came to the conclusion that he would not then be a successful author.

Several of Skinner's long-time interests now began to outshine literature: his curiosity about human beings and their actions, his liking for animals and mechanical devices, and his enthusiasm for scientific methods. Gradually, he came to see psychology as a way to combine all of these interests.

Skinner entered Harvard University as a graduate student and began his formal studies in psychology. In 1931, he received his PhD for a dissertation on the history and nature of the reflex. Skinner remained at Harvard for the next five years, supported by fellowships which allowed him to devote all of his time to study and research. For several months he worked in a physiology laboratory, but gradually his fascination with the experimental analysis of behavior came to eclipse his other scientific interests.

In the fall of 1936, Skinner joined the faculty of the University of Minnesota. Soon after arriving in Minneapolis he married Yvonne Blue, who had majored in English at the University of Chicago. His first academic book, *The Behavior of Organisms*, appeared two years later. In it he described the results of his years of research and formulated some tentative propositions. He continued to improve his experimental apparatus—which came to be known as the "Skinner Box"— and devised new methods for the objective gathering of data.

During the 1930s he worked mainly with rats, but on a war-time project he began to use other animals. During 1942 and 1943 he was engaged in research sponsored in part by the General Mills company. There he perfected efficient techniques for conditioning pigeons to perform a variety of complicated and exacting tasks. But the major project—training pigeons to guide a missile to its target—was not funded beyond the demonstration stage.

When his second daughter was born, he built an enclosed crib to provide the baby with a warm, interesting and comfortable environment. For two and a half years his daughter slept and spent several hours daily in the "aircrib." She never showed any ill effects and has lived a normal life ever since—contrary to stories that began making the rounds soon after Skinner described the "aircrib" in popular magazines.

In 1944, Skinner received a Guggenheim fellowship and devoted considerable time to his perennial project, the analysis of language. A year later he became chairman of the psychology department at Indiana University. There he continued his research projects and also ventured into a rather different area: a novel. *Walden Two* is the description of an ideal society based on the behavioral principles he had derived from extensive experimental work. It aroused both controversy and enthusiasm, and over the years has served as a model for several communal projects. The book was published in 1948, the year he moved back to Harvard University.

During the 1950s he continued his laboratory studies. He used pigeons to analyze the effects of various consequences on behavior and published his results in *Schedules of Reinforcement* (with Charles Ferster). He also wrote a textbook, *Science and Human Behavior*, and completed the book he had begun more than twenty years earlier, *Verbal Behavior*. The latter was severely criticized by linguists, largely because linguists consider language as the expression of ideas and meaning, while Skinner viewed language like other behaviors that are learned and maintained through differential reinforcement. He also spent considerable time developing systems of programmed learning. Together with colleagues he developed teaching machines, which applied learning principles to the acquisition of various intellectual and motor skills.

In his several books and a large number of articles Skinner advocated the scientific analysis of human behavior. This implies a focus on observable events and measurable relationships among them. Activities therefore, should be analyzed in terms of their relation to preceding and subsequent external events. Skinner believed that just as we do not need to consider a pigeon's thoughts to explain its pecking at a lighted button, so we can explain human behavior without reliance on mental factors. Most internal processes are inferred on the basis of one or another theory, be it Freud's, Maslow's, or anyone else's. But psychological theories are often difficult if not impossible to test, refute, or validate—they simply are *there* as long as they seem plausible. Hence Skinner has been suspicious of theories and has tried to stay away from building theories of that sort himself.

Over the years, his work has inspired an immense number of experiments with humans as well as animals, and modified versions of his conclusions have become part of modern psychology. His intellectual position—expressed in books, articles, and at scientific meetings—has upset many people, but it has also forced them to assess their own views.

Skinner's contributions lie in three areas. The most significant, and the one we are concerned with in this chapter, is his experimental research on behavior. The results can be summarized in the form of propositions which have a very solid empirical basis. Secondly, these principles have been applied in a wide range of behavior modification programs, most of them designed to reduce individuals' difficulties. Behavior principles have also been used to improve instruction through the development of programmed learning and teaching machines. Both contributions have been generally accepted and are significant aspects of the modern world.

The third area, however, has aroused considerable controversy. Skinner's outlines of the social and cultural implications of behavioral principles (e.g. in *Beyond Freedom And Dignity*) have engendered heated debates among humanists and social scientists. The principles' alleged philosophical implications, finally, have led to acrimonious discussions even outside philosophy.

Unfortunately, controversies surrounding the last area have overshadowed Skinner's significant work in the first two. When people have negative views of behaviorism today, they are usually reacting to the principles' presumed social and philosophical implications. Many of these implications, however, seem to reflect mainly the observer's own ideas and predilections.

Skinner has been careful not to build a theory of behavior or outline a philosophy of life. Instead, he has formulated a number of propositions which summarize the results of his own and other researchers' work. These behavioral principles describe important human characteristics and are ethically neutral. They do not represent a complete picture of human beings but contribute to it—as do physiological and other principles. It is unfortunate that so many people have read various negative overtones into Skinner's empirical work; such noises make it difficult to appreciate the principles and their applications to daily life.

BASIC HUMAN CHARACTERISTICS

We must consider Skinner's research not only in its own right—that is, as the study of behavior—but also as a reaction to the several approaches that prevailed when he began his work in the early 1930s. Watson's extreme position required all too many assumptions and had such a weak empirical basis that it could be easily ridiculed. The psychologist Clark Hull postulated the "organism" that intervenes between a stimulus and a response, and proposed a new paradigm: $S \rightarrow O \rightarrow R$. But while this improvement was quite acceptable to most psychologists—after all, the organism, be it animal or human being, does perceive a stimulus and does the behaving—Hull's hypotheses regarding the organism's innards met with considerable skepticism.

Skinner thought that Watson's position was too limited, and he considered Hull's formulas as little more than doubtful inferences and guesses. Most important, Skinner discovered in his early animal experiments that behavior is affected not so much by preceding stimuli (the S in the $S \rightarrow R$ formula) as by the *consequences* of behavior that had occurred previously. Other psychologists (for example, Edward Thorndike) had known about this, too, but Skinner made the study of this phenomenon his life's work.

Pavlov's dog experiments and Watson's study of Little Albert had focused on the relationship between a new stimulus (a bell or white rat) and subsequent behavior (salivation or crying). This kind of learning has come to be known as "respondent conditioning," because the organism responds to preceding events.

During the 1930s Skinner discovered that much animal behavior and most human actions follow a different paradigm. Frequently, behavior is not an automatic response to earlier stimuli. What matters, instead, is that activities are followed by certain consequences. From previous experiences in similar circumstances, the organism learned what these consequences are. The behavior influences events in the environment, it operates on the context. Hence Skinner called this kind of learning "operant conditioning."

In a typical experiment, a pigeon learns to peck at a green disk because such pecking is followed by food. But when the pigeon happens to peck at a red disk, no food comes down the chute. Soon the pigeon has learned not to peck at the red disk. When such differential reinforcement is combined with successive approximation, extremely complex activities can be established, in humans as well as animals.

Over the years, Skinner and his associates performed many hundreds of experiments on various animals and human beings. These studies have been designed to discover just what kinds of external events, and what changes in them, have what effects on a wide range of activities. A rather consistent body of knowledge has been accumulated, and it is now possible to summarize the results of these experiments in the form of propositions.

The initial supporting evidence of these propositions consisted mainly of laboratory experiments with rats and pigeons. But today there is a large and increasing number of human studies which show, on the whole, that similar propositions hold for human beings. The behaviors and their complexities differ, of course, as do the consequences, the context, and the time frames of events. Today there are enough human studies—not only experiments but also systematic observations in the real world, performed by psychologists of various theoretical persuasions—that we no longer need to rely on extrapolations from animal experiments.

The major postulate states that the most significant determinants of present behavior are the consequences which followed similar actions in the past. There are two important corollaries: when an activity has been followed by positive consequences in the past the probability of the activity being repeated in similar circumstances increases; and when an action has been followed by negative (or no) consequences in the past the probability of that action being repeated in similar circumstances decreases. The rate and schedule of reinforcement affect the frequency with which activities occur, and Skinner has devoted considerable effort to the analysis of this relationship.

In the early years, Skinner viewed "positive consequences" (or *reinforcers*) as those external events which strengthen or maintain the preceding actions, while "negative consequences" (or *aversive* factors) weaken the preceding action. Most positive and negative consequences are transsituational, in that they are effective in various circumstances and influence many different behaviors. For example, food is an effective reward for people who have not eaten for some time (i.e. when there is some deprivation), and we need not continually discover—and define—the effects of food each time an action occurs.

While deprivation in animals usually has a physiological basis, human beings are frequently affected by their culture. Thus we consider filet mignon more reinforcing than just plain food, and Levi's a greater reward than any old pants.

The second proposition holds that deprivation and satiation determine the nature and magnitude of the reinforcing and aversive character of the consequences of most activities. As general corollaries we can say that the greater the deprivation, the more significant the related consequence is likely to be, and the more likely a person will act in ways that produce the reinforcer.

Deprivation and satiation are not only matters of degree; they also vary in the ease and speed with which they can be changed. A steak dinner quickly reduces our food deprivation or "hunger" (but not for a vegetarian who would refuse the meal). An increase in wages reduces our material deprivations rather slowly because we soon discover new wants unless we focus all of our attention on the hereafter. These illustrations point to another corollary: among human beings there are a great variety of reinforcers which reflect an individual's society, culture, and historical period. Even within a culture there are likely to be differences in the reinforcers people have learned, depending on family tradition, upbringing, and idiosyncratic factors.

Behavioral consequences can also take the form of avoiding or escaping from some negative event or of losing something that we value. The brushing of teeth, for example, is reinforced by our avoiding cavities (but only if we look far enough ahead).

Most activities are affected by the situation in which they occur. An individual gradually learns through repeated experiences that a specific action is followed by positive consequences whenever a particular aspect of the context (commonly viewed as a "signal") is present. Later, when this aspect reappears, the behavior that was previously reinforced in this context is likely to be repeated. We have learned to discriminate among various aspects of our context, just as the pigeon learned to discriminate between the red and green buttons in its cage.

Similarly, a person gradually learns that some action has negative consequences when a certain aspect of the context is present. Later, whenever this aspect of the context reappears, the action that was previously punished (or at least not reinforced) is not likely to be repeated. The third proposition states that the more similar the present context is to previously learned contextual aspects, the more likely the previously learned actions are to recur—or less likely, if previous consequences were negative.

We can summarize the principles of behavior in this paradigm, where the behavior is always the central part:

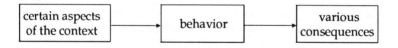

Human activities are largely determined by a) the likely consequences b) which are indicated by the present context and c) whose character and magnitude are a function of the individual's deprivation.

Over the years, Skinner has been very careful to avoid internal factors and inferred processes. He has consistently explained animal and human behavior in terms of external events and the relationship between organism and context. There is nothing strange about such efforts in the case of animals, because we cannot check our inferences about the alleged thoughts, feelings, and memories of rats or pigeons. But when we study human beings it is tempting to assume that other people think, remember, and feel in ways that are similar to the way we do, and that such processes play a role in human actions.

Skinner does not deny such internal processes. But he believes that we do not need them to understand human activities, just as we do not need them when we study animal behavior. For example, in order to predict whether or not a person will slow down after a speed limit sign we need to know her learning history—that is, her previous experiences (which include events such as her friend's traffic ticket last month). But what happens when we do not know a person's learning history? Then we either cannot predict behavior (except in very general terms), or we listen to what the individual tells us about his experiences—verbal summaries of past events that may or may not be correct.

When we look at behavioral propositions we may be tempted to conclude that they simply reflect common sense. Folk wisdom—for example, about carrots and sticks—is often similar to learning principles. We should not be surprised by such parallels, because folk wisdom summarizes some aspects of human behavior just as psychological principles summarize experimental studies of human behavior. But proverbs—such as "spare the rod and spoil the child"—are too general and do not take into account the complexity of human beings and ordinary life. The behavioral principles mentioned earlier allow us to state the necessary qualifications. Thus "spare the rod..." should not encourage punishment, for example, because experiments have shown that it is very difficult to learn from punishment alone. After all, punishment indicates only what actions are 'wrong' but does not indicate what is 'right.' The best way to establish and maintain behavior is to present positive consequences consistently and to use punishment as little as possible.

Skinner's major conclusions about behavior are inextricably linked with a vast amount of empirical data. His propositions about human activities cannot be rejected unless one denies hundreds of experiments, systematic observations, and other studies (e.g. of behavior modification) that have been performed during the last thirty years.

At the "Caminante del Mayab"

In 1962, Rice University located in Houston, Texas, celebrated its fiftieth anniversary. A number of artistic and intellectual events were scheduled to mark the occasion, one of them a symposium on the contrasting bases of modern psychology. Several well-known psychologists and philosophers were invited to present papers which were then discussed by the participants and members of the audience.

The symposium concluded in the afternoon of the third day, and Skinner felt rather tired. He left the campus immediately after the farewell dinner and planned to get a good night's sleep. But in the lobby of his hotel he met several students who invited him to a short hour of conversation.

Skinner accepted their invitation because he could not resist the temptation to talk with young psychologists. He told them that he had spent the days shuttling between hotel and campus, that he had hardly seen anything of Houston and would welcome an excursion even at this late hour.

"Not all of us are true believers," said Elena Calderón, a master's student in psychology. "I hope you don't mind."

"That's quite all right," Skinner chuckled. "I'm used to debates. Disagreements are fine as long as people are willing to consider new information."

The students discussed where they should go to show their visitor the "real southwest." Eventually Calderón suggested that they visit her uncle's Mexican restaurant which had recently opened but already enjoyed a good reputation. Skinner said that he had eaten, but would accompany the students to taste the atmosphere.

The "Caminante del Mayab" was a low building of white-washed adobe walls and arched windows of stained glass. Stone columns and heavy beams carried the red-tiled roof over a wide porch, where sheltered candles glowed on several empty tables. The flames of torches in iron brackets on the square pillars by the entrance provided unsteady light.

"What a romantic place," Skinner said to his companions as they waited in the torch light for the others in the second car. "But a rather long name for a restaurant, isn't it?"

Calderón smiled. "My uncle grew up in Mérida—that's in Yucatán," she answered. "He has always dreamed of a place like this. It reminds him of his childhood. The name means 'traveller from the lands of the Mayas.' It is also the title of a famous song by Guty Cardenas."

"Why don't we go in and get a table?" suggested Eric Olmstead, another student in psychology. "The others will find us there..."

They entered and Skinner stopped just inside the massive door. Wrought iron chandeliers hung from the dark-beamed ceiling supported by adobe columns. Large murals of Mayan scenes, especially of steep pyramids rising from dense jungle, provided an intimate yet open atmosphere.

When the maitre d' saw them he smiled: "Welcome home, Elena...Four?"

"Good evening, Antonio," she replied. "No, we'll be eight. The others are coming soon. Would you please tell my uncle that I'm here with some friends?"

The maître d' showed them to a large table in a corner.The heavy planks and simple chairs bespoke a hearty friendliness. As they sat down, a waitress approached.

"Now I don't need to visit Chichén-itzá," Skinner chuckled as he sat down on a chair against the wall. "Have you Mayan beer?"

Elena shook her head. "No, unfortunately, not yet. My uncle isn't sure about supplies. Yucatán is a long way off. 'Cerveza Corona' is brewed just across the border, and it's quite good."

"Well, then," Skinner said happily. "Let's have a round of crowns." He leaned back to enjoy a mural on the near wall and listened to the singing, guitars, and trumpets from an adjoining room.

The other four students had barely sat down when Elena's uncle joined them. He smiled broadly and welcomed the group. She introduced Skinner, and the two men shook hands.

"I've heard so much about you, professor," Francisco Gonzalez said. "Who hasn't?...But not everything I heard was good."

Skinner laughed. "It doesn't matter what you hear, but what you do. Stories are fine as long as one doesn't believe them."

"And my niece here..." the old man affectionately stroked her hair. "She tells me that at the university people respect you but worry about some of your ideas."

"That's probably because the ideas don't fit old frames," Skinner chuckled. "But—let's not think about that tonight."

"You are my guests, of course," Gonzalez said. "All of you. I want to...how do you say? ... reinforce you ... for coming. Just as your presence here makes me feel proud."

"Oh, tío," Calderón interrupted. "That doesn't sound quite right. You're beginning to talk like me."

They all laughed, and her uncle said, "I'm just trying to show you that I read some of your books, Elena. Anyway, Professor Skinner, how do you like my restaurant? It reminds me of home."

"It has a warm and friendly atmosphere." Skinner smiled. "Cozy and yet with a hint of adventure."

"And the food is good, too," the owner said proudly. "What may I get for you?"

The students ordered a light meal while Skinner requested only a *tortilla con queso*.

"I'll be back in a while," the owner said. "And I'll send you the music."

When he had left, Skinner asked Elena, "why didn't you like what your uncle said? It made sense to me."

"It made sense, of course," she replied. "But those words—for instance, reinforce—just didn't sound right."

"It would have been worse if he had talked about discriminative stimuli," James Bilden, a psychology student, said with a grin.

"There is the laboratory," Calderón continued, "and then there is life. The language of one sounds strange in the other. As if the words don't quite belong."

"It would be nice if the words we use didn't matter, as long as we recognize behavior for what it is," Skinner said. "But unfortunately, the words and concepts we use *do* matter. A reinforcer exists and operates regardless of what we call it."

"It seems to me that life would be awfully dull and our relations terribly stilted if we used technical terms on a daily basis," Bilden said.

"Perhaps," Skinner replied. "But I have never advocated that we use the words of science in the affairs of every-day life. Yet—if we did, we'd soon feel comfortable with them. Anyway, that would be a small price to pay for the advantage of using precise terms with exact meanings. Then we wouldn't get into trouble from the all-too-easy use of such words as dignity, will, freedom, hope—with all their emotional overtones."

"I'm not a psychologist," Berthold Finer said, "just a budding philosopher. But it seems to me that those concepts refer to things that are part and parcel of our humanity—and our civilization. There *is* such a thing as human dignity; and people have died defending their freedom. It seems to me that ever since Freud told us about the ego, id, and superego, we have been able to understand personality much better."

"The problem of freedom and dignity is an old and complex one," Skinner replied. "Those ideas have led people to perform noble deeds, of course—but much that is base has also been done in their name. Actually, I am thinking of writing a book on that subject; I have a few notes already.

However—those philosophical terms are dangerous when they are not handled correctly. We must be very careful if we want to live with them. But those psychological terms you mentioned and many others should be junked. Thrown out."

"Just because they refer to mental processes?" asked Henrietta Volker, an instructor of psychology.

After a moment's hesitation, Skinner said, "My objection to ego, superego, and so on is not that they are mental, but that they offer no real explanation and stand in the way of effective analysis. Experiments—mine and those of many others—have shown that behavior which seems to be the product of mental activity can be explained in other, more effective ways."

"Do we then disregard internal processes?" Bilden asked.

"Not at all," Skinner replied. "Eventually, an adequate science of behavior must consider events taking place within the skin of an organism—not as physiological mediators of behavior but as part of the behavior itself."

"Could you give us an example of this?" Finer asked.

Skinner thought for a moment. Then he said: "In a behavioral analysis, the relationship between an external event, say a green light, and the behavior, say a pigeon pecking at a disk or a person accelerating his car after the traffic signal changes, is studied directly. Traditional mentalistic formulations, however, emphasize certain way stations."

"But aren't those way stations, as you call them, part of our nature?" Bilden asked.

"Not really," Skinner shook his head. "Consider punishment. A scientific analysis examines the effect of a nasty comment, for example, while a mentalistic psychology is concerned first with the effect of the nasty comment, such as feelings of anxiety, and only later with the effect of anxiety on behavior. The mental state is supposed to bridge the gap between the cause and the effect. But it doesn't; it leads us astray. Most of those bridges are constructed by psychologists and philosophers. A mental bridge is especially attractive when cause and effect are separated by long periods of time. For instance, when the punishment occurs in childhood and the effect appears in the behavior of an adult."

"It seems to me that when we leave out these mental states the causal chain is incomplete," suggested Sidney Ramses, a student of anthropology.

"Many people think that complete causal sequences might include references to way stations," Skinner shrugged his shoulders. "But the fact is that way stations generally interrupt the account in one direction or the other. And isn't it true that these way stations, these mental states, these internal processes, often become central to the study of human beings? And some people get stuck in them!"

"Anthropologists are very fond of culture and personality," Ramses admitted.

"But such a preoccupation with mental way stations burdens a science of behavior with all sort of problems," Skinner continued. "Self-descriptions are so limited and often inaccurate. For instance, I am supposed to tell you how I feel and you tell me about your feelings. But how can we be sure *what* we feel, and that our descriptions are *accurate*?"

"So, what should one do?" Ramses asked. "Throw personality out?"

"We don't have to take the extreme position that mediating events must be eliminated," Skinner replied. "But we should certainly welcome other ways of explaining behavior."

"Just consider how we go about changing a person's opinion or attitude about something," Susan Lestrow, a student of psychology said eagerly. "When you come right down to it, we don't really alter anyone's mental state directly—because we don't know how to do that."

"Right," Skinner exclaimed. "In practice, when people speak of 'changing a person's mind' they usually talk about changing the person's verbal or physical environment."

"I'm still worried about the gap between cause and effect, between some external event and eventual behavior," Finer said plaintively. "That gap bothers a lot of people."

"But why fill the gap with all kinds of junk that's mostly words anyway?" Lestrow asked indignantly. "Why must the gap be filled now? Why not simply say: 'well, here is a mystery to be cleared up.' If all the gaps were filled, we might as well stop doing research and go dig ditches."

"Well said," Skinner agreed. "I hope you don't lose your enthusiasm after you graduate."

"Are ego and anxiety examples of what you call junk, Susan?" Ramses asked heatedly. But Skinner raised his hands in a soothing gesture.

"We are just at the beginning of the science of behavior," he said gently. "We must use all the relevant data we can. It seems to me that we should not reject any entity or process which has some useful explanatory power. It doesn't matter whether that entity or process is subjective or mental—but whatever we use has to be *effective*."

"And how do we know what's effective?" Finer asked.

"An explanation is effective if it helps us to predict future events—and if our predictions are borne out," Skinner answered. "Other researchers should be able to corroborate our conclusion when they look at similar data. A psychological principle is effective when it tells us something useful that we didn't know before, and when that information can be checked by independent observers who may not be our friends."

The students filled their glasses amidst the general hilarity brought on by the last words, but Ramses did not join in.

"I'm convinced that mentalistic ways of thinking about human behavior are barriers to much more effective ways," Skinner continued. "The major reason for this conviction is that I am certain—absolutely certain—that reports about one's own and other people's mental states and internal processes are inadequate and unnecessary."

"What you say makes sense," Olmstead said. "And when I listen to you, everything sounds reasonable. But when I hear other people talk about your ideas..."

"You should hear some of my philosophy professors..." Finer's voice trailed off.

"I think of myself as a neutral observer," Volker began. "And I have the distinct feeling that most of your critics are actually critics of behaviorism as a philosophy, rather than of experimental results or behavioral principles as such."

"People criticize the implications of these principles, especially the implications you describe for social systems," Ramses interjected. "Sociologists think you leave out too much—social systems are so complex, cultures so diverse."

"No one can object to empirical evidence, no one can deny experimental data," Lestrow said brightly. "Behavioral principles have very solid support."

"Just look at how widely behavior modification and programmed instruction have been accepted!" Calderón exclaimed. "In twenty years, they'll be as common as aspirin."

Skinner thought for a moment. Then he said: "As I see the situation, the basic behavioral principles, their social implications, and the philosophy are all interrelated. I don't see how they can be separated."

"I'm not sure—how about this?" Volker asked. "The principles of behavior have a firm experimental basis. No one quarrels with that. Some applications to individuals, say in behavior modification, have been effective for many people. But the social implications, and especially the philosophy, are mental extensions—if I may put it that way—and they don't have an empirical basis of their own."

"They have a logical basis, perhaps, but then the logic has to be checked," Finer suggested. "And," he added with a grin, "the people who do the checking should not be our friends."

Skinner laughed and nodded: "I agree that the last two don't have a solid independent base. But why should they need one? They are not separate from the basic principles."

"Perhaps the connections will become more evident in the future," Bilden suggested. "I think we need to know more about the ways in which behavioral principles operate in the real world, in daily life and in situations where many people interact, cooperate and compete."

"Speaking of real life," Calderón interrupted the discussion, "Here comes the music."

Francisco Gonzalez and the musicians had entered the main dining room and were approaching the group. "To honor you, Professor Skinner, please request the first song," the owner said.

"I don't know much about Mexican music," Skinner protested. After a moment's hesitation he asked: "what about that song you named the restaurant after?"

The musicians sang a verse and Skinner requested a translation. Gonzalez obliged and asked the musicians to repeat the verse. Then the students requested several other songs, and the musicians moved on.

"What do you think about music?" Olmstead asked. "How does music fit into behaviorism?"

"Basically, music is the result of certain behaviors," Skinner replied. "To some people the sounds are aversive, and to others they are reinforcing. It all depends on what one has learned to like."

"Do you like music?" asked Gonzalez, who had remained at the table. "What kind do you like?"

"I have always liked music," Skinner said. "When I was young I bought all the Mozart sonatas. I mean the scores. Then I played them all on the piano, at least once a year."

"Why do you play these Mozart sonatas?" Calderón asked. "Do they please you, or are they good for your soul, as some people would say?"

Skinner grimaced. "Let's just say I like them. The sounds, and the fact that I produce them, are reinforcing for me. And of course the music brings back some pleasant childhood memories. Those are reinforcing, too. I don't think one needs to go any further."

"I'm surprised at your interest in music—and classical music at that," Finer said. "Your writings, at least the ones I'm familiar with, give a rather different—one might almost say a cold and austere impression of you."

"I don't think one can—or should—draw conclusions about character or interest from a person's scientific books and articles," Lestrow said defensively. "There's no necessary connection between them."

"And we should not assess one in terms of the other," Bilden added. "But it is interesting to see what a famous author really looks like." He nodded to Skinner and smiled.

"Well, here I am," Skinner said happily.

"Yes, we can see you in the flesh now," Calderón said. "But what about the past? Could you tell us something about that? I mean, have you always been interested in psychology, and only in behaviorism?"

"That would be a long story, and perhaps boring," Skinner replied. But the young people urged him on, and he began: "In college I received no more than ten minutes of instruction in psychology—a mere whiff. From my philosophy professor, an old man who had studied under Wundt."

"At least you weren't perverted by that kind of stuff," Bilden interjected.

"Well, not then," Skinner laughed. "Anyway, after graduation I wanted to become an author. But in two years of trying I wrote very little—and wasted a lot of time."

"That's hard to imagine," Calderón exclaimed.

"Not really," Volker answered. "Remember that in those days we didn't know about self-management. One could only *talk* about will power. Even today, simply talking about will power is worth nothing compared to setting up a system of self-managed consequences that can strengthen any behavior."

"What you say is true," Skinner continued. "But you are too kind. The problem was that in those days I didn't have much to say. My discoveries and important ideas didn't come until later—much later."

"I didn't know you had been interested in writing and literature," Ramses said. "Poetry and behavioral principles don't seem to go together."

"Oh, but they do," Lestrow reminded him. "All poetry involves behavior."

Skinner raised his hands. "Let's not get into that," he suggested. "The whole area needs a lot more work."

"How did you become interested in psychology?" Olmstead asked. "Great novels contain psychological insights, of course, but it seems to me there's a big jump from novels, even psychological ones, to your kind of psychology."

"I'm not so sure," Skinner laughed softly. "Actually, I've always been interested in people and animals—and in what makes them do various things."

"What about the opinions of other people?" Ramses asked. "The many positive and negative reactions to your books, your ideas."

"I don't worry about other people's reactions," Skinner replied. "What matters is my work—my discoveries. Those have been quite rewarding. When I consider my articles and books I am quite pleased with the results of my efforts."

"How *do* you work?" Olmstead asked. "You have written so much, and when I look ahead in my life I don't see how I could write even half as much."

"I usually have much to do and am eager to present my ideas," Skinner replied. "Usually I write quite slowly, and there has been only one exception."

"What was that?" Calderón inquired.

"I wrote *Walden Two* in only seven weeks—on the typewriter rather than in longhand. And I think it shows. The book is quite obviously a venture in self-therapy: I was struggling to reconcile two aspects of my own behavior represented by Burris and Frazier. Some of it was written with great emotion. The scene in Frazier's room, in which Frazier defends Walden Two while admitting that he himself is not a likeable person or fit for communal life. Well, I worked out that scene while walking the streets near our house in St. Paul. I came back and typed it out in white heat."

"And later, how did you become interested in programmed learning?" Lestrow asked.

"About ten years ago, when my daughter was in the fourth grade, I visited her on an 'open school' day," Skinner began. "In an arithmetic class I suddenly realized that what the teachers did in that school—and in other schools—was contrary to our knowledge of the learning process. It wasn't their fault, of course, that hundreds of extremely valuable organisms were being taught in very inefficient ways. I figured out what kind of reinforcement system should be used, and then designed some teaching machines based on that system. I wanted to be sure that children would be rewarded for correct answers and be able to proceed at their own pace. Then learning would be effective—and interesting, too."

"That's fascinating," Lestrow exclaimed, "How important some days can be!"

"Actually, if I hadn't come up with that kind of individualized approach to learning, someone else would have," Skinner said. "Programmed teaching was pretty much in the air then."

"What concerns me is the use of certain words," Finer interjected. "Everything you just said makes sense. But why do you say 'a hundred valuable organisms'? There were children in the class rooms, not pigeons! Why say 'organisms' instead of 'children'? That kind of language really turns people off. And then they are more likely to reject your ideas, too."

Skinner shrugged his shoulders. "I usually say 'organism' because I want to indicate the universality of learning principles. There is a continuum from pigeons to people, when it comes to reinforcement, successive approximation, and the rest. And, to be honest, I don't much care whether people are turned off by my words or not. The facts behind the words will prevail. You know, in both my writing and research I have fought hard against deceiving myself—and other people. I avoid metaphors which are effective at the cost of obscuring issues. I want to avoid rhetorical devices which give unwarranted plausibility to an argument."

"You mentioned the universality of learning principles just now," Olmstead said. "Isn't that something we have to demonstrate rather than assume?"

"Those principles operate in all animals I've ever worked with," Skinner replied. "When I began to experiment with pigeons during the war I saw the same principles I had seen earlier in rats."

"But I think there may well be limitations—based on physiology, and especially the neurological structures of various animals," Ramses suggested.

"What would be an example of such limitations?" Lestrow asked.

"It's easy to teach pigeons to peck at a green button because they peck naturally," Olmstead said. "So, one can easily teach pigeons to peck at various things. Their genetic make-up produces a neurological structure that allows a pigeon to peck in response to lights and images. But other behaviors are more difficult for the pigeon, because they are farther removed from the pigeon's inborn neurological endowment, so to speak. I bet there are actions no pigeon can ever learn. I wonder, for instance, whether one could teach a pigeon to dig a hole and build a nest in it."

"Of course there are biological limitations," Skinner agreed. "We couldn't teach rats to fly. But my view is that within those limits—whatever they may be for a particular species—the same learning principles operate and can be applied."

"What matters is *how* animals learn, not *what* they learn," Lestrow added.

"So then we need to understand the neurological structure of each species, including human beings," Olmstead murmured. "Must we become physiologists?"

"I don't think so," Skinner answered. "The reinforcement principle is universal, and food is a reinforcer for all species."

"But only when the animal hasn't eaten a lot recently," Finer interjected with a broad smile. "Now there's physiology for you."

"Of course, Bert," Lestrow said impatiently. "But the satiation factor is already part of the theory."

"Perhaps," Olmstead nodded. "But I just have a feeling that there are more neurological limitations than we realize today. So you should be careful in your enthusiasm, Susan."

"To change the subject for a moment," Ramses said, "wasn't it about this time that you raised your own children in a glass box—what some people call the Skinner box?"

"I've heard so many stories about that," Calderón chimed in.

"Most of them untrue, I bet," Skinner said with genuine sadness. He paused and listened to the music. After a few moments he continued, "don't worry about stories. It's much better to pay attention to facts. The problem is, stories easily make the rounds while facts are hard to come by."

"Especially in such an emotional area," Calderón agreed. "But tell us, what about your children? They did not suffer from the box you invented?"

Skinner shook his head. "Of course not," he laughed. "In fact, only our second daughter was raised that way—and she greatly enjoyed it, I like to think. Before the child was born, it occurred to me that it would be best for everyone—and especially for the infant—if baby care were better organized. Perhaps through some mechanism."

"That seems like a useful extension of experimental gadgets," Bilden commented.

"Not a gadget at all," Skinner replied. "A mechanical device. Actually, I've always been interested in mechanisms, watching and building them. You know, there's nothing natural about smothering an infant in layers of cloth, or tying a baby to a board, or other methods."

"Different cultures have different customs," Ramses interjected. "What is natural to some people seems barbaric to others."

"Look at a baby's environment logically," Skinner suggested. "You would want an enclosed space to prevent injury, warmth and a minimum of clothing for comfort and freedom, and many opportunities for stimulation. So, a large box, with a glass front, heater, and other things would enable the infant to be comfortable, mobile, and have fun. Debora spent part of each day in that box for about two-and-a-half years."

"Without bad effects?" Bilden asked.

"Without ill effects of any kind," Skinner emphasized. "Many people were horrified after I wrote an article about the air crib in the *Ladies' Home Journal*. But on the other hand, by now hundred of babies have been raised in such cribs—without problems."

"It's amazing how plain the truth can be," Lestrow chuckled, and the others nodded.

"May I go back to your earlier statements about organisms?" Calderón asked quickly.

"Of course," Skinner nodded. "We still have a little time."

"Well..." Calderón hesitated. "You mentioned the word 'organism' so often—tonight, during the symposium earlier, and in your writings. I get the impression that you prefer it to 'human being.' It almost sounds as if you are more interested in animals than in people, or perhaps—as some have said—you don't like people?"

There was consternation on some faces, but Skinner smiled. "Just stories," he said kindly. "Please go on."

"I guess...I'm asking, what is your theory of human nature?"

"I have no theory of human nature," Skinner said firmly. "In fact, I don't like psychological theories in general. Look at all the mischief Freud's work has brought about. I reject verbal authority, and theory is just one expression of such authority. I have studied nature, not books, as Bacon would say. I ask questions of the organism rather than of those who have studied the organism. So you see, I get my books and articles out of life, not out of other books."

Skinner's face lightened considerably as he continued, "My view of human nature—if there is such a thing—is simply a summary of experimental results. And even today, of course, the data are still very sketchy…"

"In this connection, I was greatly impressed by Professor Koch's words at the symposium," Finer broke the silence. "Remember what he said toward the end of his lecture?" he turned to the others around the table. "Something like this: 'Modern psychology has projected an image of the human being which is demeaning and simplistic.' I think he referred to your work."

Skinner nodded. "He probably did. And I must admit that I felt quite lonely at the symposium. But an open-minded non-psychologist would not speak of my demeaning image of human beings. It is Freud's image of man that is demeaning and simplistic. On top of that, it is negative, brutal, and totally imaginary, like all mentalistic conceptions. A behavioral perspective, on the other hand, endows human beings with all kinds of possibilities—for good or bad, it is true—but nevertheless possibilities. Possibilities that are free of negative forces, brutal instincts, and other nonsense."

"But how can you be so certain you are right?" Olmstead asked anxiously.

"Because I speak about data," Skinner replied. "I only summarize experimental results. Behavioral principles are more or less—today, at any rate—working hypotheses about the nature of human learning and action. Those hypotheses may need to be clarified, but they don't need to be argued. I have no doubt that the principles will triumph. I don't mean that they'll eventually be proven right—because we know today they are valid. But they *will* provide the most direct route to a successful science of human beings."

"And what is that success?" Finer asked.

"A science that allows us to set up situations in which people can realize their possibilities," Skinner said amiably. "If a child has the potential to be a poet, we want to teach her language structure, vocabulary, and the ability to see and think. Behavioral principles allow us to do that."

"But such a science of behavior can also be used for all kinds of horrible ends, by all kinds of nefarious people," Ramses said with irritation.

"When you take out the human spirit, so to speak, aren't you building a powerful Big Brother at the same time? Or at least you are giving the Big Brother of 1984 all the power he needs to dominate everything and everyone."

Skinner thought for a moment. Then he asked: "The principles are there for all to see. Why emphasize the darker possibilities? Why not consider the positive implications? I am an optimist."

The waitress came and asked whether they wanted more beer or food. Skinner said he was tired and the others moved to leave. Skinner insisted on picking up the tab but Calderón reminded him that they were all her uncle's guests.

Francisco Gonzalez opened the heavy carved doors for them and accompanied his guests to the steps leading from the wide porch. For a moment, everyone listened to the strains of the music.

"I still would like to see behavioral principles used only by people of good will," Finer said plaintively, and Ramses nodded.

"And how would you measure 'good will'?" Lestrow asked. "Furthermore..."

"One just has to be an optimist," Calderón interrupted.

"I agree," Skinner added. "And I believe that today human beings can—must—plan their own future. The science of behavior enables us to solve the problems we have now—and those we'll face in the future."

The students thanked their host, and Olmstead volunteered to take Skinner back to his hotel.

Francisco Gonzalez shook hands with his famous guest and waved to the others: "Vaya con dios."

Notes

This imagined encounter occurs after an actual symposium held in Houston during 1962 to commemorate the 50th year of Rice University. I have chosen this occasion because Skinner's ideas were well developed by that time, but he had not yet aroused the antagonism occasioned by his later comments on social and cultural topics. Since this book is concerned with psychologists' views of human nature, Skinner's later books are largely irrelevant for the task at hand.

The setting and all subsidiary characters are invented, as are their words. I have taken care to present Skinner's friendliness and human qualities (which are often overlooked), as these became apparent in personal meetings. I also indicate the moderate and tentative versions of some major ideas—which have been overshadowed by polemics and are nowadays less evident.

I have relied primarily on Skinner's own work, beginning with his autobiography in three volumes, published by Alfred A. Knopf (1976–1979). *Science and Human Behavior* (New York: Macmillan, 1953) and *About Behaviorism* (New York: Alfred A. Knopf, 1974) are good introductions to his basic ideas and beliefs, while his *Cumulative Record*, 3rd ed. (New York: Appleton Century Crofts, 1972) is an interesting collection of articles on various applications. I have also consulted the published version of the Houston symposium, entitled *Behaviorism and Phenomenology: Contrasting Bases for Modern Psychology*, edited by T. W. Wann (Chicago: University of Chicago Press, 1964).

Over the years, a large number of commentaries have appeared, which attack and defend Skinner's position, propositions, and presumed philosophy. A good example of the many symposia devoted to the assessment of Skinners work is *Beyond the Punitive Society*, edited by Harvey Wheeler (San Francisco: W. H. Freeman, 1973). An objective treatment of the man and his ideas is *B. F. Skinner*, by John A. Weigel (Boston: G. K. Hall, 1977).

10

ALBERT BANDURA
An Afternoon in Sonora, 1982

The work of Albert Bandura exemplifies the broad range of experiments and hypotheses that characterize modern psychology. Some studies yield basic knowledge of human behavior, while others contribute to the solution of problems. Some propositions tell us about overt actions, while others describe people's cognitive processes.

Albert Bandura was born on December 4, 1925, into a family of five older sisters. He grew up in the little village of Mundare, some forty miles east of Edmonton, Alberta. The high school had only two teachers, and thus the students had considerable responsibility for their own education. After graduation he worked for a summer on the Alaska Highway, and then studied psychology at the University of British Columbia in Vancouver. In 1949 he started graduate work at the State University of Iowa.There he married Virginia Varns who was teaching at the School of Nursing. Eventually the family included two daughters.

During these years Bandura became interested in the empirical bases of clinical procedures, for he believed that one should not use therapeutic methods unless their effects are known and understood. Effective methods, of course, presuppose accurate information about the nature of the problem that is to be overcome and the ways in which possible solutions are to be evaluated. Hence, Bandura's initial interest in clinical psychology led into the laboratory, where he studied learning processes. The combination of these two interests—helping others, and the discovery of psychological mechanisms through which social influences operate—has been the hallmark of Bandura's work since then. His doctoral dissertation, written in 1952, analyzed some of the psychological processes in Rorschach tests and foreshadowed some of his later work.

Bandura then spent a year at the Wichita Guidance Center on a postdoctoral internship. A year later he became an instructor at Stanford University, where he has remained. At Stanford he began field studies of aggression and its relation to events in the individual's social context. The hypotheses he formulated in the field he then tested in the laboratory, and gradually the nature of social learning and the importance of modeling became apparent. With Richard Walters, his first doctoral student, Bandura summarized this research in the book *Adolescent Aggression*. Over the years, Bandura's focus widened to include a broad spectrum of psychological phenomena. His subjects have included the whole range of human beings, the young and the old, the neurotic and the well, children and adults enmeshed in different life pursuits.

Heretofore, psychologists had spoken of imitation as the simple mimicking of observed actions, or of identification as the taking over of another person's life style. Bandura focused attention on modeling and observational learning processes, which are quite different from narrow imitation and global identification. The results of laboratory experiments and their implications for human beings in general and developmental processes in particular, were described in *Social Learning and Personality Development*.

Together with his students and associates at Stanford and elsewhere, Bandura devoted the next several years to the study of modeling, social learning, and the ways in which behavior can be changed most effectively. He and his colleagues investigated a wide range of human activities as well as problems such as phobias, aggression, and various neurotic behaviors. The results of this work were summarized in *Principles of Behavior Modification*. He spent the following year at the Center for Advanced Study in the Behavioral Sciences, and in 1974 he served as president of the American Psychological Association.

Bandura then returned to a vexing problem that had caught his attention earlier, a problem that is significant for individuals and has implications for communities and nations as well: aggression. His own studies and those of others demonstrated that aggression is learned, usually from models within a child's or adult's social environment. In his book *Aggression* (1976) he showed that aggression can be modified in the same way that other actions are changed—when the consequences that follow an aggressive act are changed and when a person learns more effective ways of dealing with difficult situations.

Bandura's social learning theory is detailed in *Social Foundations of Thought and Action*. While it has many implications for therapy and other uses, these have been largely left for others to develop. Bandura's work is still centered in the laboratory, and he himself has been careful to draw only those immediate conclusions which have some independent empirical support. He has not burdened us with the design for a whole culture or the outline of a better society. But he provides us with principles by which people can collectively try to create the type of society they desire.

BASIC HUMAN CHARACTERISTICS

Bandura's overall view of human beings is similar to that of most learning theorists. In his words, "human nature is characterized as a vast potentiality that can be fashioned by direct and vicarious experience into a variety of forms within biological limits." The forms, of course, vary from one culture to another and from one historical epoch to the next, and psychologists have usually left the description and explanation of these forms to the social sciences. The "fashioning process," however, has been at the center of psychological research for years, and Bandura's contributions lie in this area. This process includes three major components: the determinants of behavior, the learning of new cognitive and behavioral skills, and the alteration of behavior patterns.

The results of literally hundreds of experiments and systematic observations are summarized in Bandura's basic proposition that human behavior "is mainly governed by anticipated outcomes based on previous consequences that were directly encountered, vicariously experienced, or self-administered." The consequences that were directly encountered in the past are mainly the rewards and punishments Skinner has analyzed in great detail. Bandura, however, goes far beyond Skinner.

Laboratory experiments and other studies have shown that people are affected by vicarious reinforcement: we learn from observing or hearing about the rewarding outcomes other people achieve through their actions. The opposite exists, too: through vicarious punishment we learn from the experiences of others that certain actions are likely to produce negative outcomes—hence we are less likely to perform them. Bandura also investigated the effects of self-reinforcement, as when we reward ourselves for a job well done—e.g. by treating ourselves to a good meal. The reverse, of course, also happens: self-punishment is likely to reduce the probability that the preceding behavior will be repeated. Finally, Bandura studied the effects of symbolic consequences such as verbal comments and signals that people send out deliberately or inadvertently. Bandura eventually concluded that self-administered consequences and symbolic outcomes constitute the major regulators of human behavior.

We must be sure to remember that *previous* outcomes affect today's behavior, and that the outcomes we experience, observe, or administer to ourselves today influence our actions in the future. Thus it is *not* the future that affects the present, but rather our *expectations* which are partly based on earlier experiences or observations. There is nothing teleological about Bandura's major proposition.

Our actions are also influenced by antecedent factors. When some elements in a person's context become associated with certain outcomes—through direct experience, verbal explanations, or observations of others' experiences—then these elements take on predictive value. In effect, they become environmental signals which tell us what is likely to happen if we behave in certain ways. In order to maintain their power, however, these predictive cues have to be periodically confirmed by actual experience.

Over the years, Bandura has devoted considerable effort to answer the question of how people learn new activities and cognitive skills. His experiments showed that direct trial and error experiences are not the major way in which people learn. The complex skills required for daily life, and especially activities in which errors produce dangerous consequences (such as driving a car or working with tools and machines) are *not* learned in this way. If we learned to drive a car by means of trial and error, most of us would not survive our errors to earn a driver's license. Instead, Bandura demonstrated that we learn through modeling. We observe what other people (the models) do and what happens to them afterwards, or we listen to instructions or read directions. Based on this information we form a notion of how the action is best performed. Eventually we translate this notion into action, become proficient, and feel good about our success—we might congratulate ourselves or be annoyed when we fail. It is through such observational learning and self-administered consequences that humans acquire most of their behaviors.

The general modeling—or observational learning—proposition states that after observing a model's behavior and its consequences, a person is likely to perform that action in similar circumstances if the observed outcome was positive, and to refrain from behaviors in similar circumstances if the observed outcome was negative. Thus we eventually know a large variety of behaviors while we perform only some of them, depending on the circumstances and our assessment of what the consequences are likely to be.

Bandura's research indicates that people can also learn general rules and principles by observing models, and that individuals can be encouraged to combine activities into novel ways of behaving. This is not imitation, for a person does not simply repeat an action. An individual may adapt the modeled behavior, if necessary, and learns to recognize the appropriate context in which it occurs and the outcomes it is likely to produce.

Not everyone serves as an effective model for everyone else. Rather, people consider those individuals as models who are most similar to them, or with whom they identify (perhaps because of their high status), or whom they admire, or whom they want to be like. A general corollary, therefore, is that: the more similar a person is or wishes to be to a potential model, the more effective that model is likely to be as a source of behavior.

Bandura contends that most human actions are learned through inadvertent or deliberate modeling. But whether or not the new action is repeated over time depends on the individual's experiences with them. Few if any activities are maintained over long periods without some actual positive effects—be they material or symbolic, self-produced or socially administered.

The generally accepted position that behavior changes when the consequences change has been supported by considerable research. Changes in consequences can take several forms and often involve rather complex evaluative processes. Outcomes can change in their nature and level. But more important in daily life are perceived outcomes. Bandura has described several ways in which the same outcome can take on different values. When a person expects a large reward and receives only a small one, for example, the outcome is viewed as negative rather than positive. Conversely, even a small reward when one expected none will seem large. Furthermore, a person may become aware of changed outcomes through vicarious experiences, or one can deliberately introduce changes in self-administered outcomes. Finally, old actions are likely to disappear when different actions produce better outcomes.

The nature of "positive" and "negative" consequences depends on the culture in which one grows up, the historical epoch in which one lives, and even on one's own chronological age. There are very few outcomes which are always and by nature positive or negative. Only a few consequences are purely physiological, and many are a combination of biological and cultural factors, as we see in customs regarding proper dress, acceptable table manners, and foods that are considered to be delicious or inedible. Most of the outcomes we consider in selecting the activities that make up our daily routine—as well as our unique life and achievement—are learned and have a cultural origin.

The major difference between Skinner's and Bandura's views of human behavior centers on the role of cognitive processes. Bandura pays considerable attention to cognitive factors. Observational learning, predictive cues, the evaluation of consequences, the planning and selection of activities, and especially symbolic outcomes and self-administered consequences, all involve cognitive processes.

While we observe a model, for example, we rarely have the opportunity to perform the new action then and there. We usually have to wait a while before there is an appropriate occasion to try out the modeled behavior. During the delay we carry within us a symbolic representation of what we have observed, which then serves as a guide for our behavior on later occasions. Another example of significant cognitive processes is the individual's awareness of the connection between behavior and its consequences. Humans learn much faster and regulate their behavior better if they recognize the linkage between their action and the effects it has. The connection we "see," however, is a matter of belief. Thus it is possible for people in similar situations to behave quite differently, depending on what they believe to be the relationship between possible actions and their likely consequences. Cognitive processes also underlie the evaluation of positive and negative consequences, the assessment of probabilities with which they are thought to occur, and the weighting and integration of diverse effects into a total outcome that we mentally "attach" to each of the alternatives we consider possible.

Another significant cognitive factor that affects motivation and behavior is the individual's beliefs regarding capabilities. A person's conception of self-efficacy mediates between the signals from the environment and various behaviors, and it is frequently an important factor in the selection of one action over another. If our perception is high, for example, we approach the relevant task more confidently and with less emotion. We are also more likely to do well, will not be discouraged so easily, and are more apt to try again if the first attempt is incomplete. Perceptions of competence vary from one behavior to another and are quite malleable: they are usually based on past experiences but are also affected by our observations of other people's successes and failures (modeling), verbal and other encouragement, and practice of the related action.

The Sheridan Hotel in Sonora

For several years, the Bandura family had spent at least two weeks in August hiking in the Sierra Nevada mountains of eastern California. In 1982, however, both daughters had their own obligations in Boston and Colorado. Bandura and his wife therefore invited their friends Jeremy and Dora Hawkins to join them on a tour of the Mother Lode country. Jeremy Hawkins, an eminent British psychiatrist, was visiting the Stanford Medical School for a semester and had frequently expressed a desire to see historic mining towns.

The friends drove to Auburn and then spent a day at the Donner Pass in the high sierras. From there they planned a leisurely drive south on route 49—the famous Gold Country Highway—stopping at various interesting towns and mines on their way to Mariposa.

Shortly before noon on the second day they rested at an abandoned mine just north of Sonora, a small town in Tuolumne county. They examined the old headframe and then decided to spend the hot hours of the afternoon in some cool place. A few minutes later, as they slowly drove down Washington Street, Dora Hawkins excitedly pointed to a three-story building of red brick with an imposing facade and an old-fashioned sign "Sheridan Hotel."

They parked a block away and walked back to the hotel. The doors of the adjacent "Sheridan Restaurant" stood open, and the cool interior beckoned weary guests. Jeremy Hawkins stopped to examine the corner stone with its intricate "1880" carving.

"Barely a century," he murmured to his wife, and then followed his friends into the restaurant.

The wooden floor showed evidence of a hundred years' use, but the massive bar and the ornate mirror and elaborately carved shelves behind it sparkled as if they were new. Dozens of lights on a chandelier hanging from the high ceiling gave the place a joyous and cozy atmosphere. The weary friends sat down at one of the dozen tables. The wood-paneled room was empty except for another couple with their young daughter at a nearby table.

Dora Hawkins examined the red checkered table cloth. "Real linen," she exclaimed. "Can you imagine that? Out here in the—what do you say?—boonies!"

"It's our world," a gruff voice said defensively. A large woman in a blue dress approached the tables. "And from which boonies do you come from?"

"The Bay area," Bandura smiled. "We are greatly impressed by this place. I wouldn't be surprised if Mark Twain came with you through that door."

The woman looked at them and nodded. "This is my hotel," she said in a friendlier tone. "Have owned it for thirty years—and I keep it the way it's always been. Yes, Mark Twain would recognize this room. He was here several times."

Virginia Bandura expressed admiration for the carvings and decor, and Hawkins added "it has the atmosphere of a different time—beautiful."

"I'm Dolly Heller," the woman said. "My late husband Art, rest his soul, and I bought this place just after the war. Can I get you something? To eat, or from the bar?"

Jeremy Hawkins looked at his friends, and when they nodded, he ordered a large carafe of iced tea. The bartender, a young man with blond hair, brought the tea and glasses. "Welcome to Sonora," he said with a strong accent. "My name is Peter Blissen."

Hawkins paid and asked where he came from.

"From Denmark," Blissen replied. "I study economics at UCLA."

Bandura introduced himself and the others, and invited him to sit down. A short time later Dolly Heller came with menus and took their orders.

While they waited for sandwiches, Hawkins looked around the room. "What an amazing place," he whispered. "I expect to see Doc Holliday coming through the door at any moment."

"I won't analyze your choice of character, Jeremy," his wife smiled. "But I'm just as surprised as you. It's like stepping back into Wild Bill Hickock's time."

"And I won't analyze *your* choice," Bandura laughed. Then he turned to Blissen: "Have you been to any of the big mines around here? I mean really large operations?"

Before the young man could answer, Dolly Heller brought the food.

"The tea is delicious," Jeremy Hawkins said. "I suppose you have your own recipe."

"That's right," Dolly Heller exclaimed as she distributed the plates. "And it should be good. I store the secret herbs in the cellar, where old miners' ghosts keep watch."

"Join us, won't you please?" Dora Hawkins invited her. "What's a meal without ghost stories?"

Dolly Heller sat down and asked Blissen to bring more tea. She watched her guests enjoy the food and said: "Life is hard in the winter, but now it's heaven. When the snow comes, I read a lot of books."

"The country looks just right for hiking..." Bandura began.

"And exploring old mines," Jeremy Hawkins interrupted.

"So, tell us, Peter, have you been to any big ones?" Bandura continued.

"Oh yes," Blissen answered. "I've seen several. I like the old Crown King tunnel especially."

"What's it like?" Bandura asked.

"Fascinating," Blissen replied. "Everything just abandoned—as if the miners were coming back the next day, but forgot."

"Did you go into the tunnel?" Virginia Bandura asked.

"Just a short way," Blissen said. "There was water flowing out between the rails, water dripping from the ceiling, and water trickling down the walls. The timbers were rotten..."

"Not the place for me," Mrs. Bandura shook her head. "I prefer sunny meadows."

"The worst thing, though, were those slimy yellow—how do you say, snails without houses," Blissen shuddered.

"Slugs?" Dolly Heller suggested.

"Yes, slimy slugs," Blissen continued. "Half a foot long. They looked just like banana halves, slowly sliding up and down the walls and timbers. I really felt sick when I saw them. And there were so many. Hundreds. So I didn't go in more than twenty feet or so. And then I ran out."

"I wonder about those banana slugs, or whatever they are," Dora Hawkins turned to Bandura. "Peter here seems to have a phobia, could you do anything for him?"

"My husband has been quite successful curing people of snake and spider phobias," Virginia Bandura volunteered, and Dolly Heller moved her chair closer to the group.

"How do you do that?" the Dane asked.

"In the lab we teach people to approach snakes—gradually," Albert Bandura said. "Eventually, people learn how to cope with snakes and can master what they fear."

"I'm not sure that would work with banana slugs," Blissen said.

"Why not?" Dora Hawkins asked.

"The method should work," Bandura replied. "This treatment has been successful for many people."

"But slugs are just plain disgusting," Dolly Heller interrupted.

Bandura nodded. "People with snake phobias also think snakes are repulsive. But after they master their fears, their attitude toward snakes changes. And they are no longer plagued by nightmares about snakes."

"But what's the incentive to accept slugs as friendly creatures?" Jeremy Hawkins asked. "One might show a person that there's nothing to fear, but it's hard to convince someone that a banana slug is not disgusting."

"It frequently happens that people don't like what they dread," Bandura said. "I'm sure that changing your reactions toward banana slugs might be at the bottom of your list of 1000 personal things you would like to change. But there are other benefits of overcoming a phobia. In fact, that's how I got interested in perceived self-efficacy."

"Tell us about that, Al," Dora Hawkins requested.

"It was really fascinating," Bandura began. "In our studies people overcame their phobias step by step. And they often were able to cope better in other areas of life as well. The treatment for one difficulty seemed to generalize—by strengthening people's beliefs that they can exercise some control over other things that threaten them."

While the friends ate, the conversation turned to Mark Twain's story about the jumping frog contest in Calaveras and other colorful individuals of the roaring mining camps. After the meal, the young couple from the other table approached the group.

"Good afternoon, I'm Ted Norten and this is my wife Elsa," the man introduced himself. "I hope you don't mind the interruption. I'm an accountant and don't know much about psychology..." He hesitated.

"Of course you are welcome," Virginia Bandura said. "I see your little daughter has found a good spot for her nap."

"We're lucky she still fits onto a couple of chairs," Elsa Norten said. "Actually, I'm the one who would like to talk to you. About snakes."

"You've come to the right people," Jeremy Hawkins laughed. "My friend here cures phobias, and the rest of us have them."

"That includes me," Dolly Heller said. "My Art could get along with them, but not I."

"Do join us," Dora Hawkins invited them and moved her chair aside to make room.

"Oh, thank you so much," Ted Norten said and brought two chairs from another table. His wife sat down next to Dolly Heller. "Elsa has been to a couple of therapists, but they didn't do her any good."

"What did they do?" Virginia Bandura asked.

"Not much," Elsa Norten replied. "It was all very disappointing. With one I talked about my childhood, and with the other I discussed my husband."

"But I thought your problem was snakes," Albert Bandura said with a twinkle in his eyes.

"Yes—that's why I left the two analysts. Then I started to read *Psychology Today*. Interesting, but..." Elsa Norten said.

"We overheard that you can cure such problems," her husband interrupted. "What do you do?"

"Yes, please tell us," Dolly Heller agreed.

"Well," Bandura turned to them, "the solution to the problem of snake phobias is gradual mastery of coping with snakes. The causes of the phobias lie in the past—they are no longer in the picture."

"But I think I'd want to investigate the situation a bit," Hawkins suggested.

"Can you give us an example of what you do?" Mrs. Heller asked. "I don't understand what you mean."

"Well," Bandura began. "In a nutshell, I have people with such phobias watch a person demonstrate how to cope with a snake and control it. Then we help people handle snakes in a variety of ways. People are asked to do easy things first, such as touching a snake while we hold it. Then, in graduated steps, people eventually get to hold it."

"You would never get me to do that," Dolly Heller interrupted.

"That's what everyone says in the beginning," Bandura explained. "We create a situation where fainthearted individuals succeed, despite themselves. In addition to seeing graduated tasks, people first perform the activities along with the therapist. This enables them to do things they would not consider doing on their own. Another way of gaining mastery is to perform the feared activities only briefly at first and gradually extend the time. There are other aids we can use if needed. After people have learned some coping skills, they handle snakes by themselves. And that strengthens people's beliefs in their own capabilities."

"How long does all this take?" Elsa Norten inquired.

"After a few hours of treatment, most people are able to touch snakes and be in the same room with a snake freely moving on the floor," Bandura replied.

"Has that kind of treatment been used by other therapists?" Elsa Norten asked.

Bandura nodded. "Of course. We combine desensitization with effective modeling. A client observes how other people handle snakes in various ways, and we demonstrate that the snakes don't bite. The process is actually quite effective."

"But—you are treating the symptoms and ignoring the causes. Aren't you?" Elsa Norten suggested. "So—wouldn't a new symptom replace the old?"

"There hasn't been any substitution in my experience," Bandura replied. "We have treated hundreds of people, and we have follow-up data covering several years. Actually, the notion of symptom substitution reflects the old-fashioned view that an underlying sickness *has* to show itself in some way. If not in the old symptom then in a new one."

"And yet, if a neurotic—or anyone—benefits from a symptom, for example by getting the family to do everything for him, couldn't the new symptom be explained in terms of behavioral principles? " Dora Hawkins asked. "I mean, the new neurotic actions might be followed by the same benefits as the old ones were...I would still be able to tyrannize my family, perhaps even more efficiently."

"That's possible but not likely, Dora," Bandura said. "A therapist should show the client that there are new ways to better outcomes and a generally better feeling. That's why therapy should always involve the careful analysis of the patient's social context. There always is a two-way street between individual and environment. A positive change can set in motion another positive change."

"I think that would be true in the case of snake phobias," Elsa Norten suggested. "A life without such fears would be much more pleasant, and not only for me; also for real estate agents around here, for instance."

"But something is bothering me," Jeremy Hawkins began. "Let's say that another symptom appears in a real estate agent. Now we have two very different explanations. According to one, the internal sickness, whatever it might be, reappears in the form of another symptom. According to the other, the person wants to retain the old positive outcomes—let's say, attention from colleagues and the soft job of selling only city properties."

"Don't call it 'symptom,' Jeremy," Bandura cautioned. "That betrays the psychodynamic point of view. It's more accurate to say that individuals discover another action which has the same beneficial outcomes. Beneficial for them, or in their eyes, I should say."

"Your terms also reflect a certain view, Al," Hawkins smiled. "But anyway, the question is this: how could one tell which explanation is better or more accurate?"

Bandura was serious when he said: "I firmly believe that the value of a theory is ultimately judged by the effectiveness of the methods it produces. And explanations reflect theories, of course. Psychodynamic theories provide ready interpretations of behavior that has already happened, but they are not good at predicting future behavior or in producing effective changes."

"How do you know a substitute symptom won't appear at some later time?" Dora Hawkins interjected.

"Well now, wait," Bandura said and raised his hands. "The burden of proof is on those who continue to believe in the pathology-symptom model. Anyway, we should find out whether the person has the skills to sell rural real estate. We might discover, for example, that he doesn't know how to drive on muddy roads. Once he is confident on country roads and can make U-turns without ending up in a ditch, I bet no new 'symptoms,' as you call them, will appear."

"It's interesting that the absence of a behavior, for instance not knowing how to make a U-turn, can be as much a source of difficulties as the existence of a problematic action," Ted Norten said. "That certainly broadens the area of human problems."

"We usually don't think of behavior deficits as problems because it's hard to be aware of whatever is missing," Bandura said. "That goes for observers as well as the individuals concerned."

"So, a wallflower might simply not know how to dance?" Dolly Heller sounded dubious.

"There are probably other factors as well," Bandura replied. "But I think that we shouldn't assume everyone knows how to dance well, or how to drive on muddy roads, make a U-turn, or how to get along with members of the opposite sex. Many skills that we take for granted, and that are so necessary for daily life, may be very difficult for some people to acquire. Also, people may know what to do, but they avoid the situation, or perform poorly because they distrust their capabilities."

"Going back to the hypothetical wallflower," Elsa Norten asked, "how can one be sure that taking care of the behavior deficit will be enough?"

"I didn't say it would be enough," Bandura said. "Unfortunately, depth therapies deal with symptoms and their presumed underlying causes without considering behavior deficits. I don't think one needs complex theories about unconscious causes."

"And yet, Freud's theories are immensely attractive," Norten continued. "They promise so much..."

"And deliver so little," her husband interrupted.

"In practice, yes," Dora Hawkins agreed. "But many people find them so satisfying. The same goes for Jung's theory. I don't believe everything Freud or Jung said...I accept only a little, actually. And yet...yet...It's hard to warm up to a theory that disregards human...internal...processes. We all have thoughts, memories...there's so much inner life."

"Of course," Bandura nodded. "People have an extensive inner life. But an unconscious mental life is not the source of human problems. It is people's conscious, cognitive life that creates miseries for them. I really don't know what's so attractive about viewing human beings as driven by unconscious processes they neither comprehend nor can do much about. I don't understand what's so appealing about a treatment that has difficulty alleviating human problems."

"What should one do, then?" Elsa Norten asked.

"Let's look at the social-learning approach," Bandura began. "It treats internal processes as covert events that can be assessed and changed. These mediating processes are affected by external events and, in turn, regulate our behavior. By contrast, psychodynamic theories usually consider internal processes as quite independent. These hypothetical internal causal agents—such as the ego, or some complex—have little relation to external events or even to the symptoms they are supposed to produce."

Bandura paused a moment while the others waited expectantly. He poured himself half a glass of tea and continued: "On the practical level, the problem is that psychodynamic therapies are weak. On the theoretical level, well...the problem is that they affect the way we select and interpret data. They tend to reduce one's powers of analysis. We see that in the case of Freud's Little Hans."

"I'm sorry, but I'm not familiar with that," Blissen said.

"It's the story of a five-year-old boy—Hans—who had a phobia about horses and carriages," Jeremy Hawkins began. "It's one of Freud's most famous cases, even though Freud saw Hans only once."

"And Freud wrote a case history on that basis?" Dolly Heller asked, surprised.

"The boy's father was a good friend of Freud's and knew a lot about psychoanalytic theory," Hawkins replied. "But I admit that I've always wondered about that kind of second-hand analysis."

"Anyway, what happened?" Blissen asked.

"It's a long and complicated story—like most psychoanalytic stories," Bandura said. "But the problems of presumed unconscious causes, inferences that can't be substantiated, and debatable interpretations really show up in Freud's explanation of the phobia about horses."

"Little Hans was afraid of horses—especially that they might fall down," Jeremy Hawkins said. "And he was afraid of heavily loaded wagons. The whole problem started when Hans saw a horse that had fallen in the street, apparently because it was going too fast with a loaded cart. Hans was afraid it had been killed in the accident."

"Here the specifics are very important," Bandura suggested.

Hawkins nodded. "If I remember correctly, when Hans saw the horse fall, it reminded him of a school friend who had also fallen and been hurt while they were playing horses. Freud concluded that Hans was afraid his father would die. The fallen horse represented Hans' dying father—and his mother in childbirth."

"What was that again?" Ted Norten asked.

"Freud said that, in this case, heavily loaded carts were symbolic representations of pregnancy," Hawkins continued. "...Don't look at me like that...Freud said it, not I." He paused for a moment and surveyed his table companions with a bemused smile. "Anyway, Freud wrote that when a large horse, or a heavily loaded one, fell down, Hans could see in this only one thing: childbirth. Freud said that Hans's anxiety originally had nothing to do with horses but rather was centered on his parents. This anxiety was transferred from parents to horses, as a manifestation of the Oedipus complex."

After a moment, Bandura said: "In the psychoanalytical schema, internal psychic disturbances are the basic causes of the phobic actions. The external phenomena, in this case horses, supposedly exert little or no influence over the deviant actions—except as a focus for Hans's projected Oedipal and castration feelings."

"You mentioned the fallen horse," Blissen said. "What were the other occasions when Hans showed fear?"

"If I remember correctly—good Lord, it's been years since I read the case—Hans was afraid of single large horses, heavily loaded wagons, and horses pulling wagons at high speed."

"What about just a plain horse in a pasture, or horses pulling a wagon at normal speed?" Heller asked.

"Then Hans was not afraid," Hawkins answered.

"Very strange indeed," his wife murmured. "So it wasn't a horse phobia in the general sense."

"That's right," Bandura exclaimed. "Freud didn't account for the variation in both the pattern and the intensity of Hans's anxiety and phobic reactions under different circumstances. In fact, the case material provides considerable evidence that the phobic actions were triggered by some external factors associated with the original traumatic event."

"But there might still be an underlying condition," Jeremy Hawkins suggested.

"How can a horse phobia be attributed to an underlying Oedipus complex and projected castration fears—as Freud did—when the boy responds phobically to *one* horse pulling a heavily loaded wagon but is relatively unafraid of *two* horses pulling a loaded wagon, or an empty one?" Bandura asked. "An amorphous internal causal factor cannot possibly account for the remarkable variety of behaviors, changes in their incidence and magnitude under various conditions, toward different things at different times."

"Well, then, how would *you* explain these events?" Dolly Heller asked.

"I'd start with a very different overall view," Bandura replied. "When various external factors produce diverse actions, then any internal factors must be at least equally complex. And I'd say that their activation is evidently regulated by certain signals in the environment."

"Which brings us back to the individual's learning history?" Elsa Norten asked.

Bandura nodded. "Yet...we must be very careful not to analyze without enough reliable data. The social learning approach suggests that we consider certain factors—such as the reactions of family members to Hans's phobic actions. But only careful observations over some time can give us the necessary data for an analysis of causes—and suggest solutions."

"Would that be true of social problems generally?" Ted Norten asked. "I'm always struck by the fact that what people consider social problems changes from one generation to the next, and sometimes even from one decade to another."

"The first thing we have to realize is that the essence of any social problem are activities which people in a culture label 'social problem,'" Blissen said.

"After that it becomes a straightforward analysis of the determinants of these actions," Virginia Bandura suggested. "And that includes the functions they serve."

Blissen nodded: "Many of the determinants lie in the social and economic context, of course, and so the solution of social problem implies the modification of so-called 'problem-behaviors' and deficits. And that would eventually require some changes in certain aspects of the social system or some institution."

"I might buy that," Ted Norten said. "But why do you speak of 'so-called' problem behaviors and deficits?"

"Because those actions are labelled a 'problem,'" Blissen replied. "They are not always intrinsically harmful or detrimental. Prostitution or gambling, for instance. Sometimes the behavior is simply inappropriate to a certain place or time. Taking off one's clothes, for instance, is called indecent exposure or preparing for a bath, depending on when and where you do it."

"In that case we don't have to change the behaviors, but get the person to recognize the appropriate circumstances?" Ted Norten asked. "It seems to me there is more to this problem."

"Of course," Virginia Bandura replied. "But a focus on behavior and its determinants is a good starting point."

"Let's go back to labelling," her husband suggested. "Labels are extremely significant because they stigmatize people. Labels lead even professionals astray, with serious implications for any causal analysis and for finding solutions or selecting a therapy."

"What would be an example of that?" Heller asked.

"I don't mean psychoanalysis," Bandura replied. "Although it happens there. I'm referring to the study of certain problems...such as aggression."

"I take it you don't agree with Lorenz," Blissen smiled. "He's one of my favorite authors. You don't think aggression is instinctive?"

"And you don't think much of Freud's view of aggression as reflecting a death instinct whose power builds up over time," Dora Hawkins suggested.

"You're both right," Bandura replied. "The major problem with those two theories is that they postulate a general biological process that is supposed to underlie the many different forms of human aggression. When one thinks about the great variety of aggressive acts, and the many different circumstances in which they occur, it's obvious that there can be no single causal factor."

"Obvious to you, Al," Jeremy Hawkins said amiably but with a tinge of irony.

"Well, consider what usually happens in aggression," Bandura continued. "It's an act that not only hurts a victim but creates a variety of results for the aggressor. Aggression has many causes—and it serves many functions. For example: to reduce maltreatment, to get desired material things, or to bolster self-esteem. Some people get satisfaction from seeing their victims suffer."

"Some individuals resort to aggression to gain status in a gang or the approval of friends," Blissen added.

"Aha," Ted Norten exclaimed. "So we must be careful about drawing conclusions about some presumably sadistic aspect of human nature."

"Exactly," Bandura nodded. "And don't forget the labelling process. What actions do we call 'aggressive'? Our labelling reflects all kinds of factors. First, of course, there is the behavior itself and, closely related, the injurious consequences for other people. Then we usually consider the intensity of the act—loud talk is likely to be viewed as aggressive, soft talk rarely so. We also look at the recipient's expression of pain and injury. When one boy hits another, and they both laugh, we think it's horseplay; when one cries, we say aggression."

"And when two girls hit each other—we don't even think of horseplay, do we?" Heller asked.

The group agreed, and Bandura continued: "The intentions we attribute to the performer of the act also matter. When a baseball pitcher hits the batter's head we call it an accident or aggression depending on what we attribute to the pitcher. And that leads me to another factor: the characteristics of the labeller. So many people tend to ascribe to others just those attributes that they themselves possess. A gentle baseball fan—if there is such a person—is likely to consider a "bean ball" an accident. And then there are the characteristics of the aggressor. If we know that the pitcher has a sore arm and has trouble with his control—that's one thing. If we know the pitcher hates the batter..."

"So, the observer's knowledge of the total situation is crucial, too," Ted Norten suggested.

Bandura agreed. "Don't forget°norms. If the behavior is according to the norms, or people's expectations, it's not likely to be viewed as aggressive."

"But norms vary so greatly over time and among cultures," Blissen interjected.

"That's right," Bandura continued. "And therefore what's considered aggressive in some places is not so defined in others. Many people, for instance, don't view hockey as a violent sport and don't think of players as aggressive. Fights, broken bones, and smashed teeth are just seen as part of a very competitive game."

"Well now, if we consider aggression as behaviors that are for some reason labelled 'aggressive,' what's their origin?" Dora Hawkins asked. "Do you explain them like other actions?"

"Why not?" Bandura answered. "There is every reason why we should."

"One learns to engage in aggressive acts, perhaps from models?" Hawkins continued. "But why should anyone learn such...such often beastly activities?"

"Because some people haven't developed better ways of coping with difficult situations in their life," Bandura replied sadly. "And some people don't know how to get the things they want in socially acceptable ways."

"That sounds a bit simple to me," Jeremy Hawkins said.

"The principle is simple, but the analysis of real-life situations isn't," Bandura said. "The other factor, of course, is that aggression is easy to learn and can hide the fact that the individual doesn't know of any better way to handle a difficult or vexing situation."

"If all this is true, then aggression would decline..." Elsa Norten's voice trailed off.

"When the positive consequences disappear, or when alternative ways of coping lead to better outcomes for the aggressor," Bandura completed her sentence.

"Your conclusion is the exact opposite of what most of my colleagues believe," Jeremy Hawkins said. "In fact, most psychoanalysts would recommend that a person should be given the opportunity to express his aggression, to vent his feelings, to get the violence out of his system, so to speak."

"Unfortunately, that view fits theory better than it fits the facts," Bandura replied with conviction. "By now there are hundreds of studies—

from laboratory experiments to systematic observations of daily life—which show that aggression is learned. It is usually learned from models and maintained or even encouraged by positive consequences and the absence of negative outcomes. When we allow aggression to flourish we simply reinforce it."

"There are also interesting variations among cultures," Blissen added. "Anthropologists say that the Zuni Indians of New Mexico, for instance, are much less aggressive than the Dobu of New Guinea. It is especially in people's reactions to violence and aggression that these differences show up."

"But isn't it possible that some forms of aggression have a genetic base, so to speak?" Ted Norten asked. "After all, Lorenz is quite persuasive."

Bandura smiled. "His writing is, I agree. But I don't find his data nearly as persuasive. Many animals don't follow his rules. For instance, territorial fighting does not occur in many herd animals, and for other animals it varies with population size, food supply, and so forth. The problem is that he and others use too much uncritical extrapolation. But the most damaging question is this: how can alleged instinctual mechanisms of aggression that do not apply even to all lower animals explain the behavior of human beings?" He paused to finish his tea. "No, I'll stick to human data and careful studies that can't be misinterpreted."

"You know, Al, something bothers me in all this talk about effective behavior change," Dora Hawkins said. "If behavior changes when the outcomes are changed, what protection do we have against unscrupulous manipulators?"

"Yes, psychologists seem to be giving Big Brother all the tools he'll ever need," Blissen added.

"Freud's and Jung's views were rather benign by comparison," Hawkins said. "One couldn't use their methods to manipulate a group of people, let alone a whole society."

"Wait a minute," Bandura said. "You're talking about different things. Many people have pointed out that Freud and Jung seem benign because their methods are not very effective." He turned to Blissen and continued: "psychologists are only describing behavioral principles that are already there. We *discover* some aspects of human nature, if you will. We aren't making anything up—we are not producing a weapon. I suspect that a wise and insightful grandmother knows quite a bit about behavior modification—though not the details or the processes, of course."

"But the detailed knowledge you provide..." Elsa Norten hesitated.

"Work very well in changing old behaviors and establishing new ones," Bandura continued. "But to maintain them is another matter. If the new actions are effective for the individual and congenial to the culture, the natural outcomes in the social system soon take over. In fact, therapists always try to substitute natural outcomes for artificial ones, and they always try to fade out of the picture. It is very, very difficult to maintain a new behavior that is contrary to a person's wishes, so to speak, and it is impossible to do that with a large number of people."

"So you'd say we have little to worry about?" Blissen asked, still skeptical.

"That's right," Bandura answered. "Increased knowledge of how to influence human actions does not necessarily increase the level of social control. That's because human influence is a reciprocal rather than a unilateral matter. People resent being taken advantage of, or adopting behavior that produces negative effects for them. All these factors add up to a very effective defense against unscrupulous manipulators—who presumably have their own goals and don't give a hoot about the individual's welfare."

"Russia and Eastern Europe are good examples of what you just said," Ted Norten added. "After all these decades there is still turmoil, there still are a lot of dissenters."

Bandura nodded. "Principles of behavior change are much easier to apply, and much more effective, when they are used toward generally beneficial ends than toward exploitative goals that are contrary to what people value. There is a lot of evidence that Big Brothers don't have the wisdom and insight necessary to run a national program of behavior modification. Coercive control alone isn't effective."

"Just think of the careful procedures involved in that simple snake phobia program," his wife added.

The ancient clock above the bar mirror chimed four times. "Good heavens," Ted Norten exclaimed. "How time flies."

"We're planning to take a look at Chinese Camp," his wife said apologetically. "We hear it's a fascinating place."

As the Nortens thanked Bandura for his advice and returned to their table to awaken the child, Mrs. Heller began to clear away the dishes, and Blissen collected the glasses.

"Perhaps we should go, too," Virginia Bandura suggested, glancing outside.

"Yes, it should be cooling down," Dora Hawkins agreed.

Bandura followed Blissen to the bar and admired the carved frame of the mirror. "If that wood could only talk," he murmured as he paid the bill.

Blissen counted out the change and asked: "Have you ever experimented with animals?"

"Yes, I've conducted a few studies," Bandura replied. "They showed that an animal can regulate its own behavior when it has full control over rewards. Then it rewards itself only when it achieves a certain level of performance. Even animals are capable of self-directing! But, for me, people are so much more fascinating."

"Your emphasis on human beings separates you from Skinner, doesn't it?" Blissen asked. "In fact, I think that's a fundamental difference."

"In part," Bandura answered. "An even greater difference is that I consider the role of cognitive processes in human maturation, aspirations, behavior—and distress."

"That's what always struck me about behaviorists," Blissen said. "The learning principles sound fine, but I always wonder—can they really explain the human condition?"

Bandura laughed. "Of course. We just have to add a little humanity and some thoughts. By now there is so much good research that you can bet your last dollar on the principles of social learning. I have."

Ted Norten walked over to pay his bill. Afterwards, he leaned against the ancient cash register and turned to Bandura who was admiring the carved shelves behind the bar: "Behavioristic ideas don't appeal to me nearly as much as yours."

"You have to consider their origin," Bandura said. "Behavioristic principles come mainly from laboratory experiments with animals. From the beginning of his career Skinner was fascinated by the laws of animal behavior, and eventually he extended them to cover human activities."

"And you had different interests?" Dolly Heller joined them.

"Yes indeed," Bandura replied. "From the very beginning I was fascinated by people—all kinds. The summer after high school, for instance, I worked on the Alaska highway, near Whitehorse, in the Yukon. The people I worked with really intrigued me: rough characters, most of whom had fled from creditors, draft boards, probation officers, and alimony. It was a large open-air laboratory. In graduate school I studied clinical psychology and learning theories, and I was also interested in laboratory research of various kinds."

"That's an unusual combination," Norten exclaimed.

"Iowa was a lively place at that time—and it still is," Bandura continued. "All kinds of dedicated researchers were there, investigating fundamental problems of learning. I wanted to find ways of evaluating different therapies—so we wouldn't waste a client's time with ineffectual methods. Only research can help there."

"So you've always wanted to help people?" Heller asked.

"Well, yes, at least indirectly," Bandura replied. "But I never saw myself as a therapist or clinician. I *did* see myself as a researcher who would help to...how shall I put it?...to separate the practical wheat from the hypothetical chaff...And perhaps discover some effective procedures on the way."

"Working with humans does confront one with complexities," Blissen said. "One isn't likely to come up with simplistic notions of behavior—as some of us economists should know."

"And one can't escape the importance of human thought either," Virginia Bandura added. "People remember, perceive, associate, think, predict, evaluate, choose—all in the process of behaving."

"How can radical behaviorists disregard these phenomena?" Blissen asked.

"They don't deny their existence," Bandura replied. "They would say that since we can't measure them we can't study them objectively, and so we had better not use them. At least not today. They think that we shouldn't make all kinds of inferences about internal processes."

"I believe that human behavior can be explained only if we take such processes into account," Dora Hawkins added.

"Do you agree?" Elsa Norten asked.

"To a large extent," Bandura replied. "Most human actions, and certainly most learning, can be understood much better when we recognize the existence of internal mediating processes."

"Behaviorists have called you a mentalist, Al," his wife chuckled. "And that's about the worst thing they can say about anyone."

Her husband smiled and shrugged his shoulders. "You have to have a tough hide in this profession. For me, what counts is experimental evidence. Data matter; the realities of daily life matter. One cannot fashion one's inquiries to suit other people's opinions."

The friends said goodbye to the Norten family and remained awhile in the doorway of the restaurant, unwilling to leave the cool ambience of history. Then they shook hands with Peter Blissen and wished him luck in his studies.

Dolly Heller accompanied the friends down Washington Street to the corner of Dodge, where she turned. "Come back again, please," she smiled; "you're always welcome here."

Ψ

Notes

Bandura has frequently indicated that he loves to hike in the Sierra mountains of California, and it is not unlikely that he has visited the small town of Sonora. I chose the date because by 1982 he had developed his social learning position and was exploring some of its wider implications. All but the two major participants are invented. I have selected the topics of this imaginary conversation to indicate the wide range of behaviorally oriented research, and to highlight the development of a position that illustrates the cognitive perspective in psychology.

I thank Albert Bandura for his suggestions and comments on an earlier draft of this chapter. Originally, several of Bandura's statements during the encounter were quotations from his books and articles. Most of these, however, were modified or paraphrased by their author, hence it is no longer appropriate to cite sources for them.

I have relied primarily on three books: *Principles of Behavior Modification* (New York: Holt, Rinehart and Winston, 1969); *Social Learning Theory* (Englewood Cliffs: Prentice Hall, 1977); and *Social Foundations of Thought and Action: A Social Cognitive Theory* (Englewood Cliffs: Prentice hall, 1986).

PART FOUR
THE FREE SPIRITS

11

KURT LEWIN
On a Train to Boston, 1944

Kurt Lewin is one of psychology's free spirits in the sense that much of his theoretical, experimental, and practical work was outside the main stream of research. He attracted numerous devoted followers during his lifetime and developed ideas that are still with us—although their parentage is not always recognized. Today he is remembered chiefly for his contributions to experimental social psychology (especially one branch of it, group dynamics) and the application of psychological principles to a variety of practical issues (such as inter-group relations).

The small town of Mogilno is located about 75 kilometers east of Poznan. On September 9, 1890, when Kurt Lewin was born there, the area was part of West Prussia—today it is in central Poland.

Leopold Lewin owned a general store with living quarters above it, and was a sociable member of the middle class. His wife, Recha, worked by his side and raised a family of four; Kurt, the second, was the oldest son. The Lewins also owned a farm near town, and there Kurt loved to wander through the forests and meadows. He also learned to garden and became adept at woodworking and mechanics—but in school he was an average student.

The boy attended the gymnasium (high school) in Poznan until 1905, when the family moved to Berlin. In the new surroundings he became an excellent student and was especially taken by Greek philosophy. He intended to become a physician and upon graduation in 1909 studied medicine at the University of Freiburg. But after one semester there, and another in Munich, he became interested in biology. In 1910, Lewin decided to become a professor and began to take courses in biology, philosophy, and psychology at the university of Berlin. There he was especially impressed by the philosopher Ernst Cassirer. Within a short time he was a noteworthy student at the Psychological Institute headed by Carl Stumpf.

In the summer of 1914 he completed his work for the PhD (which he received in 1916) and volunteered for army service. The year 1917 was quite significant for the aspiring professor: his first two papers were published (one written while he was convalescing from a war wound), and he married Maria Landsberg.

After the war (in which he received the iron cross) Lewin returned to work at the Psychological Institute in Berlin. These were exciting times—the Gestalt school was developing, and luminaries such as Kurt Koffka,

Wolfgang Köhler, and Max Wertheimer gave the Institute a world-wide reputation.

Lewin participated fully in all aspects of life. By 1922 there were two children, he had bought a house, and he had become a *privatdozent* (instructor), teaching classes in psychology and philosophy. Unlike most German professors, Lewin was democratic in his relations with students. During the 1920s he became a popular teacher who attracted students from other countries. His friendly and gregarious attitude encouraged discussions and often led to lasting friendships with former students. For years, he regularly met with several students and colleagues to discuss all sorts of psychological matters, usually on Saturday mornings at the Schwedisches Café.

In 1922 Lewin published one of his best-known articles, on the Aristotelian and Galilean views of science and their implications for psychology. Foreign students, especially from the United States, were greatly impressed and disseminated his views overseas. During the 1920s Lewin also became renowned for the designing of experiments that were at once ingenious and simple (using little apparatus). More than a dozen doctoral dissertations, practically all of them written by women, were based on experiments designed to test one or another of Lewin's ideas. Many of these studies have become famous. Bluma Zeigarnik, for example, analyzed the effects of incomplete tasks on the recall of those tasks—and today we speak of the Zeigarnik effect (rather than the Lewin effect).

But the long hours and hard work took their toll, and the Lewins were divorced. In 1929 Kurt married Gertrud Weiss and eventually two children were born into the new family.

The ties with his homeland also weakened. Lewin spent the fall of 1932 as a visiting professor at Stanford University, and, upon his return to Germany in the Spring of 1933, concluded that Hitler could not be trusted. He resigned his position during the summer and accepted a two-year appointment as a child psychologist in the School of Home Economics at Cornell University. In September 1936 he accepted a similar position at the University of Iowa's Child Welfare Research Station. Both positions were initially supported by foundations, since the Depression made regular university positions impossible.

At Cornell and Iowa (with visiting appointments at several other universities) Lewin divided his time between experimental research and the development of field theory. He summarized his ideas in the 1936 book *Principles of Topological Psychology*. The natural democrat in Lewin brought out the best in students who flocked to him from across the country. As in Europe, free-wheeling discussions with students benefited everyone, and many of his students eventually became colleagues and friends.

Again, some of the experiments originally performed in connection with dissertations, became famous. At the Iowa research station, for example, he supervised studies which analyzed the effects of frustration on children's regression to earlier stages of development. He also participated in experiments to determine the nature of democratic and authoritarian groups, and the implications of each for individual members and their performance.

During the war years Lewin was extremely busy and frequently traveled to Washington, where he served as consultant to several government agencies. He also performed experiments relevant to the war effort, such as changing the food habits of families and improving labor-management relations in factories.

As a result of his work at Iowa, Lewin became interested in the structure and workings of human groups in various settings. This interest gradually developed into what is now known as "group dynamics." His open attitude toward human phenomena eventually led to the invention of T-groups. Over the years, Lewin's research interests changed as well, from testing propositions relevant for his theories to the discovery of effective policies and action programs (e.g. to reduce prejudice).

As he became involved in action research and spent more time on the East Coast, his position at Iowa became rather tenuous. In the summer of 1944 Lewin resigned from the university and spent four months in Washington. In the following Spring, after founding the Research Center for Group Dynamics at the Massachusetts Institute of Technology, he moved to Cambridge. There he gathered several former students and associates, and for the third time in his life began a fruitful career as teacher and researcher. He devoted long hours to experiments in social psychology, especially group dynamics, and to the development of practical applications in such fields as community relations. In the midst of his work he died prematurely in February 1947.

BASIC HUMAN CHARACTERISTICS

Kurt Lewin's lasting contributions lie in three areas: the nature of psychology as a science, individual human characteristics, and the relations of individual and group. Although his name appears in few books today, many "common sense" ideas in modern psychology were developed or elaborated by him.

In his day, Lewin was best known for his "field theory" and experimental studies of individual and group phenomena. While "field theory" as such has been superseded by other explanations, some aspects of it have become part of psychology's conventional wisdom. In this section I will outline those ideas which still have relevance today.

To a considerable extent, Lewin's contributions were obscured by his use (some would say abuse) of terms from physics and mathematics. Most of his ideas were part of what he called "topological psychology," an ambitious attempt to bring the insights of physics and the rigor of mathematics into the formulation of psychological propositions. Were such an effort made now it would be called premature—and during the

1920s and 1930s when Lewin worked out his principles of topological psychology the science was much less developed than now.

While the original statements of these principles are often awkward, we can grasp their essence quite easily. Indeed, the elements of physics and mathematics Lewin introduced are not necessary for understanding his basic principles; hence we will disregard those elements. During the last forty years, psychologists have accumulated considerable supporting evidence for many of Lewin's propositions—while most of his concepts from physics and mathematics have fallen by the wayside.

According to Lewin, human beings are complex, thinking organisms in constant interaction with their social and physical environment. The individual is not simply a collection of parts but a system. To understand a person, therefore, it is improper to study the several parts in isolation, for example perception and memory, and to add the pieces later. The whole of any "individual" is more than the sum of the parts. Complex psychological forces (e.g. tension, frustration, and satiation) operate within the individual. Other forces are involved in a person's relations with the context (e.g. goal attainment). In most of these relations the individual plays an active role—unthinking, automatic responses are rare indeed.

Psychologists, then, are called upon to perform extremely complex analyses, involving the whole person, the context, and the relations between the two. These three phenomena constitute the "field" which should be the focus of psychological analysis. In an experiment it is impossible to study such a complex "field" of elements and forces simultaneously—one can analyze only a part of the field. But as long as one is aware of the system to which the part belongs, and of the relations which operate even as the study is being performed, the results will increase our understanding of the forces at work. Most of the experiments which Lewin helped to design and run had the goal of increasing our knowledge of the complex field of psychological forces that underlies daily human events.

Any human action is determined by several factors; some lie within the individual, while others are characteristics of the context. Hence any explanation or prediction of behavior must be based on the analysis of individuals and their relations to their surroundings. Here Lewin introduces the concept of "life space"—the totality of factors that influence a person at any one time.

Some elements of an individual's life space are objectively real (i.e. part of the physical world), others are cognitive (e.g. a person's knowledge and ideas), and a few are imaginary (e.g. illusions of what might happen in the future).

Lewin's major postulate is that any activity is determined by several causal factors within a person's life space. The life space usually has a time frame that covers the activity's duration, and its complexity varies with the relevant activities. Thus my life space can be short and simple (e.g. when I buy and eat an ice cream cone) or quite long and complex (e.g. when I paint my house during the summer). A significant implication of this postulate is that any action's causal factors lie only in the present, not in the past or future.

Lewin's emphasis on the present has been frequently criticized, especially by people who misunderstood him. But his "neglect" of the past and the future is more apparent than real. What determines behavior now is an individual's present view of the future, and his present view of the past. When a person's views of the past and future change, his behavior is also likely to change—even though the actual events of the past do not change, of course, and the actual events of the future remain in limbo. Furthermore, while it is true that whatever people do now depends partly on the activities they have learned in the past, what really matters is how well they remember and perform those actions now.

Lewin's concern with the present was in part a reaction against psychoanalysts' emphasis on childhood events and the teleological view that the future affects the present. But his position also makes eminent sense on its own. As our present memories of the past and present hopes (or fears) for the future change, our actions will probably change accordingly.

The life space of children is typically quite simple; it includes only a few individuals and events. As children grow up, their life space becomes progressively more complex. Regardless of age, however, a person's life space includes not only actual people, events, and things, but imagined ones as well; not only accurate knowledge but errors. If my life space includes a ladder leaning against a wall, for example, I will go around it—because walking under a ladder brings bad luck (I believe). That is a superstition, but to me it may be a definite possibility. Thus Lewin talks about life space components on two levels: reality and irreality. Both are part of the total situation which the psychologist must know in order to understand a person's behavior.

Lewin devoted considerable time to the analysis of two crucial aspects of human beings: goals and tensions. Throughout their lives, normal people have several goals they try to achieve. The power of goals (or, in Lewin's words, their "valence") varies and may be positive or negative. A particular goal's power depends on its significance for the individual and the perceived probability of attaining it. Again, what matters is the goal's momentary significance and probability—both can exert their influence only in the present. For example, "eating lunch with friends" is a positive, powerful goal for me, even at 10 o'clock in the morning, if I skipped breakfast and have been alone since yesterday. Even though the goal lies two hours in the future, it exerts its power on me NOW—as I think about my friends and listen to my stomach growl.

Although goals are focal points of an individual's life space, they can change from one moment and situation to the next. The goal of having an ice cream cone is easily subordinated to that of answering the door when the bell rings, for example, unless I am very hungry or afraid of bill collectors.

The other important aspect of human beings is tension (or disequilibrium) and the tendency toward equilibrium. Tension is aroused not only by deprivations (e.g. insufficient food or companionship) and various unmet needs, but by other situations as well, for instance incomplete tasks. This latter phenomenon is illustrated in Zeigarnik's classic experiment (repeated many times since 1927): people tend to remember incomplete tasks better than completed tasks, and are likely to finish them when they have an opportunity to do so.

While Lewin used the term "life space," "valence," and "force" very frequently and for many years, few psychologists do so now. The terms, however, are not as important as the underlying ideas—and these are still with us. Today we recognize that human beings are always enmeshed in a "total psychological situation," and we speak of "outcomes" and "cognitive processes."

We can see now why Lewin's orientation was so popular and appealing. His views of people and their actions were essentially humanistic, and he frequently used data from real life. At the same time, he maintained scientific rigor, both in the formulation of his ideas and in the testing of specific propositions.

Today it is "common sense" to speak of psychological situations. But it was Kurt Lewin who showed us that in order to understand a person and to explain both routine and special activities, we must know the person's total psychological situation—which includes the individual, the context, and various cognitive processes.

On a Train to Boston

In the summer of 1944 many threads of Kurt Lewin's plans were finally coming together. For several years now his substantive interests had been undergoing gradual changes, from a focus on individual characteristics to a concern with group phenomena. His favorite methods of investigation were also changing, from laboratory experiments to research in ordinary settings such as a factory or community. Recently he had become especially interested in what he called action research—the developing and testing of hypotheses through deliberate interventions in a community's or group's ongoing affairs. He was particularly enthusiastic about the opportunities for significant research presented by labor-management problems in factories and intergroup relations in heterogeneous communities.

As yet there was little solid information about the most effective means for changing people's actions, ways of thinking, and relations with others. He had some ideas, based on his field theory and preliminary research by his students, but these ideas still had to be tested, and he was sure that more ideas were yet to be discovered.

Lewin was convinced that a special research center was needed to develop and test effective ways of improving relations between individuals and groups, and among disparate groups. Such a research center would also lay the theoretical foundations for solving the many problems in the world that arose from the hostilities among racial, religious, and ethnic groups. But there was no point in starting a research center unless there was a good chance that it would develop into an effective tool of sociaL change—and that would require money.

By August, the Commission on Community Interrelations had decided to fund the newly established Research Center for Group Dynamics. In Cambridge, the Massachusetts Institute of Technology had offered to house the researchers. The former students, colleagues, and friends he had asked to join him were enthusiastic about the prospects.

One morning in late August, Lewin and his wife boarded the Union Pacific's City of Los Angeles on their way East to tie up the last few ends of the great move to Boston. He expected to sign the necessary papers there and in New York, and to look for a house near MIT. Then the couple would return one last time to Iowa City and he would resign from the university—finally, to everyone's relief.

The bright yellow Pullman cars were as cheerful inside as they had appeared when the train pulled into the ornate station. And although their sleeping compartment was small, the Lewins looked forward to an enjoyable and relaxing journey—without children, household duties, or student reports.

They decided to eat an early lunch and made their way to the dining car soon after eleven. The head waiter seated them at one of the few empty tables and asked whether they would mind company—the train was quite full and the diner not as large as it should have been. They agreed and ordered a light meal.

A few moments later another passenger was escorted to their table—a balding man of about Lewin's age with his empty left coat sleeve tucked into the pocket.

The couple looked at the newcomer. Startled, they rose and smiled broadly. "Kunkel," Lewin exclaimed. "Fritz Kunkel—what in the world—sit down, please. Welcome."

After a warm greeting, Gertrud Lewin beamed: "Such a pleasant surprise! What are you doing on this train? We heard that you were in the States—alone—but we never thought we'd meet you."

"I got the big kids out in time," Kunkel said wistfully. "But the little ones are still in Europe. I couldn't get them out... Right now I'm on a lecture tour; a week in Chicago, and so on. And you?"

"We're preparing to leave Iowa," Mrs. Lewin said, and her husband continued: "I'm finally starting my Center, at MIT."

Kunkel looked surprised: "A psychology Center at an engineering institute?"

"Of course," Lewin said. "It's the logical place for a scientific enterprise. And as you know, my psychology..."

Kunkel nodded. "How well I remember. Our discussions at the Berlin Psychological Institute were really something, weren't they? You're still into physics and mathematics, life space and all that?"

"In a much more sophisticated way, of course," Lewin replied. "Those Institute discussions really helped me—Köhler, and you, and the others." After a pause he added: "And you, still into therapy and all that?"

"I have a good practice in Los Angeles," Kunkel answered. "My books do well, I lecture..."

"You had no language problems?" Mrs. Lewin asked. "Your patients understand?"

"No big problems," Kunkel said. "Idioms still give me trouble, sometimes..."

"I know what you mean," Lewin laughed out loud. "I always want to use idioms when I talk, so I can be really American. My students help..."

"Wellll..." Mrs. Lewin interrupted with a smile.

"So, one day, they told me that if you want to say that someone made a profound point, you say: 'you really slobbered a bibful.'"

"Oh, no," Kunkel laughed.

"Oh, yes," Lewin grimaced. "So, at a recent meeting of the APA I was a discussant at a session. I said about Terman's presentation—in public, mind you—that he had really slobbered a bibful."

The three laughed heartily. "Everyone was very gracious," Mrs. Lewin said, wiping her eyes. "But now Kurt always gets a second opinion before he uses a new idiom."

"Yes, it's amazing how much trouble language can cause," Kunkel said. "I have friends read my manuscripts, but errors still creep in."

Lewin agreed and told several stories of printers' devils invading his articles. During the meal the old acquaintances toasted each other and the future of the Center at MIT.

"Even when there are no errors," Lewin picked up the earlier thread, "people can still misinterpret ideas—and they do."

"Wilfully or otherwise," his wife added.

"Yes, I remember how we used to argue in Berlin—about your neglect of the past and future in a life space," Kunkel said. "We therapists were especially hard on you."

"I still can't understand what's so difficult about that idea," Lewin said. "There is no logical or material connection between the past—any past event—and the present."

"Many therapists would argue with you there," Kunkel suggested. "Patients, like everyone else, are greatly affected by their past, especially their childhood. The past often appears in their dreams, too—and the future as well."

"But look at it logically, scientifically," Lewin urged. "Your clients remember NOW what happened to them ten years ago. Right? They dream NOW about some event in their childhood. They hope NOW that something will happen in the future. Their actions NOW are greatly influenced by their memories NOW and their hopes NOW."

Kunkel nodded. "That's true, of course. And so the past and future become part of the life space."

"But not directly," Lewin insisted. "The past and future become part of the present through a cognitive process."

"And that cognitive process is the link between present and past," Kunkel said.

Lewin nodded.

"So, the past and future are there, they play a role in daily life," Kunkel continued.

"Our present memories and hopes," Lewin repeated.

"I think that many people don't really care about the nature of the link between present and past, as long as you have a person's history in the life space—somehow, somewhere," Kunkel suggested. "It really seems to me that you and your critics talk past each other..."

"Today just as years ago," Mrs. Lewin said. "Kurt is used to it by now, but it's still disconcerting."

"What do you do with your patients?" Lewin asked. "You discuss past events, for instance some traumatic happening in childhood. Eventually the patient may develop a different interpretation. For instance, let's say she realizes that her mother did not really reject and hate her, she was just too busy with the new baby."

Kunkel nodded and was about to speak.

Lewin raised his hand and continued: "The actual events of the past do not change, only the interpretation, the memory. And what really matters—from the very beginning—is that interpretation of certain specific events. Those specific events are NOT part of the life space—but the memory of those events, no matter how distorted, most certainly is."

"That makes sense," Kunkel said. "But it seems to me that one could then say two things that would be equally true. It would be correct to say that a person's history is not part of the life space, because there is a distance of ten or twenty years. But it would also be correct to say that history is there, in the form of a memory."

"So, you are right, Kurt, and the critics are right," Mrs. Lewin turned to him. "It's just a matter of perspective."

Lewin shook his head. "I think it's more or less wilful misunderstanding. This matter of past and future is just a convenient focus of attack, it seems to me."

"That could be," Kunkel nodded. "Your orientation is so plausible, and basically so appealing, that it just cries out for some people to take a whack at it."

"A good idiom," Mrs. Lewin smiled. "And I think you're right. I hope that when we get to Cambridge things will be different."

The waiter brought apples for dessert. Kunkel, who had lost his left arm in the First World War, held apple and knife in his right hand and deftly began to peel the fruit. The Lewins watched him, fascinated by his dexterity.

"That's really amazing," Gertrud Lewin said. "I had forgotten how well you manage with just one arm—and hand."

"Well, I've had almost thirty years to adjust my life," Kunkel smiled.

"You mean your life space, don't you?" Gertrud Lewin asked.

"If you want to put it that way," Kunkel agreed.

"Why not?" Kurt Lewin asked. "It seems to me that the world is different for a person with only one arm. There are challenges no one else can see. Take shoe laces, for example, or cutting one's fingernails..."

"Well, yes," Kunkel agreed. "But after you learn to tie your shoes and cut your nails, life goes on—in the old way."

"But the life space is different, it seems to me," Lewin persisted.

"I would say 'life is a bit different,' that's all," Kunkel said. "I'm not sure one needs to bring life *space* into this—or into everything."

Lewin pursed his lips. "But I think one should—one must," he insisted. "I'll tell you why. The word 'life space' implies the unity of the world in which a person lives. That unity of the individual, the processes within, and his context. If one doesn't use the term 'life space' there is a real danger that one will forget that unity."

There was a pause. Kunkel looked out the window, and after a while he nodded. "I see your point. I suppose it depends on one's original perspective. I always think of that unity, and so I don't need to be reminded ot it. But there are many people who see only bits and pieces—and they should think of their life space."

"That's right," Lewin smiled. "And you just wait. In a couple of years all kinds of studies on that topic will come from us at MIT."

"Please don't become too scientific—in the bad sense," Kunkel cautioned. "I'm still not convinced that you have to bring all that baggage from physics and mathematics into human affairs."

"Really?" Lewin asked. "Isn't psychology a science?"

"Of course it is," Kunkel replied. "And someday we'll know enough about people to make formalization a reality. Then the right mathematical notations and formulas will make sense. But at this moment—I don't think we know enough about either."

"Well, I don't agree," Lewin said firmly. "There's no point waiting until we know all we should. I think that the topological formulation of ideas helps research, it helps one to think clearly, it leads one to discoveries. We should prepare students for organizing the facts they'll discover."

"Perhaps," Kunkel said. "Only time will tell..."

"And speaking of time, I really feel like a nap," Mrs. Lewin said. "I got up very early today, with the baby sitter coming and all those last minute chores..."

Lewin shook his head: "I'm going to the observation car. One gets a different perspective of the country from there."

Kunkel agreed. "I would love to join you there, Kurt, but I really must work a bit on my lectures. Otherwise I'll feel guilty. But of course we'll see each other later, no?"

"Of course," Lewin said. "We'll have dinner together. Then we can talk about new ideas and good old days at the Berlin institute."

"No doubt your new one at MIT will be as exciting and fruitful," Kunkel said as they rose from the table and shook hands.

Kurt Lewin accompanied his wife to their compartment and then made his way through several Pullmans to the observation car. The climate control system was quite effective, and the air was cool in spite of the early afternoon sun. The tables and comfortable chairs on one side were bathed in bright light, and only a few passengers braved the rays.

Lewin looked for a seat on the shady side of the car and finally selected a plush chair next to a middle-aged couple engaged in low conversation. He was about to take the latest issue of *Time* from the low table in front of him when one of the passengers from the sunny side of the car approached him.

"Excuse me," the young woman smiled at him. "You look like one of my favorite psychologists."

"Really?" Lewin chuckled and introduced himself. "There may be others who look like me."

"No, you're the one," she said happily. "I'm Myrna Kenten, a school psychologist from Long Beach—that's in California." After an exchange of greetings, she continued: "I've always wanted to talk to you, Professor Lewin."

"Well, here's your chance," Lewin smiled and pointed to the chair next to him. "What can I do for you?"

Kenten hesitated. "You know, I've always been fascinated by those experiments of yours..."

"They're not really mine, you know," Lewin broke the silence. "I have some ideas, some hypotheses. But the actual work of designing and running an experiment—my students do most of that."

"What fascinates me is their origin. The original idea, not just the work itself," Kenten said. "For instance, the Zeigarnik experiment. How in the world does one think of that?"

"That idea came to me in a café," Lewin said. "Some students and I had spent a whole afternoon with coffee, cakes, and conversation at the Schwedisches Café. I then asked the waiter for the bill. He could remember exactly what everyone had ordered, and how much everyone owed—without writing anything down. And of course there were many customers besides us."

"Remarkable," Kenten observed.

"After we paid, Bluma commented on the waiter's prodigious memory," Lewin continued. "But I said it was just part of his job, and that he wouldn't remember the numbers ten minutes after we had paid."

"So Zeigarnik asked him again, a little while later?"

"Exactly," Lewin nodded. "And the waiter didn't remember the parts of the bill. In fact, he became angry when I asked him whether he remembered only unpaid bills."

"Your idea of tension," Kenten suggested.

"Precisely," Lewin replied. "The waiter felt some tension while the bill was unpaid, so he remembered the figures. After payment, the tension disappeared, and with it the memory of the precise amounts each of us owed."

"That certainly makes sense," Kenten said.

"But we can't know anything for certain until we run laboratory experiments..." Lewin began.

"Excuse me," the man next to Lewin interrupted. "I couldn't help overhearing your conversation. Why do you insist on experiments? I'm a farmer, and I think real life is what counts. It does in my line of work."

Lewin turned to him and smiled. "But in the laboratory we can control the important variables—in life we can't. Or at least not as well."

"My name is Daniel Potter," the man introduced himself and shook hands with Lewin. "I own a farm near Springfield, in Missouri. And this is my wife, Dorothy. She is a painter."

Lewin introduced himself and Kenten, and asked why he worried about experiments. "I think we need to discover a lot more about people than we know today," Potter said. "And I worry about information we get from labs—they seem so artificial, compared to everyday reality."

"And what about the essence of human beings?" his wife asked. "I'm afraid it gets lost in the lab."

"Artificiality can be a drawback," Lewin agreed, "but it's the price we pay—quite willingly—so that we can vary and measure the important factors that operate. That's the only way we can discover what causes what."

"Could you give us an example?" Dorothy Potter asked.

"Well..." Lewin thought for a few moments. "Consider mood swings in children. I mean, how they seem to lose and gain years in just a few minutes."

"Yes, it's amazing, how children's age can fluctuate," Daniel Potter said. "Our daughter is seven years old—but she can act like a four- and even three-year old within a few seconds."

"That's one of the really fascinating aspects of working in a school," Kenten added. "We see such things all the time."

"Have you discovered what produces that regression?" Lewin turned to Potter.

The farmer thought for a while. "It happens in various places, at various times, in various circumstances..." He paused again. "No, I haven't figured out why it happens—but then, it doesn't happen all that often."

"That's why we need experiments, to systematize observations," Kenten said with a smile.

"So you have discovered the reason?" Dorothy Potter asked.

Lewin nodded. "At least, we have a pretty good idea. The underlying factor seems to be frustration."

"Really?" Daniel Potter sounded doubtful. "Our Elizabeth seems to regress in so many different situations that it almost looks—well—random."

"But in the future, please observe the situations carefully," Lewin advised. "I'm sure that you'll see that the regression comes after some kind of frustration."

"Can a child be randomly frustrated?" Mrs. Potter asked.

"It only seems to be random," Lewin replied. "Especially at that age, a child encounters all kinds of novel situations, and all kinds of problems that it would like to solve—but can't quite..."

"Aha, I see," Daniel Potter interrupted him. "I remember the last time this happened. Betsy was in the barn, trying to move a bale of hay. She's quite strong, and proud that she can take care of Taña, her horse. But the bale was too heavy—so, after several attempts, she just sat on the bale and began to suck her thumb."

"Yes, I remember," his wife added. "we were quite worried about the thumb sucking. But it hasn't happened since."

"There's no need to worry," Lewin smiled. "Regressions are quite temporary, just like frustrations. In fact, you might say that both are part of growing up."

"How did you discover that link between frustration and regression?" Daniel Potter asked.

"We observed children in a laboratory. They played in a room full of toys, with a barrier across. After a while we lifted the barrier, a net, and the children could play with some really fascinating toys in the other half of the room. Then, we lowered the barrier again, so the children could no longer play with the new toys—just the old toys. We observed the children during the three periods and noted how creatively they played and what other things they did."

"What else did they do?" Dorothy Potter asked.

"I remember the study," Kenten broke in. "The children tried to get through the barrier, they became a bit aggressive, and they started to do things they had not done for a long time."

"Yes," Lewin added. "It was almost as if some of the children had lost two or three years of their age."

"How can you be sure that such a frustrating experience would not leave a mark on their spirit?" Mrs. Potter asked somewhat testily. "I'm not sure one should play such games. Especially with children."

"It's not a game, by any means," Lewin said with a friendly smile. "It's a means of discovering human nature. How else would we have discovered the link between frustration and regression? And now that we know the link, we can help."

"Whom, and in what way?" Mrs. Potter asked.

"Well, you and your husband, for example," Kenten said. "Now you know that you don't have to worry about Betsy's thumb sucking, or whatever else she does when she doesn't act her age. That experiment helps me in my work as well…"

"To set your mind at ease," Lewin turned to Dorothy Potter, "after the third period in that experiment we lifted the barrier again and allowed the children to play with the new toys until they tired of them. So you see, the whole experience was satisfying to them."

"I'm glad you did that," Kenten said. "I still feel sorry for Watson's Little Albert who's walking the earth afraid of white furry things."

"I doubt that," Lewin chuckled. "By now Little Albert is—what—in his early twenties? I'm sure he has outgrown those fears Watson gonged into his head."

"I admire your optimism," Kenten said.

Before Lewin could answer, another passenger from the sunny side of the car approached and introduced himself as James Hanson, a businessman from Indianapolis.

"I heard what you were saying about experiments," he began. "A good friend of mine owns a textile company, Harwood Manufacturing. They just hired a researcher to do some studies in a factory."

"Oh yes," Lewin smiled, "I participated in the discussions…"

"Really?" Hanson interrupted. "I heard that a Professor Levine was involved."

"That's I," Lewin said amiably. "But it's Lewin as in shoe-in. For a while now I have been using the American pronunciation of my name. Now that I'm a citizen I feel my name should be consistent with my feelings."

"Without a change in the spelling some people may be confused," Kenten suggested.

"I don't think so," Hanson replied. "If your name is spelled L-e-w-i-n it's pronounced loo-in, that's simple enough."

"What about those studies in the factory?" Daniel Potter asked.

"If I remember correctly, there was a problem with getting employees to change their ways of working…" Hanson began.

"Productivity and morale were very low because of the work changes," Lewin continued. "But my theory is that when people become involved in the change process, those difficulties will disappear."

"So you are going to gamble on the theory?" Dorothy Potter asked.

"Well, it's not really a gamble," Hanson replied. "My friends at Harwood are convinced the project will be successful."

"But theories are so—how shall I say?—so vague, so ephemeral, so, so—theoretical," Mrs. Potter continued and wrinkled her nose.

The group was silent for a while, until Kenten said: "Well, not always."

"Actually," Lewin continued after a moment, "there is nothing as practical as a good theory."

"Sounds like a contradiction in terms," Dorothy Potter murmured.

"Not at all," Lewin smiled. "Consider: when we do something new—anything new—we do it on the basis of some idea of why we do it and what's going to happen. In other words, we have a little theory. The better our theory, the greater the chance of success in whatever we're doing."

"That's right," Hanson said. "Without a theory the Harwood people wouldn't know what to do about group morale, or where to start."

"They would just try different things, willy nilly, without rhyme or reason," Kenten added.

"I admit that some theories are mostly hot air," Lewin laughed. "Especially in psychoanalysis. But my theories have an empirical basis. That's why I say—about my theories and others, too—there's nothing more practical than a good theory."

"You sound as if you don't think much of psychology," Kenten said to Mrs. Potter.

"You're right," she answered, without regard for her husband's disapproving glance. "I think psychology is a lot of—humbug, frankly. I think that artists, painters like me, composers, and poets, know a lot more about human nature than psychologists ever will. Grandmothers also know a lot more, I think."

"You have a lot of faith in conventional wisdom," Hanson commented.

"And much of that is contradictory," Lewin added. "What about proverbs like 'look before you leap' and 'he who hesitates is lost'?"

The others mentioned more proverbs, and for a while they played a game of coming up with contradictory pairs.

"That's the trouble with observations of everyday life—they give us only hints of psychological laws," Lewin continued. "What we see is usually so unsystematic that we can't draw any conclusions. Too many factors confound the situations we observe in daily life. We need experiments to make systematic observations and separate the causal and irrelevant factors."

"Ah yes," Daniel Potter agreed. "And yet I wonder whether there might not be some really important issues and questions that are simply too big for the laboratory?"

"I share your concerns to some extent," Lewin said. "That's one reason I'm looking for other places in which to do research—such as a factory or community."

"Can the laboratory tell us anything that's significant for the world?" Dorothy Potter asked. "What you said earlier about the regression experiment has implications for a few individuals—parents like us, for instance. But what about the larger scene? War, for instance. Working away in some little lab—what does that do for mankind caught up in a desperate war?"

Before Lewin could answer, Kenten said testily: "The same comments hold for artists, it seems to me. Painting away in some little corner of Missouri—what does that do for mankind caught up in a desperate war?"

"It depends on the painting, I suppose," Hanson interjected. "Goya's work is one thing, modern works are another..."

"Especially if you can't even tell which way to hang them," Kenten snorted.

Lewin raised his hands. "Please, let's leave the gallery and go back to the lab. I'll give you an example to answer your question," he turned to Dorothy Potter.

"Two former students of mine, Ronald Lippitt and Ralph White, did a fascinating study on group structures and their effects on members' actions and feelings. We worked with small groups of eleven-year old boys who were doing various things, like making masks, building models, and so on. We had four groups, twenty boys altogether. The groups were led by adults; those students I mentioned, and some others. We observed the kids carefully, made notes of what they did—we even took some movies, hidden behind a burlap curtain..."

"Really?" Kenten's eyes sparkled.

"There were three kinds of leadership," Lewin continued. "Some groups were led in democratic fashion, some in an authoritarian way, and some had a laissez-faire leader."

"I suppose you switched the boys around?" Hanson asked.

"Yes, we did," Lewin answered. "All the groups experienced all three kinds of leadership."

"That's really interesting," Daniel Potter exclaimed. "You almost duplicated the world..."

Lewin nodded happily. "Yes indeed, although at the beginning we weren't really interested in that. Anyway, we discovered that the different leadership styles affected the boys' behaviors in many ways—and rather quickly, too. The group atmosphere was affected, the tension level of the individuals..."

"Any specifics?" Hanson asked eagerly.

"Well, in the authoritarian groups the boys quickly lost their initiative, some completely. The boys also became aggressive and discontented, many were restless and fought with each other. Cooperation just about ceased—the boys worked alone and no longer cared much about others or the group. There was a lot of scapegoating. The boys also destroyed more of their own projects and the materials they worked with; they demanded more attention from the leader, and the only boys who left the experiment did so while they were in authoritarian groups."

"All the boys were volunteers?" Susan Potter asked.

Lewin nodded and continued: "We considered the boys' personalities, upbringing, and so on, to make sure that the groups were comparable. And they were, because at the beginning of the experiment, all the groups behaved the same. Differences came about because of the different styles of leadership."

"What about the laissez-faire group?" Hanson asked.

"In those groups the boys did a lot less work, and they also had fewer discussions," Lewin replied. "Some of the boys became rather frightened when they entered that group, especially when they came from the authoritarian group."

"And when it was all over?" Dorothy Potter asked.

"All but one of the boys preferred the democratic groups," Lewin replied. "The boys were happiest in those groups, accomplished the most…"

"So, what's your conclusion?" Hanson asked, leaning forward.

"On the whole, I think that there is ample proof that the difference in behavior in autocratic and democratic situations is not a result of differences in the individuals. I was really amazed when I saw the expressions on children's faces during the first day under an autocratic leader. The group that had formerly been friendly, open, cooperative, and full of life, within a short half hour, became a rather apathetic-looking gathering, without initiative."

"That's really sad," Kenten interjected.

"The change from autocracy to democracy seemed to take somewhat more time than that from democracy to autocracy," Lewin continued.

"I wonder why that is so?" Daniel Potter asked.

"Autocracy is imposed on the individual," Lewin replied firmly and without a smile. "Democracy one has to learn."

"Ah, yes," Hanson agreed. "But I'd like to have some confirmation from field studies, at least."

"Those will be coming," Lewin said with enthusiasm. "At MIT we'll be doing all kinds of new studies. In the laboratory, in communities…"

"Always laboratories," Dorothy Potter interjected unhappily. "Isn't there anything else?"

"Psychology is more than laboratories, experiments, and theories," Lewin replied as the bartender approached the group.

Daniel Potter offered to buy a bottle of California wine and the others accepted.

When the wine was poured, Lewin said: "I think of the psychologist as exploring a rich and vast land full of strange happenings: a toddler is trying to say his first word; a child is playing; a youth has fallen in love but is unhappy in a situation he can't escape; men are killing each other in wars. There is the mystical state called hypnosis, where the will of one person seems to govern another person. There is a reaching out for higher and more difficult goals; loyalty to a group; dreaming; planning; exploring the world; and so on without end. It is an immense continent full of fascination and power, and full of stretches of land where no one has ever set foot."

His companions were quiet, waiting.

"Psychology is out to understand and conquer that continent, to find its hidden treasures, to investigate the danger spots, to master its vast forces, and to utilize its energies."

"Yes, indeed," Kenten murmured.

"How can one reach this goal?—That is the question," Lewin said softly.

"Don't forget, we want to know the real world, not some individual's illusions," Hanson added.

"As long as we concentrate on the whole individual and the context we'll avoid illusions," Lewin said.

"Yes," Kenten chimed in. "Problems arise when we concentrate on one or another part and disregard the rest. I can see that in school children every day."

"But aren't some parts more important than others?" Hanson asked.

"That would be hard to prove," Lewin replied. "I am absolutely certain that one cannot understand a human being—or any activity, for that matter—without considering the total psychological situation of the person."

"Why do you say 'psychological situation' instead of simply 'total situation'?" Hanson asked.

"And aren't human beings independent creatures—I mean, beings with a soul, a spirit, if you like, that has nothing to do with their situation?" Dorothy Potter added.

"Perhaps we should say something about life space," Kenten suggested.

"What's that?" Daniel Potter asked.

"A person's life space consists of all the factors within a person and in the social and physical environment that affect him at the moment," Lewin answered. "I use that term because I want to show that any person is always inextricable involved in his surroundings."

"And every person affects her surroundings as much as the context affects her," Kenten added.

"So, my life space would include my farm?" Daniel Potter laughed. "Then it must be pretty big."

"Well, not necessarily the whole farm," Lewin replied. "Only those parts which are immediately relevant for you at this moment. And those could change from one day to the next."

"For example, one day you may think of yourself as a farmer in terms of acreage," Kenten added. "Another day you think mainly of cows, and the next you worry about rain. So, different aspects of the farm would be part of your life space at different times."

"I can see that," Mrs. Potter said. "But why must we bring in the 'psychological situation'? The farm, cows, rain and corn, are all real enough."

"In that case, yes," Lewin answered. "But there are many parts of an individual's life space that reflect a limited or distorted perception—for instance, when a farmer thinks of his place as his grandfather's legacy that cannot be sold for any price..."

"Aha," Daniel Potter turned to his wife. "We know someone like that. Remember Rob Hempstead last year?"

"The fellow was in real trouble, but he wouldn't sell a hundred acres, even though he had no use for them," his wife explained.

Lewin nodded. "A person's life space includes the total psychological situation. All the things he sees and is aware of—whether they really exist or not."

"What about illusions, delusions, and so on?" Hanson asked.

"If the individual takes them into account in his actions, then they are real, actual, for him—and therefore part of the life space," Lewin replied. "And if you want to understand the person, or predict his actions, you have to take into account the whole life space—no matter how bizarre."

"Where 'whole' is in the eyes of the acting person," Kenten added.

"That makes psychology a very complex exercise," Hanson murmured.

"The complexity of our field simply reflects the complexity of our subject matter," Lewin exclaimed.

"Children, of course, have a less complex life space," Kenten said. "The person is less complex, the goals are less complex, and the environment is less complex as well."

"But the 'unreal dimension'—if you want to call it that—is perhaps more complex," Lewin added. "After all, we have to consider a child's imagination and fears."

"What about a person's goals?" Daniel Potter asked. "Where do they fit in?"

"And people's needs?" Hanson asked. "Are they part of one's life space?"

"Of course," Lewin answered. "In fact, they are extremely significant parts. After all, much of what people do is designed to satisfy their needs, and to reach their goals. Regardless of barriers."

"Why is that?" Dorothy Potter asked.

"On the basis of all kinds of evidence—circumstantial, anecdotal, experimental—it seems reasonable to postulate that human beings strive for equilibrium," Lewin replied. "An unsatisfied need, an unmet goal, or different degrees of tension in various parts of a life space, they all produce some disequilibrium. The person attempts to re-establish equilibrium."

"But is that possible?" Hanson asked. "It seems to me that when a person tries to meet one need others may arise—all kinds of things change over time."

"Yes," Lewin replied. "That's why I talk about a dynamic equilibrium. To catch the time dimension, the sense of movement, of change, that is so much a part of human life."

"What about goals that are not very clear?" Mrs. Potter asked. "I can see how a person might do various specific things in order to achieve a certain goal, say buying a car. She has to save money, talk to dealers, and so on. But what about vague goals, such as a person's sense of fulfillment?"

"That's a good point," Lewin smiled at her. "Too many of my colleagues think of specific material or social goals, for instance a car or status. But I think there are more significant goals that people seek to attain..."

"Like what?" Hanson broke the silence.

"Self-fulfillment, developing one's capacities, and so on," Lewin suggested.

"Rather difficult to measure, or even define," Kenten said.

Lewin nodded. "But that's no reason to deny those goals, or to disregard them."

"You would say they are part of a person's life space?" Daniel Potter asked.

"Of course," Lewin answered. "Not everyone has such goals, but when a person does have them—say, an artist—those goals are part of her life space, just like any other goal."

"What about robbing a bank?" Hanson asked.

"If it's a goal, it's part of the life space," Kenten replied. "But in that case we might want to change the person's goals."

"Just as we try to change people's goals in a community torn by racial conflict," Lewin added. "In fact, that will be the point of several projects for the coming years."

Lewin was more than happy to describe the program at MIT to his new acquaintances, and the conversation ended only when Gertrud Lewin en-

tered the car and suggested that they enjoy the Illinois corn fields from
the open platform.

$$\boxed{\Psi}$$

Notes

I have chosen this encounter's time and place to illustrate Lewin's peripatetic
life—here he is preparing for the third time to begin a new life in a new place.
His ideas are fully formed, and he is ready to do research in novel areas. The characters in the dining car are real, those in the observation car are invented. My
father knew Lewin at the Psychological Institute in Berlin during the late 1920s,
and had numerous lengthy discussions with him. It seemed appropriate to let
them meet again in 1944, when my father was a psychotherapist in Los Angeles.

I have relied primarily on Alfred J. Marrow; *The Practical Theorist: the Life and
Work of Kurt Lewin* (New York: Basic Books, 1969); and on Morton Deutsch's
"Field Theory in Social Psychology," in Gardner Lindzey and Elliott Aronson
(eds.), *The Handbook of Social Psychology,* 2nd edition (Reading: Addison Wesley,
1968). Lewin's theoretical books are sometimes difficult to understand; the major
one is *Principles of Topological Psychology* (New York: McGraw-Hill, 1936). His articles are more interesting and still applicable; several of them have been collected
by Dorwin Cartwright in *Field Theory in Social Science* (New York: Harper, 1951).

12

JEAN PIAGET
A Hike on Mont Salève, 1966

Jean Piaget is probably the best known European psychologist outside the psychoanalytic tradition. Since the early 1920s his prolific writings on the cognitive development of children have exerted a profound influence on the field of child psychology as well as on parents and teachers. Unlike the other European giant, Sigmund Freud, Jean Piaget encountered relatively little opposition to his ideas, and even his critics respected his empirical work.

Jean Piaget was born on August 9, 1896, in Neuchâtel, Switzerland. His father was a historian at the local university, and, from an early age, the two had intellectual discussions on historical, scientific, and religious topics. The boy developed an early interest in biology and showed considerable talent for observing natural events. He was barely ten years old when his first article (about an albino sparrow) was published. By the time he graduated from the "Latin School" (high school) he was curator of the local museum's mollusc department, had written several articles on molluscs, and had become a recognized authority on that subject. Throughout his life Piaget retained a fascination with the life of molluscs in the ponds and streams of western Switzerland.

As a teenager, Piaget developed another interest which persisted to the end of his life: philosophy. Initially he was greatly affected by Henri Bergson's "creative evolution," and in later years he was drawn to epistemology (the study of the nature and limits of human knowledge). A concern with religious questions provided the third basis of Piaget's intellectual life.

After graduation in 1914, Piaget spent several months in the mountains, where he wrote a philosophical novel, and then entered the University of Neuchâtel to study biology. Four years later he received his doctorate for a thesis on the life of Valais molluscs. After a year's study of psychology in Zürich, Piaget moved to Paris, where he attended lectures at the Sorbonne and worked on the standardization of intelligence tests.

Piaget became intrigued by the systematic errors that children made on these tests. He talked to children of various ages, analyzed their typical errors, and wrote his first papers on cognitive development. On the strength of this work Piaget was invited in 1921 to become "director of studies" at the Rousseau Institute in Geneva (organized in part to train teachers).

For the next several years, Piaget studied children between the ages of four and six who attended the kindergarten of the Institute. In these studies, he employed what came to be known as the "clinical method." This was an adaptation of methods he had observed in Zürich (used by Bleuler and Jung), centered on friendly but systematic conversations with children. Strange as it sounds today, before Piaget's time psychologists had not talked much with children.

While a child performed various motor and mental tasks at the kindergarten, Piaget would talk to her about her thoughts regarding the task. In these conversations, Piaget set out to determine the child's views of the physical and social world. In addition, he tried to find out what was wrong with these conceptions (from the adult's point of view). On the basis of numerous conversations he concluded that when children grow older their thought patterns change—and they can think in ways they could not have done before. His first professional book, *The Language and Thought of the Child* (1923) made him famous and gave the field of child psychology a new direction.

In 1925 he married one of his former students, Valentine Chatenay, who became a valued coworker for life. By this time Piaget believed that cognitive processes which exist in older children are absent in infants. He proposed that cognitive skills develop as the child interacts with the physical and social world. To test this hypothesis, he began the systematic study of his own children, beginning at birth. Jaqueline (born in 1925), Lucienne (1927), and Laurent (1931), became the most closely analyzed babies of Europe. For years, the three Piaget children were the major sources of information regarding cognitive and other changes in infants.

The books on child development he published during the 1920s made him the leading authority of that field, and he was invited to lecture in several countries. Indeed, for a while child psychology was almost synonymous with Piaget. His international stature was recognized in 1936, when he received an honorary doctorate from Harvard University.

From 1925 to 1929 Piaget held positions at the universities of Neuchâtel and Geneva and divided his time between the two cities. During these years he continued working with children from birth up to the age of about 14 and formalized his theory of intellectual and moral stages. In 1929 Piaget settled in Geneva, as the assistant director of the Rousseau Institute and professor of history of scientific thought. After 1940 he was also professor of experimental psychology. In the following years he accepted positions with several national and international associations.

For many years Piaget and his associates had access to hundreds of Geneva children at the Rousseau Institute. In addition, he played a significant role in teacher training programs there. Hence he was able to perfect his theory and to test its applications—advantages enjoyed by few other modern psychologists. He was not interested in studying children in other cultures because he was convinced that the range of neurophysiology within populations is the same all over the world. His "little Genevans," as he liked to call them, represented the human species.

In 1955 the Rockefeller Foundation agreed to underwrite Piaget's lifelong dream: the Center for the Study of Genetic Epistemology. In the following years Piaget devoted considerable time and effort to his work at the Center, as well as to the study of perception. Many of his later articles and books, however, continued to focus on various aspects of cognitive development.

Piaget remained physically and intellectually active until his eighties. He continued to travel widely, lectured at universities all over the world, and retained the respect of psychologists regardless of orientation.

BASIC HUMAN CHARACTERISTICS

Piaget has contributed to our knowledge of human nature in two related areas. First, he described the nature and operation of several important cognitive processes. Second, he described children's cognitive development and its implications for various aspects of daily life. While Piaget did most of his pioneering work between the 1920s and 1940s, later studies have necessitated only relatively minor changes in the original formulations.

Piaget's early and continuing interests in biology and philosophy influenced his work with children in two significant ways. The scientific training he received in his youth led to a lifelong emphasis on careful observations, empirical data, and the repeated testing of ideas. His philosophical concerns with the nature and limits of knowledge led him to the analysis of children's ways of thinking about their relations to the world. Thus Piaget combined science and philosophy into a fruitful conceptual and methodological blend.

The conclusions which Piaget drew from his studies of children are often considered to be a theory of cognitive development. But it is actually more a description of how children of various ages think about various aspects of the physical world that surround them. In his books, Piaget gives us a detailed classification of children's ideas at various ages. These sets of categories help us understand children's thoughts— and actions—of daily life.

While Piaget emphasized children's cognitive development, he also described the reasoning processes that characterize adults (i.e. his "last stage" that begins at about 11 or 12). Piaget's careful descriptions of the sequence of stages through which children pass help us understand adult modes of thinking as well, for at times we may "slip back," and a few people do not attain the final stage at all.

In order to understand children's cognitive development, we must consider three important mental processes in which all human beings engage. Regardless of their age, individuals view their surroundings (and themselves) in terms of *schemas,* and these schemas involve *assimilation* and *accommodation.*

These three concepts are important aspects of today's cognitive psychology. They were used in 1906 by the American psychologist James Baldwin, whom Piaget met in Paris just after the First World War. Today we use these terms as further developed by Piaget and others. A "schema" is the way we organize our impressions of the world (or various aspects of it) so that they make sense to us. In daily life, we frequently behave in terms of our schemas of people, things, and events—rather than objective reality.

For example, I may organize many observations over a long time and in different situations into one schema: my aunt is a "kind person." When we meet, I act toward her in accordance with that schema. On a much larger scale, I may see the world as an inherently just place, where people ultimately receive what they deserve. This "just world" schema allows me to be content even when criminals sometimes go free, because I know (from my schema) that justice will be served—if not now, then later, and if not here, then somewhere else.

The schemas of children are necessarily simple in structure and limited in content and scope. As children mature physically and develop mentally, they tend to use progressively more complex and complete schemas.

When a child or adult interacts with the physical and social environment, the resulting experiences are *assimilated* into the relevant schema. In this way individuals are able to understand what is going on around them. When new experiences do not fit the old schema, a person may misinterpret events so that they will still fit. When I see that my usually kind aunt is very angry, for example, I may conclude that this "kind person" has been provoked by someone's terrible deed.

But when an individual has a great number of new and different experiences, these may be difficult to fit into the existing schema. Then the schema *accommodates* to the new environment by changing enough so that it can accept and fit in the new information. After many new experiences the "new" schema that gradually emerges through accommodation may be quite different from the "old" one. Thus I may come to think of my aunt as a "kind but human person."

Piaget believes that people have a need for a satisfying conception (or view) of the world. Indeed, he assumes that there is a human need for cognitive equilibrium. Furthermore, he postulates that individuals strive to have schemas that are internally consistent and reasonably congruent with the world. Whenever there are problems with consistency or fit (as seen by the individuals concerned), people tend to reinterpret the world or modify their schemas.

These processes play significant roles throughout a person's life. The simple schemas of our childhood gradually develop into the complex schemas that serve us reasonably well throughout adult life. Over the years, the cognitive equilibrium children reach tends to become more complicated as well.

Today, Piaget is best known for his description of children's cognitive development. His most general postulates state that 1) cognitive development occurs in a fixed sequence of four qualitatively different stages, and 2) all physiologically normal human beings pass through these stages, regardless of the culture or historical period in which they grow up. While recent research indicates that there may be a few exceptions to the second postulate, empirical evidence in general supports both.

Piaget's third major proposition is that thoughts follow from action. The child learns to think and begins to formulate ideas on the basis of manipulating physical objects in the immediately surrounding space. Indeed, the crucial aspect of any child's life is its interaction with the physical, and eventually the social, environment. As a child grows older, these interactions become more complicated, systematic, and future-oriented. Progressively larger segments of the environment are successfully manipulated, and cognitive processes become more complex. During the first dozen years of life, individuals gradually develop capacities that enable them to move from concrete views to abstract thought, from an emphasis on the here and now to concern with possibilities and the future.

It is useful to think of cognitive development as an undulating slope which trends upward from infancy toward adulthood—with three relatively short periods of rapid change separating four longer periods of relatively slow growth. Piaget gives only approximate ages for the three periods of rapid change (which separate the "stages"). Some children develop more quickly than others, and some children remain longer in one "stage" than in another. What matters to Piaget is the sequence of mental capacities, not their timing.

STAGE I. A child's cognitive development starts with the *Sensory-Motor* stage which begins at birth and lasts to the age of about 18–24 months. Piaget believes that at birth the infant considers himself and the world as one unit, and that only those things exist that can be seen or touched. During the following months the infant develops a sense of "self," an individual who is a distinct unit that differs in various ways from the rest of the world. There also develops a sense of the world as consisting of elements that have their own characteristics, independent of the child's sensory impression and physical manipulation. At the end of this period, for example, the child knows that a ball still exists, even though it may be hidden under a blanket, and can be found by looking under the blanket. The mental processes involved in such "simple" knowledge actually involve several cognitive procedures which are beyond the newborn's capacity. By the age of about two years, however, a child is capable of "representational thought"—she can think of things and processes that cannot be immediately seen or touched.

STAGE II. The *Pre-operational* stage begins when the child has learned how to speak reasonably well and is capable of symbolic thought. It lasts

until the age of about 7. At the beginning, the child is still greatly influenced by immediately visible properties and events, and cannot
"properly" take into account more than one characteristic of objects at a
time.

Two of Piaget's famous experiments on the conservation of quantity
and number illustrate the young child's limitations. When liquid is
poured from a wide glass into a thin one, the child thinks that the quantity increases (because the level in the thin vessel is higher). When two
rows of, say, six buttons are arranged so that one row is longer than the
other (with larger spaces between the buttons), the child thinks that the
longer row has more buttons.

Two other characteristics of thinking are important at this stage.
Children tend to be egocentric—they have considerable difficulty imagining another person's view, be it of a landscape or social event. Furthermore, children believe that many objects are alive and can move and
think much as they themselves do.

During these five years the child is gradually freed from the limitations of his own immediate experiences and develops a conceptual system of thought. As she engages in increasingly complex interactions with
the physical (and social) world, she rises above immediate perceptions
and begins to see the relations of several characteristics of objects. For
example, the child begins to recognize the importance of a vessel's height
and diameter, or the number and spacing of buttons.

At the end of this period the child sees the world as a well-ordered
(rather than chaotic) system of people and things governed by certain
(simple) processes and rules.

STAGE III. The stage of *Concrete Operations* lasts until the age of about
11. During this period the child acquires the capacity to manipulate ideas
about concrete things and events in the present. She can use some general
rules and is less dependent on what is actually before her eyes. But the
child has considerable difficulty thinking of future events. It is still hard
to imagine hypothetical situations and to consider a number of possibilities.

The fact that most of the child's thoughts remain tied to observable
events is illustrated in a classic experiment. Children are asked to determine what makes a pendulum go fast or slow. They are given a string
and several weights. The typical child proceeds by trial and error, varying the string's length, weights, and force of push in random combi-
nations. Because the child proceeds haphazardly, the "right answer"
appears accidentally, if at all.

STAGE IV. The final stage of *Formal Operations* begins at age 11 or 12.
From now on children engage in essentially adult modes of thinking.
Teenagers can use symbols, think abstractly, reason logically, envision
future possibilities, and make conceptual judgments. All of these perfor-
mances and capacities do not differ qualitatively from those of adults.
Indeed, the major remaining differences between adults and children

exist in the content of thoughts. Teenagers have less knowledge and fewer experiences than adults, but their mental operations and logic are the same.

The classic task for this stage is, again, the pendulum problem. But now the youngster proceeds systematically, varying one or another factor while keeping the others constant. As a result of taking the kind of well-ordered logical steps that a scientist might follow, the youngster discovers the solution. Indeed, the typical cognitive processes of the fourth stage are those of the scientist.

Piaget believes that cognitive development is crucially affected by the child's manipulations of the physical environment. Hence one would predict that the richer the physical context—in terms of opportunities for varied interactions with it—the easier the transition to the next mental stage is likely to be.

Piaget also proposes that cognitive development leads to changes in a child's social relations, emotional life, and moral reasoning. The young child's limited communication and inability to think logically, for example, necessarily affects other aspects of behavior—including the use of rules (e.g. in a game of marbles) and notions of what is fair and just. As yet it is not clear, however, whether changes in a child's moral views are determined by cognitive development or are merely parallel to it.

During the last thirty years, Piaget's ideas have inspired hundreds of studies. Together, they have raised questions about some aspects of Piaget's categories, but on the whole the results have supported the existence of cognitive development as described above. Only a few modifications are necessary.

There is now considerable evidence that young children are more capable than Piaget indicated. When children's logical procedures are tested with different (and more familiar) tasks, for example, they often do better than Piaget thought they could. The tasks he had children perform seem to have led to a general underestimating of children's intellectual capacities. In addition, there is greater variability in the timing of the stages, and of capacities within human populations, than Piaget originally believed. Indeed, Piaget did not perform systematic studies of how individual differences among children might affect their cognitive development.

The major problems that remain concern the mechanism behind cognitive development. Why is there such a sequence of logical thought? What are the determinants of cognitive development? On the one hand, the maturation of the child's neurophysiological system is part of the answer. On the other hand, learning, experience, and especially the child's interaction with the physical environment, are of great significance. The exact nature of the relationship between these two sets of factors remains to be analyzed in detail.

A Hike on Mont Salève

In the morning of a sunny day toward the end of August 1966, Jean Piaget prepared for a leisurely hike to his favorite mountains near Geneva, the Salève. It was just a few days after his seventieth birthday, and he was eager to re-establish some equilibrium in his life by spending a day in the wilderness. He good-naturedly accepted the celebrations arranged by his friends and students, but with each passing year he thought that this price of fame was perhaps getting to be a bit high.

Piaget sat in the hallway of his modest home in the Rue du Rang, putting on his hiking boots. He smiled as he thought of the isolated farm house on the high meadows of the Valais, where he had spent most of the summer. Those mountains of southern Switzerland had charmed him since his youth, when he had roamed the valleys looking for molluscs. How many glorious hours he had spent in the company of streams and lakes of that region! And how fascinating to watch their shell-clad inhabitants! Even now, almost fifty years later, he could recall the thrills of observing their life.

Just before ten o'clock his young hiking companion arrived. A few days earlier Piaget had met the young man during an afternoon reception at the Rousseau Institute. The old psychologist had been charmed by the eager questions which reminded him of his own youthful enthusiasm. And so it was only natural that the two would arrange a day's outing to the mountains. Piaget shook hands with George Sherman and asked him to carry pipe and tobacco in his rucksack. After a short farewell to Valentine the two men left the house. Piaget stopped for a moment in the garden to show his visitor the flowers and other plants he used for his biological studies. Then they drove off, eastward to the mountains with the crocodile silhouette.

"It's good to drive slowly," Piaget said as they crossed the Arve river at Bout du Monde on his favorite road to Veyrier. "Then one can almost touch mother nature—and in comfort, too."

"One of my professors used to say that one can easily be seduced by philosophy," George Sherman murmured. "I suppose that can happen in biology as well."

"Of course," Piaget nodded vigorously. "I think that's true of any field. But such seduction is very dangerous."

"Really?" Sherman asked. "I can't think of anything better than to devote one's life to an interesting subject—and to work on some important question until the day one dies."

"Ah, yes," Piaget agreed. "But the danger I'm thinking of is—well, to be one-sided. There's nothing worse than being just a poet, for instance. Or just a psychologist or philosopher, for that matter."

"Well…" Sherman winced.

"A person should have several interests," Piaget continued. "How else can one feel part of this complex universe? How else can one really appreciate the world? If one is only a philosopher one gets a lop-sided view of the world. And if one is just a psychologist, one is bound to end up with a one-sided view of human nature. As Freud did."

"But not everyone can be good in two or three fields," Sherman said. "How many people are there like you, with achievements in biology, philosophy, and psychology? Most people have a hard time being good in one area."

"Yes, I have been lucky," Piaget said and let his hand trail out the window to feel the rushing air. "But I think that even if one is good enough to accomplish something in one field—one should have an understanding of other areas as well. Otherwise one lives in a hole, so to speak."

"A psychologist, for example…" Sherman hesitated.

"Should know something about biology, be interested in philosophy, appreciate poetry—and so on," Piaget continued.

For the next several kilometers Piaget called Sherman's attention to interesting aspects of the landscape, until the car entered Veyrier. Just beyond the village they crossed the border into France. The guards recognized Piaget and waved them through, barely glancing at his companion's papers.

"I've been thinking about the question you asked me the other day," Piaget began. "But I'm not sure of the answer, because I don't know your attitude toward empirical facts."

"I thought that since you are interested in philosophical issues you'd be the best person to ask," Sherman said. "Ever since I graduated from college I've been wondering whether to become a philosopher."

"I've been called a philosopher—and worse," Piaget looked at his companion with an impish smile. "But I'm a philosopher of a certain kind—that's the important qualification. Like many others before me, I seek universal laws. Laws that govern human knowledge. But unlike most philosophers, at least today, I emphasize facts and collect hard data. I look at the world empirically, with the eyes of a scientist. Most philosophers don't. That's why I left philosophy as such—oh, some forty years ago."

Sherman nodded. After a moment he asked: "Can you give me an example of what turned you away?"

Piaget thought for a while. "In my early study of children I often had ideas—about various aspects of logical development, for instance, their intellectual processes, and so on. As soon as possible I started to look for hard data. And if there was no information—well, I designed an experiment to test the idea. I always wanted to find out how good my ideas were—or any ideas about nature. The only way to establish the validity of an idea is to test it. That's why experiments are absolutely essential. And philosophers? More than likely they will think about an idea, look at it logically, and so forth. Most philosophers have no respect for facts and don't care about empirical tests. When I discovered that—I said 'good-bye' to philosophy."

"And yet you have devoted your life to important questions—philosophical questions, about the nature and limits of knowledge," Sherman persisted.

"That's true," Piaget admitted. "I've had that interest because I'm convinced that the basic problems, or questions, in biology are essentially of a philosophical nature. But the answers, and the best methods for getting at them, are basically empirical. So, I've been using empirical methods for more than fifty years. And I'll continue for another twenty."

"Why don't philosophers use your methods?" Sherman asked.

"I'm not sure why they don't," Piaget replied. "Part of the answer is that they haven't been taught to be empirically oriented. Another part of the answer is that—well, you know, empirical work can be very hard, long, dirty, and sometimes boring. In the late 1920s, for instance, I wanted to finally answer some questions about evolution. So I took off a few months from my psychological work and went back to my favorite molluscs. I studied 80,000 of them. In rivers and lakes. I watched their behavior, I made notes of their habitat. Can you imagine those long hours? All that work, the mud and wet feet are simply part of a scientist's life and discipline. How many philosophers would do that?"

"None of the ones I know," Sherman grinned.

"I believe that discoveries are made by doing," Piaget continued. "Just as thoughts arise from interacting with our physical and social world. It's not the other way around. Discoveries—thoughts—don't just come into being. They are the results of human action."

"So, what would you do in my place?" Sherman asked.

Piaget shrugged his shoulders and drew on his pipe. "I had a glimpse of science and what it stands for, before undergoing the philosophical crises of adolescence. I'm certain that those early experiences protected me against the daimon of philosophy. Perhaps you should look for similar protection. If it's not too late."

When the car entered the little village of Pas de l'Echelle Piaget suggested that they stop at a juice bar on the other side of the railway underpass.

"The lady there makes her own juices from assorted fruits," Piaget enthused. "I don't know whether it's the exotic taste or the nearness of the trains—but I always get the feeling of distance and far-away places at that juice stand. Besides, we can take a liter of something along for later."

Sherman parked the car at the kiosk, and Piaget got out and bought two large glasses of what he called his "tropical concoction." They enjoyed the cool drinks while sitting at a small wooden table shaded by a multi-colored sun screen.

"And I thought that our 'Orange Julius' at home was something special," Sherman murmured.

"It all depends on the context," Piaget smiled.

"On my frequent trips to America I often go to an 'Orange Julius.' It's a pretty good place, and there aren't many others."

A passenger train passed, southward bound, and Piaget counted the cars. "I've always done that, since I was a child," he explained to Sherman. After a pause he continued: "You are thoughtful. Have I said anything I shouldn't have?"

"Oh no, no," Sherman murmured. "It's just that—your words stuck in my mind."

"Which ones?" Piaget inquired.

"You spoke of the daimon of philosophy," Sherman said. "That sounds strange—at least to my American ears."

Piaget laughed. "Yes, I know. You Americans don't recognize daimons. But of course you have them. Like everyone else."

"But the daimon of philosophy?" Sherman wondered.

"What I meant is that philosophy can be very seductive—and quite overpowering," Piaget replied. "It *was* for me. When I first came into contact with Henri Bergson's ideas, oh, how I was seduced. Delicious. I was just a teenager then. But as I told you earlier, I was inoculated—by my earlier scientific pursuits. And because I had that protection, I could enjoy the seduction without paying for it—no horrible consequences."

"What consequences?" Sherman wondered.

"Becoming a philosopher," Piaget laughed. "That would have been a disaster! Thinking all day, changing my mind at night, and *doing nothing* all week—for years."

"You're exaggerating," Sherman suggested timidly.

"Of course," Piaget exclaimed happily. "But there is a kernel of truth. Whatever I have accomplished is due to one thing—that I am interested in facts, empirical data. Before anything else, I am a scientist."

"But so many of your writings are in philosophy," Sherman protested.

"That's true," Piaget admitted. "But what I am doing, and have done for more than fifty years, is bring empirical data and scientific methods to bear on philosophical questions."

"In your psychological research," Sherman said.

"And in other areas. For example..." After a moment's pause Piaget exclaimed: "Hola! Look at that adventurous lady!"

Sherman looked in the direction of his companion's outstretched arm. A tall girl of about nineteen was approaching, dressed for a mountain hike and carrying an enormous rucksack. She ordered some juice and smiled at the two men.

Piaget waved to her, and she came over, a glass in her hand.

"Good morning," she said with a heavy German accent. "What a beautiful day."

"Yes indeed," Sherman replied and asked where she was headed.

"Across the mountain," she smiled. "To Mornex and then on to Arbusigny; I'll visit friends there."

"Perhaps we can take you a little way up this side," Sherman volunteered. "Until the end of the road."

"My name is Inge Brandt," she said pleasantly. "I'm almost ready for the second year of medical school at the University of Konstanz."

"A beautiful city," Piaget said. "Do join us. You have a long day's climb ahead."

The girl hesitated. Sherman introduced Piaget and himself, and after a moment Brandt accepted their invitation. She sat down and looked at Piaget.

"I have heard of you," she said. "And your work. But as long as I don't have children, I don't think I can use it."

"Oh, don't be so sure," Piaget chuckled. "The stages of development also tell us about the logical thinking of adults."

"You were going to say something about research in other areas," Sherman suggested.

"Ah, yes," Piaget smiled. "You know that I've always been interested in molluscs. Well, in 1913 I wrote a paper on a mollusc, *Limnaea stagnalis,* and variations in its forms. In 1928 I transplanted some eggs of one variant to a small lake on the Vaud plateau that had no such molluscs. Just to see what would happen. I've been back to that little lake many, many times. For almost forty years I have observed the development of variations there."

"That's amazing," Inge Brandt exclaimed. "Such tenacity. But toward what end?"

"I'm looking for answers to many questions," Piaget replied. "There are some questions about evolution, for instance."

"Ah, I see," Sherman said. "The biologist in you."

"Yes indeed," Piaget nodded. "Evolution is an extremely fascinating subject. For instance, Darwinians rely too much on chance mutations, it seems to me. And they treat the organism as something passive, that only reacts to the environment."

"That sounds all right to me," Brandt said.

"But think of the probabilities," Piaget urged. "If the mutations necessary for the development of the human eye had been brought about simultaneously, they would have had the probability of only one in 10 to the 42nd power. In other words, practically none."

"Wow," Sherman exclaimed.

"On the other hand," Piaget continued, "if it had been a question of successive mutations, in which new ones were simply added to preceding mutations, so that a cumulative effect was achieved, then it would have taken as many generations as there have been in the age of the earth—or even more."

"Hmmm," Brandt murmured. "That's really—quite amazing."

"And that's just the human eye," Piaget continued. "Now consider the whole neurophysiological system, its complex structure, the way it operates in even the simplest tasks of a child..."

"Yes, I see," Sherman broke the silence. "Philosophy doesn't help much here."

"But why worry about such—such, well, mysteries?" Brandt asked. "As a physician I'll be interested in curing a patient's inflamed eye. What does evolution matter there? And when you study a child's cognitive development, aren't those larger questions irrelevant?"

"Not to me," Piaget shook his head. "Of course, I don't think about evolution, or even biology, when I talk to a six-year-old to see whether he understands the conservation of juice in different sized glasses. But my whole life's work has been devoted to discovering principles that tie many things together. Biological phenomena and psychological processes, for instance."

"Universal laws?" Brandt asked.

Piaget nodded. "The four stages of cognitive development—that's just one small piece of the larger puzzle."

"And what's that puzzle?" Brandt asked. "Pardon my naïveté."

"The puzzle of how the various aspects of biology and psychology fit together," Piaget replied. "The puzzle of evolution."

"I'm glad my life is simpler," Brandt emptied her glass. "Although it won't be as interesting, I suppose."

"Those or similar questions may get a hold of you some day," Piaget smiled. "Then you'll be glad you have a scientific background."

"I'm beginning to understand your message," Sherman said after a moment.

"I have no message, really," Piaget shrugged his shoulders. "People use my work, my ideas, in whatever way suits them. That's the point of my writing. Why else would anyone write? Ideas can't be forced on anyone."

Inge Brandt peered around the edge of the sun hade to determine the sun's position. Piaget also looked and suggested that it was time to continue the journey.

George Sherman stowed the rucksack in the car's trunk and commented on the weight.

"I'm carrying two books along with all the necessities," she explained. "Isn't that a dumb thing? But I feel that I have to review anatomy."

"I know how you feel," Piaget chuckled. "When I was your age I also carried books everywhere. Bergson, and zoology. Ah, those were the days..."

"The days of adventure aren't over," Brandt said as the three entered the car. Then she and Piaget talked about the biological curriculum of medical schools.

Slowly and very carefully, Sherman drove along the winding gravel road that climbed part way up the western slope of Mont Salève.

"With your interest in philosophy and biology, how did you ever end up in psychology?" Brandt turned to Piaget. "Your studies of molluscs, and your early expertise—what good reasons to spend a lifetime wandering across Switzerland!"

"Well, actually, that possibility never entered my mind," Piaget smiled at her.

"But it's a very logical possibility," Sherman interjected. "I can easily imagine myself doing that sort of thing."

"Such ideas never occurred to me because by the time I graduated from high school, I was hooked on philosophy, as you say in America. In fact, I started a philosophical novel in my last year and finished it during several months' stay in the mountains."

"Really?" Sherman was surprised. "I have to read it as soon..."

"Oh no, don't," Piaget interrupted him. "It's awful. Juvenile stuff. Somewhat autobiographical, too, I'm afraid. I just had to get something out of my system."

"Might I ask what it's about?" Brandt asked.

"Well," Piaget hesitated for a moment. "It's about a young man, Sebastian, whose major problem is the relationship between science and faith."

"Really?" Brandt was astounded. "Faith?"

"In those days I was quite interested in religious issues and questions," Piaget turned to her. "You see, my mother was a devout Protestant. As a budding zoologist I had problems with religious doctrine, dogma, faith..."

"What happens to Sebastian?" Sherman hesitated.

"Eventually he discovers that faith and science are complementary. Steps, if you will, toward—well—happiness. Or perhaps today I would say that together they constitute a new, higher equilibrium for the thoughtful individual."

The two young people looked at each other, while Piaget smoked his meerschaum.

"May I return to the earlier point?" Brandt asked after a long silence. "How did you get from philosophy to psychology?"

"The way Wundt and James did," Piaget laughed. When he saw Sherman's surprised look he continued: "No, don't believe it. I was just joking. Actually, I was interested in epistemology..."

"As a teenager?" Brandt asked, incredulous.

"Yes, I did a lot of things in my youth," Piaget smiled. "Perhaps the most important was that I started to look for universal laws of human knowledge."

"Why in the world..." Brandt began.

"I was convinced that the basic problems of biology, indeed of all the sciences, were problems of knowledge and of logic," Piaget replied. "Most of the arguments that biologists were getting into, I thought, were due to inadequacies of logic. And especially ignorance of the limitations of knowledge."

"What about biological facts?" Brandt asked. "Sometimes we disagree about those, too."

"Of course," Piaget agreed. "And I was very much interested in facts and ways of getting them. That's why I have always emphasized careful observations and clear experiments."

"And psychology?" Brandt interrupted the silence.

"Well, even before my days in Paris I began to see that psychology was a way of combining my passion for empirical data with my passion for epistemology. Even before I entered university I realized that between biology and the analysis of knowledge I needed something other than philosophy. That need could be satisfied only by psychology. I was looking for facts—facts about the development of human knowledge. And those facts can be collected only by experimental psychology."

"So, it was a passionate love affair?" Brandt raised her eye brows.

"Yes indeed," Piaget nodded. "Almost from the beginning."

"I wonder, then, why you have neglected biological factors in your theory, except for genetics," Brandt asked. "At least, that's the way it looks to me."

"It only looks that way," Piaget replied. "The human being's biological structure is a given element. The fact that an infant's neurophysiology matures is also a given element. But maturation by itself does not matter much. What does matter—and I have said it so many times—is the human being's interaction with the physical, and also the social, environment. That interaction exercises our cognitive powers, so to speak. That conscious, deliberate interaction, which involves a host of cognitive processes, s the essence of the human being."

"And genetics?" Brandt persisted.

"I use that term in two rather different senses," Piaget said. "There is the usual meaning of a person's basic physiological inheritance. And of course genetics is implied by the neurophysiological basis of human thought. The other sense of 'genetic' refers to development, more or less systematic changes over time. I'm interested in both."

"I think that perhaps medical school courses lead students to overemphasize the biological," Sherman suggested to Brandt.

The girl shook her head. "People who study cognitive development can't escape biology, because the brain is there. Period."

"A semicolon, at most," Piaget chuckled. "I let other experts study the brain and body of babies, children and adults. Because the brain doesn't interest me. What interests me is what goes on within the whole neurophysiological system. How the individual, with that system, manipulates objects in space and interacts with the environment."

"Wouldn't the brain give you the mechanism that explains a child's passage from one stage to the next?" Brandt asked.

"I don't think so," Piaget replied. "A child of, say five, has certain schemas of the world. As she interacts with the world, new information is assimilated by the schemas. The schemas accommodate and change as the child experiences a great number of new interactions. So, by the age of eight, the schemas she has are fundamentally different from what they were at five."

The car had reached the end of the road, and Sherman parked. He took out Brandt's rucksack, but she remained beside the car, looking down the tree-covered slopes.

"I don't want to seem ungrateful," she turned to Piaget beside her. "But I still don't understand the mechanism behind the transition from one stage to the next."

"Assimilation and accommodation..." Sherman began.

"That's quite all right," Piaget said pleasantly. "You are not alone. It's only natural that one answer shouldn't satisfy everyone, just because it satisfies me." He lit his worn meerschaum pipe again and smiled at her. "In my youth there were many answers that didn't satisfy me. So, I looked for better ones. And you must do the same."

Inge Brandt smiled at the old psychologist, and they shook hands. Piaget showed her where the path across the mountain began, and described the two places where forks might be confusing. Sherman held the rucksack for her, and when she was ready for her journey he wished her good luck.

She thanked the two for the ride and began to climb the steeply rising path toward Monnetier-Mornex.

"She's quite a girl," Sherman said with a tinge of disapproval.

"She has a lot of courage," Piaget chuckled. "Crossing the Salève alone, and crossing swords with an old man."

"Perhaps I should have said something..." Sherman began.

"Oh no, no," Piaget soothed him. "Questions like hers are good for me." He smoked his pipe for a few minutes, enjoying the scenery. Then he continued: "I sometimes wonder what would have happened to my theory if more people had asked me searching questions. What if I had had more critics?"

Sherman was about to answer when Piaget said: "let's get started. There is a path from here to Collonges. Along the mountain side, with gentle gradients. Just right for someone like me."

"And for a novice like me," Sherman agreed and put on his rucksack.

After an hour and a half the two hikers reached a small clearing. They were about to cross it when they noticed a young woman at the upper edge, who was packing her brushes and paints into a box. She returned the hikers' greeting, and they approached her. Piaget praised the partially finished painting on the easel. She smiled at him and blushed.

"I don't believe in the old proverb that one should be quiet until the painting is born," Piaget said kindly. "I can tell already that you have captured the atmosphere of this meadow."

"I am Sylvia Neroux," the painter introduced herself. "On a holiday from Lausanne."

Piaget introduced himself and his companion. "Which way are you going?" he asked. "Shall we help you carry your things?"

"I'm going to the Capri Inn," she answered, pointing across the meadow.

"I know it well," Piaget said. "Jules Hetier serves a good meal."

"I'm meeting some friends there for lunch." Neroux smiled. "I was planning to carry my things, as always, but if you want to take the canvas and easel I would be more comfortable."

The three walked along the edge of the meadow and followed the path into the forest. After a few minutes they could see a white building shimmering through the widely spaced trees ahead.

"Perhaps you would join us for lunch?" Neroux asked her companions, and Sherman eagerly accepted.

"If your friends don't mind the company of an old man," Piaget chuckled.

"As long as he's famous," Neroux laughed.

The Capri Inn stood on the upper end of a narrow, gently sloping meadow that afforded a splendid view of the countryside and the village of Troinex in the far distance. Half a dozen wooden tables and short benches stood under a great oak tree next to the small whitewashed house. Three teenagers sat at one table, drinking iced tea. At another table sat a middle-aged couple, engrossed over a map.

Sylvia Neroux approached the couple and placed her painting materials on the next table. Then she gently put her hands on their shoulders.

"Here I am," she said sweetly. "With some guests."

The man rose and shook Piaget's hand. "Herbert Dillingham," he said. "From Plymouth."

"My godfather is a dealer in old coins," Neroux added. She was about to introduce Piaget when Mrs. Dillingham cried out "Oh, Professor Piaget! What an honor to meet you!"

Piaget smiled at her: "I'm just a human being, please."

Neroux had barely completed the introductions when the inn's owner appeared.

Jules Hetier greeted Piaget like an old friend and asked: "the cider, as usual? And we have some fresh bread, just out of the oven."

Piaget smiled happily and nodded, and the others ordered the same. Then the guests re-arranged the benches so that everyone could have a view of the meandering Arve on the plain far below.

"I never thought I'd sit at the same table with you," Mrs. Dillingham turned to Piaget. "So much of my teacher training was based on your theory. And now here we are. Together. Marvelous!"

"Beatrice, dear…" her husband cautioned.

"Oh, Professor Piaget," Mrs. Dillingham continued excitedly. "As a music teacher I have so many questions. May I ask you some questions? If it doesn't bother you."

"Go ahead, please," Piaget smiled. "But we shouldn't bore our company."

The others assured him that they would be interested, and Herbert Dillingham pointed out that ancient custom encouraged the joining of food and good conversation. "Besides," he added, "I have some questions, too. I'm interested in music and my wife's work."

Mrs. Dillingham took a few moments to gather her courage. "I have seen quite a few exceptions to your rules," she said. "I think there are children who don't seem to follow the timetable you set out. But on the whole…" She blushed and her voice trailed off.

"Don't worry," Piaget smiled. "Of course there are exceptions. After all, I have described only the general situation. The human race is at once the same and quite diverse. And with all that marvelous diversity—one must expect some variations in development."

"I wonder whether potential painters and architects progress faster than normal children?" Neroux asked.

"But how would you measure such potential in children?" Sherman interjected.

"I just think that painters and architects, when they are still children, may have a better feeling for space than kids who later become—what, booksellers," Neroux continued.

"Perhaps children with such talents simply do better on spatial tests," Sherman suggested. "Just as some people do very well in mathematics and others do poorly."

"That would be an interesting study," Piaget replied. "One would have to keep good records, follow people's careers for two or three decades. But it could be done."

"Would it be necessary, though?" Herbert Dillingham asked. "If I remember correctly what you told me, Beatrice, the ages at which these stages begin and end are quite flexible and vary from one person to the next."

His wife nodded: "All those figures are approximations."

"What really matters is the sequence of stages," Piaget said firmly. "All children, no matter what their culture or race, pass through the same sequence of cognitive development. My little Genevans follow the same path as children everywhere. That's the important point."

"In my experience there have been quite a few children who do better than your descriptions would indicate," Beatrice Dillingham continued. "I don't know whether that's because I deal mainly with children in music classes…"

"There are some studies which make precisely that point," Piaget said. "But what worries me is that most of those studies were done in America or Britain. I wonder whether that's a reflection of Americans always being in a hurry and trying to speed things up."

"Well," Sherman said, "it's a good question whether one can accelerate a child's passage through the stages. After all, today children have to learn so much more than they did a hundred years ago."

"But isn't it also true that today children don't have to learn the fallacies of the past?" Herbert Dillingham asked. "We don't have to burden chemistry students with phlogiston and other silly things, for instance."

"There are a lot of unanswered questions about cognitive development," Piaget said. "Why shouldn't there be? After all, these processes have been studied for barely forty years. And how many investigators have worked in the area? Just a few. So we have to be patient."

Jules Hetier appeared with a jug of cider and a round cheese. He was accompanied by a woman almost hidden behind a white apron bordered with intricate needlework, carrying a tray of glasses and loaves of bread. "My sister, Alicia Verdoni," he introduced her to the group. "She is helping me this summer."

The inn keeper began to slice the bread and cheese, while his sister distributed the glasses and filled them with cider.

"May I join you for a few moments?" she asked pleasantly, with a tinge of Italian accent.

Everyone welcomed her. Hetier brought a bench from a nearby table and sat down beside her. She looked at Piaget, but hesitated to speak.

"I can see you have something on your mind," Piaget said pleasantly as he helped himself to some bread and cheese.

Alicia Verdoni smiled shyly. "Well, yes," she said finally. "I have always wondered—ever since I read some articles about your work—how you can discover so many things about children. You seem to be able to read their minds—almost."

"Not by a long shot," Piaget chuckled. "It's basically hard work. Although I must admit it's less difficult now than when I started. You know, I sit down with a child, I show him a puzzle or some interesting little task, and then I ask questions while he is busily working at it."

"And you make a note of what the child says?" Verdoni asked.

Piaget nodded. "Some tasks are simple. For instance, I pour juice into two glasses and ask the child whether the same amount is in each glass. She says yes. Then I pour the juice from one glass into another that is taller and thinner, and ask her whether those two glasses now have the same amount of juice in them. The child usually says no, that there is more in the tall, thin glass."

"Why is that?" Hetier asked.

"Because the child under a certain age, about five or so, pays attention only the higher level of the juice. A child cannot understand conservation of volume until the age of about seven or eight."

"What happens if the child herself pours the juice from the wide glass into the narrow one?" Neroux asked. "Shouldn't that make a difference?"

"I never say what 'should' happen," Piaget replied with a smile. "I am out to discover the laws of mental development, I am not making them."

"Does it matter whether the children talk to you, or to some other man, or to a woman, or a relative, or another child?" Verdoni asked. "My children talk differently to different people. And they talk differently in different situations."

"I suppose that could matter," Piaget replied. "But by now a great many people have been using this 'clinical method' as I call it, in different settings and with literally thousands of children, and the results seem to be quite consistent."

"But isn't there a danger that children might not report their thoughts accurately?" Neroux asked. "What if they don't know the right words to make the point that's in their head, so to speak? Or maybe they just can't express what's really going on in their minds."

"What about children who don't tell the truth, or fudge a bit?" Hetier asked. "How does one know whether a child's words reflect what he is really thinking?"

"That's a good question," Beatrice Dillingham interjected. "In the lower grades especially I have the feeling that children sometimes don't even know that they aren't telling the truth."

Piaget looked out over the clearing and said: "Those are good questions. I admit that there is a possibility that children's reports may not reflect their thoughts with 100% accuracy."

"It seems to me that when you ask a child to explain the rules of marbles to you..." Beatrice Dillingham hesitated.

"Go on," Piaget encouraged her.

"Well, do they really believe you when you say that you don't know the rules?"

"If they think you're kidding, then perhaps they won't tell you the truth either," her husband added.

"A good point," Piaget chuckled. "I have thought about this problem, of course. The answer is, again, consistency. By now there are hundreds of observations, studies, and experiments that show pretty much the same results. So one would have to suppose that many and perhaps most children tell the same kind of fibs. That's not likely, is it? Besides, I have watched children play marbles—and I have observed that what children say is what they actually do. In the laboratory and on the playground."

"What about the other moral issues?" Sherman asked. "When you ask children questions about hypothetical events—for example, breaking one dish or fifteen, and so on. Might not children say one thing and do something different in the actual situation?"

"The answer is, again, consistency of experimental results," Piaget replied. "I just can't imagine all my Little Genevans telling the same little white lies. In so many different situations and to so many different people. And why would my Little Genevans want to deceive me, my many students and associates? But the most important point is that the experiments which are crucial to my theory don't depend on complicated verbal reports from children. Those experiments depend on what the child actually does—or can do, or cannot do."

"Such as the simple report of how much juice there is," Herbert Dillingham suggested.

"Exactly," Piaget said. "Or consider the experiment on egocentrism. We ask a child of five which of several photographs shows the view that someone would have who looked at mountains from a different position. The child points to a photograph, and it's either the right or a wrong one."

"That assumes a child understands what she's supposed to do," Neroux interjected. "But it's not all that easy to imagine what a landscape would look like from a different position. Even adults might have difficulties there. As a painter it took me quite a while to learn about perspectives."

"But we create a very simple situation," Piaget replied.

"I think I remember a study where children were supposed to place a picture so that someone else could see it correctly, and they did it, even at that age," Beatrice Dillingham said.

"When my five-year old Vittorio talks to his two-year old sister, he uses words in Violetta's vocabulary," Alicia Verdoni said. "Doesn't that show he can put himself between her ears?"

"Perhaps he has simply learned that he can communicate with her in only that way," Sherman suggested.

"But that would indicate he isn't all that egocentric," Neroux suggested.

"Mental processes have several dimensions," Piaget said. "What I call egocentrism no doubt has several dimensions as well. So one should not be surprised that there are differences in performing various tasks. Nevertheless, general egocentrism is a part of every child up to the age of about seven."

"You know, it sounds strange to hear that word—about—so often," Beatrice Dillingham said. "In so many articles I've read the ages at which cognitive stages begin and end are quite rigid."

"That's foolish and a big error," Piaget remarked. "Those age divisions are quite broad—after all, some children develop faster than others. And our instruments to measure cognitive development aren't perfect, either. I don't know why people seem to prefer imaginary precision to real variability."

"I wonder about something else," Beatrice Dillingham said. "I remember a very few children—no more than two or three in the last half dozen years—who seemed not to get into the last stage, Do you think they were just slow, or is it possible that some people never make it into formal operations?"

Piaget furrowed his brow. "That's a good question," he said finally. "I've heard of a few such cases. But one can't be sure of the data. Yet. Actually, someone at the Rousseau Institute is working on that question."

"What about adults?" Herbert Dillingham asked. "Do adults always live in the last stage—formal operations? Some people I know seem to have great difficulty thinking abstractly, and I suspect a few can't—or at least they don't, as far as I can tell."

"I used to think that all physiologically normal individuals reach that last stage," Piaget answered. "But lately I've come across some data that suggest there may be some exceptions."

"The problem is that the stages emphasize more or less logical thought," Neroux said. "If I were a scientist, the content of the stages would make sense to me. But as a painter—well, I wonder whether there are other thought processes..."

"Such as...?" Piaget asked.

"Well, I'm not sure. What about, say, artistic or creative thoughts?"

"Don't those processes—whatever they are—also involve relations with the physical world?" Piaget asked. "The cognitive processes I have studied concern the relationship between an individual and the world he lives in. Those thoughts summarize the interaction between human being and the physical universe. In childhood the universe of concrete, physical things. In adulthood, the universe of things and ideas, of the actual and the possible, of the concrete and the abstract."

"Yet—it seems to me that painters see things differently," Neroux persisted.

"Or at least the great painters," Sherman added.

"Not so," Piaget shook his head. "Painters see the world just as we do—only better. They see things in perspective, in color, in composition with other things. Painters have gone through the first three stages and are perfectly at home in formal operations. I bet that the great painters could think like scientists—and did. Just look at Da Vinci's drawings."

"And great composers?" Beatrice Dillingham asked.

"They too, of course," Piaget replied. "Formal operations are the basic tools of any art."

"What about the child Mozart?" Herbert Dillingham asked.

"How I would love to talk with him!" Piaget exclaimed. "What I would give if I could have him in my experiments from birth to fifteen."

"I bet Mozart would be far ahead of other children," Sherman suggested.

"Probably," Piaget agreed. "Unfortunately, I haven't tested genius in any systematic way."

"What would that do to the theory of stages?" Sherman asked.

"Nothing," Piaget replied. "The crucial test concerns not the timing of the stages, but their sequence."

"What about you yourself?" Sherman asked. "I understand you published your first article at ten. So you must have been far ahead of other children."

"Not necessarily," Piaget chuckled. "I think that people make too much of that first piece. It wasn't really an article in the usual sense, of many pages and with references. Just three short paragraphs, barely a typed page these days. Though I didn't have a typewriter, of course. I just wrote down what I had observed, a sparrow who was partly an albino. It was not the same as Mozart's first symphony."

"Your teachers must have encouraged you," Alicia Verdoni suggested. "Did you skip some grades?"

"I did not skip any grades," Piaget answered. "I think that education should not be rushed. Cognitive development cannot be accelerated—much as the Americans would like to do it," he smiled at Sherman. "A child—or neurophysiology, if you will—has a natural pace of development. Practice through interactions with the world is essential for cognitive development, but everything happens at its own rate."

"So, teachers can only encourage," Beatrice Dillingham repeated. "They cannot push children?"

"Encourage is the right word," Piaget emphasized. "My observations for more than fifty years indicate that logic is not inborn; it develops little by little. My studies have taught me not to explain the whole of mental life by maturation alone. The human brain needs opportunities to work and exercise—in the form of interactions between the individual and the world. The tragedy is that schools often don't provide enough opportunities for such interactions. A child needs to do things, perform, interact, manipulate—not just read books."

"Don't forget 'thinking'," Herbert Dillingham added.

"I omitted that on purpose," Piaget said. "Thinking is a natural consequence of doing. Or better, thinking occurs while one is doing something. While a child interacts with her surroundings, she thinks. Without such interactions there wouldn't be any thought. I mean, what would she think about?"

"She could simply think about herself," Neroux suggested.

"That's possible," Piaget replied. "But then I would ask: what is this 'herself' she's thinking about? The sense of self comes from interactions with the world—both things and people. When the little girl thinks about herself she is really thinking about various things she did, what happened to her, and so on. In other words, she is thinking about past interactions. She might even produce a new reality. Without past interactions she wouldn't have anything to think about—there would be no 'self'."

"But I can think about stars..." Sherman began.

"Because you have seen them," Piaget suggested. "And that is a kind of interaction. As a child you tried to touch them, perhaps. You have watched their coming and going on cloudy nights. You have talked with your parents and friends about the Milky Way, the evening star, the moon.

You have interacted with the sky in many ways, and that's why you can think about the stars."

Notes

This encounter is based on Piaget's well-known love of mountain hikes. Although he is seventy years old at the time, his stamina is that of a much younger man. I concentrate on Piaget's psychological work and disregard his biological and philosophical interests, except insofar as these are immediately relevant to cognitive development. All secondary characters and their words are invented.

Biographical information comes mainly from Piaget's chapter in *A History of Psychology in Autobiography* vol.4, edited by Carl A. Murchison (Worcester: Clark University Press, 1952). For Piaget's major ideas, I have relied primarily on the immense collection of his articles edited by Howard E. Gruber and J. Jacques Voneche, *The Essential Piaget: an Interpretive Reference and Guide* (New York: Basic Books, 1977). I have also used *Piaget: Critique and Assessment* by David Cohen (New York: St. Martin's Press, 1983). A good introduction to Piaget's basic ideas is contained in Philip A. Cowan, *Piaget With Feeling: Cognitive, Social, and Emotional Dimensions,* (New York: Holt, Rinehart and Winston, 1978).

13

ABRAHAM H. MASLOW
A Welcome to Menlo Park, 1969

The psychologists we encountered in the preceding chapters have held rather consistent views throughout their careers, and it is difficult to discern fundamental shifts in their intellectual development. The analysts were not interested in laboratory science once they had begun to build their systems, and the experimenters were not interested in analyzing the splendors of the inner life. Abraham Maslow was interested in both and equally at home in the academic and psychodynamic traditions. These two roots explain his unique contributions.

Abraham Harold Maslow was born on April 1, 1908 in a slum section of Brooklyn, New York. His father, a cooper, had immigrated from Russia and gradually worked his way up in the business world. As he did so, the family of seven children moved into progressively better quarters, and by the time Abraham entered Brooklyn Borough High School they lived in a middle-class neighborhood. As the eldest child, the young Maslow felt rather neglected and did not get along well with his mother. He was not close to his father either and spent much of his time in the home of an uncle.

Maslow was a shy and awkward youngster, skinny and concerned with his presumed poor looks. For years he had almost no friends and spent many hours in libraries. After graduation from high school in 1926 he attended City College of New York, initially studying law to please his father. There he discovered classical music, went to the theater, and gradually made a few friends. He took full advantage of New York's lively atmosphere, attended Will Durant's lectures on philosophy, and went to New York Philharmonic concerts at least twice a week.

For a while he went to Cornell University, but after a few lonely months in Ithaca he returned to City College. In the fall of 1928, Maslow transferred to the University of Wisconsin, where he first became interested in psychology. In December of that year he married his cousin Bertha, and eventually two daughters were born. In Madison he studied psychology with Clark Hull, Harry Harlow, and William Sheldon; but he also pursued his own interests which now included anthropology.

After receiving a bachelor's degree in 1930 he began graduate studies. Initially he had been captivated by the promises of behaviorism extolled in John Watson's books, but he soon became disillusioned and turned to the laboratory study of primates. Maslow's careful experiments on learning and food preferences of primates soon brought him to the attention of the profession. After his doctorate in 1934 he remained another year at Wisconsin as a teaching assistant. In 1935 Edward L. Thorndike invited Maslow to become his research assistant at Columbia University, and the young psychologist spent two years as a Carnegie Fellow in Thorndike's laboratory, with considerable freedom to work on his own projects. During this time Maslow continued his careful studies of dominance and submission in pairs and small groups of primates. A series of articles on this subject soon made his name.

In 1937 Maslow accepted a teaching post at Brooklyn College where he remained for fourteen years. His contacts with eminent anthropologists and psychologists gradually expanded his views, and the darkening political situation in Europe persuaded him to forsake the laboratory for the study of human beings in real-life situations. These new concerns and his continued optimism are illustrated in his *Principles of Abnormal Psychology*, which appeared in 1941. Two years later he published the article that made him famous: "A Theory of Human Motivation." Here he postulated a hierarchy of needs ranging from physiological requirements to the need for self-actualization.

The idea of self-actualization—developing one's capacities to fullest measure—had been around for a long time, and psychologists as diverse as Kurt Goldstein and Carl Jung had written about it. But Maslow expanded this concept and made it popular. The basic idea originally came to him as he attempted to understand two people he admired greatly: the anthropologist Ruth Benedict and the psychologist Max Wertheimer. He concluded that these individuals had developed their potentials more than most other people. Yet he believed that a similar state could be reached by just about everyone else. In later years Maslow presented his readers with a vision of what a healthy society would be like, a social system that would encourage rather than thwart the human being's need for self-actualization.

Maslow devoted the next several years to the elaboration of the needs hierarchy and the analysis of self-actualization. While the former task was relatively easy and successful, self-actualization remained an elusive process that was difficult to analyze. He published the results of his work in a series of articles which brought him to the attention of psychologists outside universities and concerned individuals everywhere.

In 1951 Maslow accepted the position of chairman of the psychology department at Brandeis University. But he was not happy there, for he could not get used to administrative duties and the new generation of students. During these years he came to emphasize the whole person and to study the individual as a totality rather than as a sum of perceptions, memory, learning, and all the other aspects studied in laboratory experiments. He also began to advocate—eventually with considerable passion—that psychologists should study normal, healthy people rather than draw conclusions from the characteristics of neurotics and stunted personalities.

His 1954 book, *Motivation and Personality*, showed that Maslow was no longer a mainstream academic psychologist. The articles he wrote later as well as his subsequent books led the way into new areas. Years earlier he had left behaviorism, then he had left psychoanalysis, and now he was discovering another kind of psychology, a humanistic psychology. This Third Force, as he called it, would go beyond the limitations of the other two approaches but build upon their insights.

Maslow's studies of the most creative and effective individuals of his time and throughout history had shown him what human beings are really like when society does not inhibit the expression of their innate fine qualities and rob people of opportunities to develop their potential. His vision of a psychological utopia—which he called Eupsychia—in which all people would be psychologically healthy by actualizing their potentialities, has appealed to many.

That vision is based more on plausible assumptions than on empirical evidence, however, and many academic psychologists have looked askance at Maslow's later writings. Yet his life-long efforts to discover human characteristics through systematic observations, and his intellectual honesty and audacity were recognized by his peers in 1968 when they elected Maslow president of the American Psychological Association.

In the summer of 1969 Maslow resigned from Brandeis University and moved to Menlo Park, California, to accept a fellowship from the Laughlin Foundation. There he continued his work in humanistic psychology until his death on June 8, 1970.

BASIC HUMAN CHARACTERISTICS

Maslow's high reputation among academic psychologists was based on his early laboratory experiments, especially his studies of learning, food preferences, and dominance-submission patterns among primates. Gradually his interests shifted to the study of human beings, initially to the human counterpart of dominance. Maslow broadened this concept considerably and eventually transformed it into the human concept of self-esteem.

In the course of his work Maslow came to realize that the need for self-esteem is only one of several basic human needs, and gradually he came to the conclusion that these needs are arranged in a hierarchy of prepotency. That is, needs exist in a sequence from the most powerful to the least powerful (although these latter are still significant). Under the right circumstances, any need in the sequence can be powerful. The most important "right condition" is that the needs which rank lower in the hierarchy are relatively well satisfied.

The two terms which Maslow uses so frequently—motive and need—are not interchangeable because they describe quite different phenomena. A need refers to an element that must be present for a person's well-being and even life. Thus we speak of an individual's need for oxygen, sleep, or protein,—and Maslow would add various psychological needs. The latter are necessary for psychological health, just as nutritional needs describe what is required for physical health.

Motives, on the other hand, are psychological urges that push us to do or say certain things. Thus we are motivated to visit relatives, make a living, or wear "proper" clothes. In a nutshell, needs usually refer to something that is momentarily absent but necessary, while motives usually refer to forces that push us toward a particular goal. Thus Maslow described his postulated hierarchy of needs in an article on motivation, and his book *Motivation and Personality* describes and analyzes human needs in great detail.

Psychologists had studied needs and motives for quite some time before Maslow began to write about these topics, and they had spoken of "higher" and "lower" needs. But psychologists had usually assumed that the higher (emotional and intellectual) needs are derived from the lower (physiological) needs. Maslow's proposals were quite different.

There are very few empirical studies that have been specifically designed to test Maslow's major hypotheses, largely because these ideas are so broad in scope and complex in content. At the same time, however, there is no solid evidence against many of his ideas. The most plausible statements—and the ones most likely to be supported eventually by empirical evidence—concern the hierarchy of needs, and especially self-actualization.

First, Maslow postulated that human beings are characterized by a set of independent, innate needs which individuals strive to reduce or satisfy. Each need reflects a basic requirement of human existence and presents the individual with a dominating goal—to do whatever is necessary to satisfy or reduce that need. At the same time, the person is likely to have a particular world outlook, a philosophy of life, and a vision of the future that reflects the dominant need. All of these change as the individual's basic needs change, and thus we should expect considerable variations as human beings grow older or find themselves in new or difficult situations that activate new needs. The psychological importance of any behavior then, depends on its relation to the basic need that is dominant at the moment.

Maslow's second postulate indicates that these basic human needs are naturally arranged in a hierarchy of prepotency along several related dimensions:

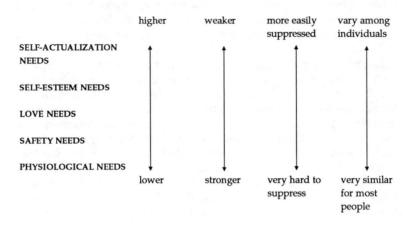

In his third postulate, Maslow states that any particular need is most powerful and effective when the needs below it are satisfied to a considerable degree. As a corollary, a person is sick when any one of the higher basic human needs is thwarted or left unfulfilled. Conversely, healthy individuals are motivated to develop their capacities to the fullest.

When one of the basic needs is relatively satisfied (about sixty percent, according to Maslow's illustrations), the next higher need becomes active. While it is dominant, the 'previous need' still plays a minor role, especially if it was insufficiently reduced, and the 'next higher' need begins to emerge. These needs are sometimes conscious, but they are often largely unconscious. Furthermore, needs are modified by culture, the surrounding social reality, and by the opportunities we encounter. Thus cognitive factors, especially our views and interpretation of what surrounds and awaits us, play a crucial part in bringing one or another need to the foreground.

The higher and more social needs emerge only when the lower and more physiological needs are satisfied to a large degree. We can see this in the gradual development of an individual's life: jobs and marriage typically are the major interests of youth, while concern with potential and life's meaning usually appear somewhat later. We see a similar situation during momentary conditions: it is difficult (though not impossible) to enjoy a concert when one has not eaten for two days. Here we must be careful, however, because daily fluctuations are only superficial and not indicative of whatever basic need may affect us.

Maslow has another interesting idea: the lower needs typically involve deprivations, as when we are motivated by a lack of food and shelter or are surrounded by uncertainty and danger. The higher needs, and especially self-actualization, usually involve a striving toward some goal, such as the fullest development of one's potentialities.

Maslow assumes that human beings naturally strive to satisfy their needs, and that in the normal course of life they will naturally come to center on progressively higher needs. In some circumstances, however, our daily life may momentarily revert to earlier and lower needs which then define what is significant. During a war, for example, safety needs may be at the center of our life, and during economic misfortune our major concern is likely to be the satisfaction of physiological needs. At such times self-esteem and self-actualization are likely to play decidedly secondary roles if indeed any at all.

People's needs are not identical. For example, individuals differ with regard to the amount and type of food needed to keep the body functioning, depending on such factors as metabolism rate, insulin production, and so forth. It is plausible to suppose that similar individual differences exist in the other basic needs. While most people devote much time and effort to the satisfaction of their physiological and safety needs, for example, a few become poets and live in garrets. The recognition of such individual differences regarding the higher needs, however, does not invalidate the basic postulates.

Maslow recognizes the existence of many exceptions, of people who are more interested in their reputation than in love or their family, for instance. But he cautions us to look beneath surface phenomena: a person might believe that he is lovable and acceptable only if he has a high income. The self-actualization need, described by Carl Jung in the 1920s, is Maslow's most troublesome proposition. The basic idea makes intuitive sense, especially to people who devote their lives to excellence in poetry, music, mountaineering, cooking, books, scuba-diving, or philosophy. A mundane job and a drab environment do not necessarily interfere with these devotions. Yet we can see problems: just how do we know what an individual's potential is, and when is she on the way toward developing it? Is a bounty hunter, a heroin dealer, or a ruthless dictator, developing his potential? Who is to say—and on what grounds—that these individuals are not in the process of self-actualization?

The essence of the self-actualization need is that whatever human beings can be they eventually must be. Maslow's optimism leads him to the assumption that the vast majority (if not all) of the potentialities—ranging from cooking to hunting to composing—are positive and have a beneficial impact on other people. He considers exceptions, such as criminals or dictators, as the results of early misfortune, environmental conditions, or events the person could not control.

An implicit conclusion is that self-actualization is a natural process that requires little guidance from the individual and—most important—little effort or work. Maslow takes great pains to describe the many characteristics of self-actualizers (famous contemporary and historical figures) but says very little about the road toward that goal of full actualization. The long hours of work, the many disappointments, the hard labor and years of preparation—the nitty-gritty steps on the road—receive little attention. No wonder that many people have assumed—mistakenly—that self-actualization is natural in the sense that growing up is natural, that it is not concentrated labor but rather a "letting go" that leads to the easy, painless goal.

In spite of these concerns and reservations, however, we should consider the self-actualization postulate as an intriguing possibility. As yet we do not know enough about human beings to accept Maslow's version—but at the same time we do not know enough about human nature to reject his views.

A Welcome to Menlo Park

I n the spring of 1969, the Laughlin Foundation of Menlo Park, California, offered Maslow a fellowship which would allow him to engage in whatever research he wished. The complete freedom of this opportunity appealed to Maslow. He decided to move to Menlo Park, south of San Francisco, and resigned from Brandeis University.

In the early days of October, members of the psychology club of La Cañada College decided to invite Maslow to a welcoming get-together. Although he was still recovering from his big move across the continent, Maslow agreed to address the students.

Late one Thursday afternoon, Maslow talked in one of the lecture halls about the work he intended to do in the years ahead. He expressed the hope that psychology's "Third Force" would become as powerful as the other two. After the lecture, the students invited him to meet with them for some refreshments. They walked down the hall to a large, airy room whose open windows afforded a splendid view of the Stanford Hills.

Elizabeth Durkheim, the club's president, welcomed Maslow and accompanied him to the table with coffee and donuts. There he exchanged pleasantries with several students and commented on the life-style he had observed during the past month, so different from Massachusetts.

Maslow refilled his cup and walked over to the windows. "What air," he marvelled, "and what a view. I'll be happy to spend the rest of my life here."

Durkheim joined him. "The job you described is big and will take years. I had always thought that psychologists have been quite successful looking into all the nooks and crannies of the mind."

"Not by a long shot," Maslow shook his head vigorously. "Just consider what therapists are doing. Psychoanalysis is quite unsatisfactory, especially as the source for a general psychology. The picture of humanity it presents is a lopsided, distorted puffing up of human weaknesses and shortcomings—which is then supposed to be a full description. That's simply not true. Practically all the activities that people pride themselves on, and that give meaning and value to life, are either omitted or pathologized by Freud. Work, play, love, art, creativeness, religion in the good sense, ethics, philosophy, science, learning, parenthood, self-sacrifice, heroism, saintliness, goodness—Freud and his followers handle these so weakly ...if at all."

"You will provide a balance?" Durkheim suggested.

Maslow nodded. "Yes...I am carrying on in the spirit of the young Freud—while the psychoanalysts are merely pious, and loyal to the old man. I have eaten all that material and digested it and have made it into my flesh, so to speak. But now I'm eager for the next meal...I'm not content to regurgitate and chew and re-chew on the same psychoanalytic cud. I've already gotten the nourishment out of it, discarded the parts that are not nutritious. Now I'm going on to build something myself."

"I can see your point," said Joseph Mellon, another student who had come over from Stanford. "That's why I'm interested in research. I think laboratories have given us a lot of important discoveries."

"Well, to a limited extent," Maslow hesitated. "Many of the greatest discoveries in psychology have come from outside academic psychology, not only from a few psychiatrists and other psychologists, but also from philosophers and educators. The history of academic—I mean 'scientific'—psychology is largely a saddening story of futility and of very careful and painstaking exploration of one blind alley after another."

"But I think each exploration tells us something about mankind," Mellon replied. "It seems to me that simply knowing a blind alley narrows the field by telling us what the human being is *not*."

Before Maslow could answer, Durkheim interjected: "And where do *you* come in, Professor Maslow? It's hard for me to imagine an alternative to those two major approaches in psychology."

"Ah, look at it this way," Maslow said eagerly. "I respect both psychologies, but I am also impatient with them. On the one hand, psychologists consider the neurotic and the sick. On the other, psychologists study minute parts of laboratory subjects. But there is another world! It's not a *new* world but the *rest* of our world! I mean, the more than ninety percent of the population that is not sick, not in a clinic, not in the laboratory. The millions of healthy and *whole* people living a decent life in the real world, unaware of psychological concepts! And you know—all those normal people have not been studied before!"

"That's quite a big job," Durkheim marvelled.

Maslow nodded and sighed. "Huge. Right now I'm busy finding out what the best aspects of human nature are. I think that by analyzing the best people in depth, we can discover the values by which mankind must live, and for which mankind has always searched. Under the best conditions and in the best individuals, I can see what these old human values are: truth, goodness, and beauty, and some others as well—for instance, gaiety, justice, and joy."

"That's a marvelous project," said Alice Collingwood who introduced herself as a student from La Cañada. "I'm really amazed that such work hasn't been done before."

"I think that it was probably tried and thrown aside," Mellon suggested. "Joy is hard to analyze scientifically ..."

"And perversion is more interesting than goodness," Durkheim added.

"I'm finding many beautiful things," Maslow said enthusiastically. "Average, normal human beings—how different they are from the picture painted by Sigmund Freud and John Watson."

"How do you account for that difference?" Collingwood asked.

"It's mostly a matter of perspective and method, I think," Mellon suggested.

"The main problem is bigger than that," Maslow said firmly. "Unfortunately, most of what we know today about human motivation doesn't come from psychologists. It comes from psychotherapists who draw conclusions from their patients."

"Obviously not a random sample of the population," Mellon said with a trace of sarcasm.

"It's worse than just a poor sample," Maslow added. "Neurotics have all kinds of emotional problems..."

"Otherwise they wouldn't be going to therapists," Collingwood interjected.

"Right," Maslow nodded. "Therefore, a theory of motivation derived from neurotics leaves out a great deal. It cannot help but emphasize negative aspects and various problems. Such theories reflect the jaundiced views of crippled spirits..."

"And what's left out?" Durkheim asked.

"Whatever is characteristic of healthy individuals," Maslow replied.

Mellon looked surprised: "What is health, then?"

"A lot more than the absence of illness or pain," Maslow said. "A positive, optimistic outlook, helping others, a sense of humor, creativity, and so on."

"Symptoms of illness are easier to study, perhaps, and more interesting," Collingwood suggested.

"But they are an aberration, by definition," Maslow continued. "An adequate theory of human beings must also be concerned with what is good in them. We should look less at neurotics and mental patients and more at great people in history and the finest people alive today. Unfortunately, so far that hasn't been done—or even attempted."

"We should get our theory of motivation from them?" Durkheim asked. "Wouldn't that give us another partial view?"

"That should be the basis of our theory, yes," Maslow enthused. "It's not really a partial view, though, because it reflects more than ninety percent of the population—at least to some degree. Those people I mentioned represent the typical human being much more closely than any patient of Freud or Adler ever did. To understand human phenomena we must study the whole range of normal people, including the very best among us. As a result of this shift in emphasis, psychologists will become optimists. And their theories will be more realistic."

"But we must be careful that they don't end up with an optimistic bias," Mellon suggested.

"Yes, of course," Maslow agreed. "We don't want a Pollyanna approach. We simply have to realize that *really* healthy people are very different from the average neurotic patient. These two groups differ in many ways. They think and behave differently, they see themselves, other people, and the world quite differently. When a therapist analyzes the crippled, stunted, immature and unhealthy individuals who come to a clinic seeking help, the inevitable result is a cripple psychology—and even a stunted philosophy."

"Oh, brother," Durkheim murmured.

"When we study normal individuals, including self-actualizing persons and those who are just beginning the process, we are much more likely to come up with a truly scientific psychology," Maslow said.

"But what is health?" Mellon persisted. "You said it's not simply the absence of disease. How can one tell a healthy person from a sick one?"

"Well," Maslow began, "I've been thinking about this for quite a while. It seems to me that a person is sick when the basic human needs are not met. When the lower needs are not met, for example a malfunctioning liver or the lack of some trace element, the person is physically sick. Similarly, when higher needs are not met, an individual is psychologically, or even spiritually sick. I believe that a lack of love is just as important as a lack of vitamins and the effects can be just as detrimental."

Maslow paused and looked at his empty cup. With a broad smile he continued: "Right now my body needs something, and I am motivated to do what is necessary." He walked to the refreshment table for some coffee and a donut. There he met Robert Smucker, a history major, and invited him to come along.

When the two rejoined the group, Collingwood asked: "Are the motives of healthy persons different, then?"

"I believe so," Maslow nodded. "The major motives of healthy people focus on developing their capacities. Healthy individuals want to actualize what is potentially within them."

The conversation was interrupted by several guests who welcomed Maslow and wished him a happy stay. Maslow thanked them and expressed a liking for his new home town.

"I gather from what you have said that you do not call yourself a Freudian," Mellon began when the guests had departed. "And not a behaviorist, either. Then…what *do* you call yourself?"

"I leave labels to others," Maslow laughed. "I believe that I am carrying on the real spirit of Freud, the spirit of inquiry and discovery. So…well, I consider myself a Freudian, but not as *exclusively* Freudian—because I am going beyond Freud, just as I am going beyond Watson. Our job—yours and mine—is to integrate these various truths into the *whole* truth, which should be our only loyalty."

"What made you want to go beyond psychoanalysis and behaviorism?" Collingwood asked. "Where are you going *to*?"

"Yes," Mellon agreed. "What else is there, besides those two major approaches?"

"It all started when I became a father," Maslow said with a smile. "When I watched my babies…well, they made my psychological training look ridiculous and blind. To this day, I simply cannot understand how it is possible to live with a healthy and well-loved baby and be a literal behaviorist or a textbook Freudian. I bet that these philosophies are shed like masquerade costumes as one enters one's home and greets one's spouse and children. Every baby is an individual; idiosyncratic and different from every other baby. I can see no evil in a baby, no malice, no sadism, no joy in cruelty, no guile, no phoniness or hypocrisy. I can see no persona, no role playing, no trying to be anything other than a baby. I see many of these same wonderful qualities in certain adults, the self-actualizing people I have studied. One of their great achievements is to become childlike again, in a kind of second innocence."

"And what about behaviorism? Perhaps you are a bit harsh," suggested Doris Verber, an assistant professor of psychology who had just joined the group. "Some interesting work is being done by young psychologists who have gone far beyond Watson."

Maslow smiled wistfully. "Behaviorism has done a lot," he nodded. "In fact, it was Watson's beautiful program that brought me into psychology during the late twenties. But its fatal flaw—as far as I can see it today—is that it's good for the lab and in the lab, but you put it on and take it off like a lab coat. It's useless at home with your wife and kids and friends. It does not generate an adequate image of man, a philosophy of life, a decent conception of human nature. It's not a useful guide to living, to values, to making choices. If you try to treat your children at home in the same way you treat your animals in the lab, your wife will scratch your eyes out. In fact, my wife ferociously warned me against experimenting on her babies—I was working on monkeys at the time…" He joined in the laughter of his companions.

"I agree as far as Watson's ideas are concerned," Verber said. "But so much work—and different work, on humans—has been done since Watson's time. I think that much of Skinner's work is quite useful ... in the real world of normal people."

"I don't know," Maslow chuckled. "Walden Two is not a pleasant place. I don't see any self-actualizing people there."

"Perhaps not in the novel," Verber persisted. "But I bet that self-actualizing people have learned a lot of skills and other actions through the kind of operant conditioning Skinner describes."

"Only time and a lot more studies will tell," Maslow said.

"Wouldn't it be possible to see whether behavioral principles are important—in your own studies of self-actualizing people?" Collingwood asked. "It seems to me one should be able to discover the importance of learning in the life histories of these people. And—actually, there might be a lot of learning, even if the self-actualizing processes are natural, as you say—like growing up."

"Yes, I'd like to do such studies," Maslow said eagerly. "Unfortunately, I just don't have the time that would be necessary to do all the careful experimenting myself..." He paused, and then continued, apologetically: "Experiments, even if they were possible, would take too long, considering the years I have left and the many other things I still want to do. So, I do only 'quick-and-dirty' little pilot explorations, mostly with only a very few subjects. That's inadequate for publishing in academic journals, but enough to convince myself that the results are probably true and will be confirmed some day—probably by someone else. Today I must be modest about the applicability of my data."

"How many people are working in the same area as you are?" Durkheim asked. "Big projects usually require the co-operation of many people."

Maslow smiled wanly: "I had a couple of graduate students, and a few others helped out once in a while. But on the whole, my approach doesn't appeal to young scientists—and certainly not to established academic types."

"The major concepts are awfully fuzzy and the variables just about impossible to measure," Verber suggested. "Self-actualization is so terribly amorphous—obviously it varies from one person to another. So, how can one derive any principles about it? A musician, a painter, a cab driver—there you have three different potentialities already."

"And yet the idea makes intuitive sense," Smucker said. "As a historian I feel that there have been such self-actualizing people—who carried civilization forward, so to speak. But I agree the topic is hard to analyze from a scientific point of view."

"Science as viewed by academic psychologists," Maslow interjected. "People outside universities are probably more broad-minded."

"Yet less likely to make significant discoveries," Verber said defensively. "What good is an idea if you don't know whether it's true or false?"

"It all depends on where you are," Collingwood said. "At the beginning of a project there are a lot of half-baked ideas, and one should have an open mind about them. Later on one needs to be scientific, of course, and rigorous."

"I agree with that," Maslow said pleasantly. "Whenever I start something, I give up the inhibiting effects of logic, proof, reliability, and so on, and all the cautions and criticisms of my careful and critical friends. I dash on ahead into the unknown, using only my own intuition of what is right and significant. Otherwise I'd never get anything done or discover anything."

"Such methods make it rather difficult for scientists to follow you," Mellon said. "I bet that'll be true especially of your ideas regarding self-actualization."

Maslow nodded sadly. "The concept of self-actualization has been consistently misunderstood and misread and misused by scholars and by laymen, especially young ones. Scholars have often dismissed it as 'optimistic' wish-fulfillment or as unworthy of scientific analysis—and of a scientist. I grant you that my work here is a first-stage investigation that has all the faults of any beginning. Yet, I wonder at the 'scientists' who demand that truths be born equipped with a full set of statistics. To demand rigor, exactness, and complex details from the first exploration of a wilderness is just plain silly. I refuse to be apologetic about discovering a gold mine."

"Does that mean you reject scientific methods and empirical data?" Mellon raised his eyebrows.

"By no means," Maslow replied with vigor. "I want to preserve the empirical, testing, checking, conservative emphasis of science and its methods. But also—I want to build upon this emphasis and go beyond it. Because a simply negative checking, and a perpetual looking for what's wrong, amount to nothing. In fact, they are worse than nothing."

"This also means, I suppose, that at the beginning of a project one works alone," Smucker suggested. "At later stages, other people help in the testing of ideas. Oswald Spengler wrote his *Decline of the West* pretty much alone, and Einstein developed his theory of relativity in isolation. Later, of course, many physicists all over the world tested his theory with all kinds of experiments."

Maslow nodded. "I try to remember pioneers like that. Right now I have nobody in the whole world to talk with about my own work. I'm a lonely worker. In fact, I don't even get into many arguments. The closest approximation to a friendly discussant, in that real sense of having a constructive argument, is Frank Manuel, and he thinks all my work is a lot of shit. Pardon me. But our talks are very good debates, nevertheless. I learn something from him even if he doesn't learn much from me."

Several guests who had been standing nearby now came forward to wish Maslow well. Again there were a few minutes of talk about the Bay area as Maslow shook hands with everyone.

When the guests had left, Mellon changed the subject: "May I ask you a specific question?...About your need hierarchy."

Maslow smiled. "Of course. But it's not *my* need hierarchy. A hierarchy of needs is inherent in every human being. But go on—what's the question?"

Mellon blushed slightly and said: "Right...Now...how do we know when another need is ready to emerge? It seems to me that people are—well, or at least, I am—subject to several needs or motives at the same time."

Maslow nodded. "Most normal people in our society are partially satisfied and partially unsatisfied in all their basic needs, at any one time."

"And when does a new need emerge?" Mellon persisted.

"Emergence is not sudden, it's not a jump, but rather a gradual process by slow degrees, from nothingness. For instance, if a need is satisfied only 10 percent, then the next higher need may not be visible at all. But when the first need becomes satisfied 25 percent, the higher need may emerge five percent, and as the first need becomes satisfied 75 percent, the higher need may emerge 50 percent, and so on."

"I suppose there would be individual differences in those percentages," Collingwood suggested.

"Yes," Maslow said, "and that's why the whole subject of needs and human motivation is so terribly difficult to study. And terribly important, too."

"All of these problems are compounded in the study of self-actualization," Smucker added. "Do you have any results so far?"

Maslow hesitated. "I work in three areas: historical figures, people I know and others alive today, and students. I have some good data about historical figures, like Goethe and Beethoven, but not enough specifics, really. Living self-actualizers are often reluctant to talk about themselves. Ruth Benedict warned me about that problem, but I'm going ahead anyway. Again, the major difficulty is that it's hard to get enough details. So I thought I would be able to get at specific factors and processes by looking at young people who are just beginning their self-actualization. But there I ran into tremendous obstacles. I have studied almost 3000 students by now. The vast majority are quite reluctant to talk, they are apathetic, just not interested in this topic."

"How many self-actualizing students have you caught in your net?" Collingwood asked.

"So far, only one," Maslow said with some dejection. "Either my search methods don't work, or there are very few actualizers. I almost fear for the future."

"But that's just what I would expect," Verber said firmly. "One isn't likely to find something when one doesn't have good measures or definitions of it. But even if you did, I wouldn't expect many undergraduates to be on a definite path toward self-actualization. You say that's the highest need. I presume that it appears slowly, and last. At first only a little bit, as you just told us. So it seems to me that one couldn't really expect to find many self-actualizers under the age of—well, say thirty."

"But I think I know some," Collingwood said brightly.

"Could it be self-indulgence?" Verber asked pointedly. "A young poet who misspells half his words and calls it 'free English,' a teenaged painter who puts blotches of color on cow-hides, a twenty-year old composer who produces noise because he rejects counterpoint which he doesn't understand in the first place—they all might argue that they are actualizing their unique potential, but their doings look like amateurish self-indulgence to me."

"The same thing could be said about some artists in their forties," Smucker added. "I'm afraid that self-actualization and self-indulgence are quite similar. Perhaps they exist mainly in the eyes of the beholder."

"At least until we have clear measures of self-actualization," Mellon said. "And of self-indulgence ..." he smiled at Verber.

"In addition to that, there is another major problem, in my mind at least," Verber continued. "It seems to me that self-actualization requires all kinds of skills, ideas, attitudes, and other behaviors that many people don't have. These must be learned, must they not? How and from whom? I think in your articles you overlooked the hard work, the practicing, the sheer drudgery that eventually results in self-actualization."

"I never said self-actualization was easy," Maslow replied. "The implication of hard work is certainly there."

"Along with the implication that self-actualization is a sort of natural process about which we can't do much," Verber persisted. "I think that might lead some people astray—into easy self-indulgence, for example. If one doesn't know much about the lives of the great self-actualizers one might think it's an easy and natural process—not much of a task."

"I thought all of that was implied in my descriptions of self-actualizers," Maslow repeated. "But I am also convinced that it *is* a natural process—such as looking for safety and love."

"And I would say—*working* for safety, *learning* to do and say the right things at the right times so that one will be loved—and lovable," Verber said gently.

"Yes, all those things," Maslow agreed.

After a moment, Verber continued: "In fact, I see a real danger here. Self-actualization may well become an excuse for self-indulgence, unless you point out how much laborious and tedious effort and time are involved. Self-actualizers have to learn more than just to read and write well—they must also learn to work and to reason. They must learn the complicated skills required for their creative endeavors. And that implies discipline..."

Maslow nodded. "Go on," he said kindly.

"All the great actualizers you mentioned—the great artists, composers, writers, and so on—they all had great skills and a tremendous amount of discipline, especially self-discipline. How else can the inner glory that one is actualizing develop, how else can it be expressed?"

"I might not use those exact phrases," Maslow said, "but I would agree that self-actualization requires a lot of work. But too much discipline might stifle it."

"When people let themselves go, they don't develop the skills needed to actualize their potential," Verber insisted. "When individuals spend their days contemplating their navels and picking raspberries—all in the name of self-actualization—they end up with stiff necks and jam. Young people move to California to do just that. But I think that most human beings have potentials that go far beyond philosophical navels and artistic raspberries."

"That's a bit sarcastic, isn't it?" Maslow grumbled.

"Perhaps," Verber replied. "But I don't think it's far-fetched. Let's wait a few years and see what happens."

After a moment, Collingwood turned to Maslow: "Your descriptions of self-actualizing people scare me a bit. I don't think I can ever be as good as they."

"Ah, yes," Durkheim joined in. "Those people intimidate me, too. I don't see how anyone can achieve those good qualities—and keep them, too."

Maslow laughed. "In my articles I emphasize only one side, the side that is important for my illustration of the self-actualization process. But there is another side, too. These people make mistakes, they lose their tempers, they have regrets, they get lost in a new city, they can't fix their cars. They are human, just like you and I."

"I'm glad to hear that," Durkheim sighed, and Collingwood smiled with relief.

"Actually, this study I'm doing on self-actualization is teaching me something we should all learn," Maslow continued. "There are no perfect human beings. The self-actualizers exist, even if not by the hundreds. That should give us hope for the future. But—to avoid disillusionment with human nature, we must first give up our illusions about it."

"Positive illusions as well as negative illusions," Smucker added, and Maslow emphatically agreed.

"But is it possible to escape from illusions—or avoid them—when we talk about such important matters as human nature?" Mellon asked. "So much of the future depends on what we think people are *really* like."

"Not to mention a person's self-image," Collingwood added.

Durkheim turned to Maslow. "What do *you* think human nature is like?" she asked. "I mean...specifically...is the human being good or evil? When I look around the world today—or study history—I feel so sad."

"It's much too simple to say that people are basically good or basically evil," Maslow replied. "I would say that the individual can become good, probably, and better and better, under better and better conditions. But also it is very easy, even easier, for people to become bad or evil or sick, when they are deprived of the conditions that are fundamentally necessary for a decent life. I think it's a good idea to stress that social conditions are means or instruments and that the only *ends* are the fulfillment of human nature. By that I mean the satisfaction of the basic needs, and especially the highest: self-actualization..."

"Then it seems..." Mellon interjected.

"Wait," Maslow interrupted him. "Let me finish. A correct statement would be: it is within the nature of human beings that, granted increases in the levels of need satisfaction through whatever conditions are necessary, individuals may be expected to become 'better and better' or then to appear to be 'basically good.' Similarly, people do evil things when the social conditions are such that their basic needs, and especially the higher ones, are thwarted. I don't think humans are evil; some are schlemiels. Most of the evil is done without malice. Yes, evil comes less from malice and sadism than from good intentions that are stupid and low-level."

"The problem with the initial question is that it did not define 'good' and 'evil,'" Mellon said rather loudly. "Another problem is that a person does so many things during the year, in the course of a life-time, that it's impossible to make a comprehensive judgment."

"It's hard to say what a person—any person—really *is* apart from what he does or says," Verber added. "Don't we think of a person as 'good' or 'evil' on the basis of what he does? So I would agree with you, Professor Maslow, that social conditions are of paramount importance. After all, they do affect behavior so strongly."

"Perhaps one should not speak of 'good' and 'evil' with all the semantic and logical problems. We should look for another standard," Smucker suggested.

Maslow nodded: "Right. I like to think in terms of human potentialities and the degrees to which they are developed. Then a person's only failure, so to speak, is failing to live up to one's own possibilities. In this sense every individual can be a king and must therefore be *treated* like a king, in the sense that every person is sacred and transfinite. Ultimately, like beautiful sunsets or beautiful flowers, they are not comparable. Each one is the most beautiful, the most sacred, the most perfect in the world."

"What you say sounds very good—even inspiring," Mellon said. "But when I look around me—many of the people and their actions make it difficult for me to really *understand* your optimistic position. I guess I'm just a bit too skeptical."

"But consider this," Maslow said enthusiastically. "Individuals can solve their problems by their own strength. Only a few have done this so far, because most people have not yet developed their full strength. And the forces of 'goodness' within a person have not yet developed fully enough either. So they can't be seen as the hope of the world—except by a few in rare moments of exaltation. But now that we know what people's needs are we can build a society, a culture, in which the basic needs can be gratified enough so that everyone can develop their potentialities."

"I don't see many signs of that society yet," Smucker said. "And I can't think of any time or place in history where human possibilities could flower."

"What about ancient Greece?" Durkheim asked.

"In Athens there were slaves, and Sparta treated its peasants abominably," Smucker replied. "No, it seems to me that even in the best of times only a few people were able to develop their potentialities."

"But the past does not set limits for the future," Maslow said loudly. "We learn from history what *not* to do, and we learn from psychology— *my* psychology—what *should* be done…After all, every baby born is capable, in principle, of self-actualization. We should never give up on anyone, ever; and certainly not on the future and our ability to guide and shape it. Human beings have a higher nature. It's possible to tend it and foster it, or to stunt it. Society can do either."

There was a pause, and Smucker looked around the now empty room. "We are the last ones here," he said.

"Bertha will begin to worry if I don't get home soon," Maslow laughed. More seriously, he continued: "We may be the last ones in this room, but in a wider sense we are among the first—the first people who have the knowledge, and perhaps the desire, to help build a healthy society that produces healthy individuals."

Notes

This encounter is an imaginary welcoming party, which might well have been organized by enthusiastic students at a community college near his new home town of Menlo Park, California. All secondary characters and their words are invented.

I have taken information about Maslow's life and ideas from *A. H. Maslow: An Intellectual Portrait*, by Richard J. Lowry (Monterey: Brooks/Cole, 1973) and from *New Pathways in Psychology: Maslow and the Post-Freudian Revolution* by Colin Wilson (London: Gollancz, 1972). Additional material is based on the private notes which were published in *Abraham H. Maslow: A Memorial Volume*, prepared by the International Study Project (Monterey: Brooks/Cole, 1972). An excellent introduction to Maslow's major ideas is his *Motivation and Personality*, 3rd edition (New York: Harper & Row, 1986). The derogatory remark concerning his work (on page 271), which Maslow considered the opinion of a good friend, is quoted by Colin Wilson (1972, p. 148). I include the phrase to illustrate Maslow's modesty, and his capacity to view his work from the perspective of others.

CONCLUSION

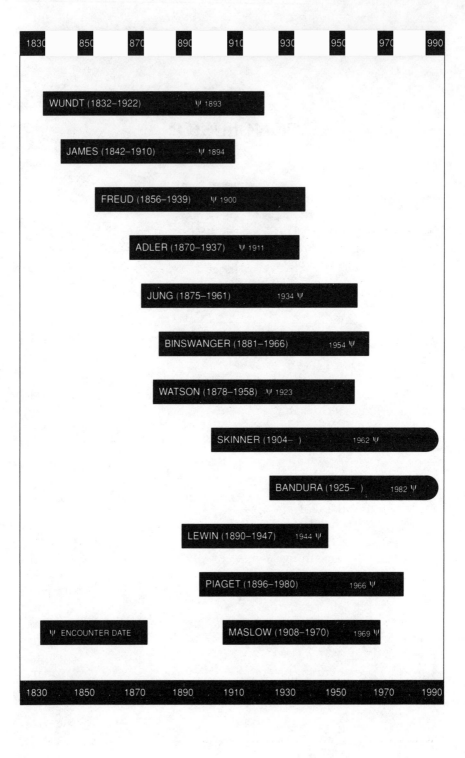

| 1830 | 850 | 870 | 890 | 910 | 930 | 950 | 970 | 990 |

WUNDT (1832–1922) Ψ 1893

JAMES (1842–1910) Ψ 1894

FREUD (1856–1939) Ψ 1900

ADLER (1870–1937) Ψ 1911

JUNG (1875–1961) 1934 Ψ

BINSWANGER (1881–1966) 1954 Ψ

WATSON (1878–1958) Ψ 1923

SKINNER (1904–) 1962 Ψ

BANDURA (1925–) 1982 Ψ

LEWIN (1890–1947) 1944 Ψ

PIAGET (1896–1980) 1966 Ψ

Ψ ENCOUNTER DATE   MASLOW (1908–1970) 1969 Ψ

| 1830 | 1850 | 1870 | 1890 | 1910 | 1930 | 1950 | 1970 | 1990 |

14
DISCOVERING THE HUMAN MOSAIC

One of this century's grand adventures is the discovery of human nature. Throughout the encounters we have seen how formidable a task this is, what difficulties must be overcome. Since the human being is immensely complex, no one researcher can hope to be an expert on all dimensions, and no one method can hope to capture all splendors of human events. Hence psychology is essentially a co-operative effort of investigators who study one or another human characteristic with a variety of tools.

In these chapters we have met twelve psychologists who made significant contributions to our understanding of human nature. We have become familiar with several perspectives and methods, and we have seen how these channeled the researchers' work. Yet it is interesting that so many "old" ideas—for example what Wundt, James, and Adler said about cognitive factors in daily behavior—sound so modern. Indeed, there seems to be a considerable overlap of ideas. Such continuity is not surprising when we realize that most psychologists analyze essentially the same phenomenon: the human being. It is comforting to know that, although researchers pursue their work in several different directions, so many of their discoveries fit together reasonably well. This is especially true when we make allowances for differences in language and emphasis, and consider various hypotheses rather than complete theories.

The psychologists we met lived in different social, cultural, and historical settings and came from diverse intellectual backgrounds. No wonder they asked different questions, sought answers in sundry ways, and emphasized a variety of human attributes! After barely a century of wide-ranging scientific research, psychologists' knowledge of human possibilities and limitations is quite impressive. Although it is sometimes difficult to see how the results of thousands of studies meld into a living portrait, the pieces that have been gathered by honest, hard-working investigators are beginning to coalesce into a multidimensional human mosaic.

During these encounters we have noticed at least five major recurring themes. Psychologists have used different terms to describe them and thereby obscured the similarities, and sometimes these ideas have remained implicit. Yet regardless of the researcher's general perspective and specific theory, the common elements are inescapable.

First, all of the researchers have indicated that most human activities are learned. Some psychologists did not pay much attention to the process itself, while others (e.g. Freud) developed elaborate terminologies. However, as yet there is no general agreement on the nature of learning.

Most of the psychologists we have met concluded from their research that human beings have goals and consider the future. Even researchers who do not use these particular terms, for example Skinner, hold that the consequences of earlier actions have profound effects on subsequent behavior.

A third recurring theme is the tendency for human beings to "construct" the reality in which they live. For example, the optimist views people and the world in one way, the pessimist in another, as each selects certain aspects and explanations of the social and physical system. We see different versions of this idea throughout the encounters, sometimes explicitly as in Piaget and Binswanger, sometimes implicitly as in Wundt and Lewin.

The postulate that human beings strive for "equilibrium" (or balance, consistency) is another element we saw in most encounters. Some researchers state this explicitly (e.g. Freud and Piaget) while others imply such a characteristic (e.g. Bandura and Lewin). We also saw that there is a wide range of areas in which equilibrium is important. Balance may be physical, as when food is a reinforcer for a hungry person, or cognitive, when people prefer a view of the world (or schema) that is consistent (in their estimation).

Finally, several of the psychologists we encountered discussed the development of a human being's potential. We saw that Adler's terminology differs from Lewin's, for example, and that Jung and Maslow approached this need from different points of view. Yet these and other investigators came to rather similar conclusions.

How do these recurring themes and other ideas we encountered in the previous chapters contribute to a general conception of human nature? In the following sections I outline one way of drawing together the significant contributions of researchers who studied human beings from different perspectives.

LEVELS OF ANALYSIS

When we try to understand individuals, and especially when we want to explain their actions or to predict what they will do tomorrow, we usually consider three quite distinct phenomena. We look at people's activities and situations; we infer their thoughts; and we may want to deduce some deeper motives. Similarly, psychologists analyze human beings and events on three levels, each with its own perspectives:

1. observable activities,
2. cognitive processes (e.g. thoughts), and
3. psychodynamic elements (e.g. motives and feelings).

Since this book focuses on psychological attributes and processes, I will pay little attention to their biological foundations.

Just as the events on each level are rather different, so the methods used to study them differ. The most effective ways of gathering and analyzing data on one level may not work well on another. Hence a researcher's favorite method will depend to a considerable extent on the level at which the phenomenon under investigation occurs.

Many events of daily life involve processes that take place on all three levels, often simultaneously. For example, when I drive home in the afternoon, I perform a great number of interrelated activities. If it is close to five o'clock, I probably select a route that I deem to be free of rush-hour traffic. This is especially important because I intensely dislike being caught in a traffic jam. Thus my actions (level one) are the results of assessments (level two) which in turn may be related to deeper motives (level three).

The complex factors and processes that constitute human events have led to an unavoidable division of labor. Today, most psychologists specialize in the analysis of one or another phenomenon and use whatever methods are appropriate. The study of learning new skills, for example, or of typical human errors, or motivation, is a full time job. Unfortunately, such an inevitable division of labor eventually leads to the diversity that gives modern psychology its fractured look.

This diversity is maintained, in part, by the continual building of new theories and by the relatively few attempts to integrate existing explanations. Indeed, it sometimes appears as if psychology consists largely of conflicting theories and their devoted, combative adherents.

As long as we consider only complete theories, there is little hope of bringing together the discoveries and insights of researchers who study human beings from various perspectives. But when we focus mainly on propositions with firm empirical foundations and disregard the other parts of theories, many pieces can be fitted together and a coherent image of human nature begins to emerge.

When a theory has a tight logical structure—as so frequently happens in physics and chemistry, for example—one cannot simply take one piece of it and disregard the rest. Most psychological theories, however, and in particular the early global attempts to explain all of human behavior, have a rather loose structure. Hence we can take one or another well-founded proposition and need not accept other hypotheses, especially if the relationships among them are vague or unstated.

THE SCIENTIFIC STUDY
OF HUMAN BEINGS

Until the latter part of the nineteenth century, psychology was generally considered to be a part of philosophy. By the time Wundt established his laboratory in 1875, the wars of disciplinary independence had been just about won, but skirmishes continued to liven up the intellectual scene for some years to come. Both Wundt and James, whom we met in the first two encounters, fought in the battles for psychology's autonomy. They lived long enough to enjoy the pleasures of independence—although James, as we saw, returned to the other side and became a famous philosopher.

In their laboratories, Wundt and James demonstrated that various actions are systematic and predictable rather than capricious. One of Freud's major achievements was to show that complex activities are determined as well. In his own way, each of the three helped lay the foundation of the new science by elaborating psychology's fundamental postulate: human behavior is governed by laws which can be discovered through systematic empirical analysis.

From the very beginning, however, practitioners of the new science followed two rather different roads to the discovery of human nature. These differences persist to this day, and debates as to which is preferable show no signs of ending, as we have seen in several encounters.

Some researchers worked in laboratories. They carefully designed experiments in which conditions were systematically varied, collected data with increasingly sophisticated instruments, and tried to be objective in their analysis of information. Replication of experiments by other researchers, in other laboratories and with other subjects, was always an important consideration. Thus Wundt was a forerunner of modern experimenters and would probably feel quite comfortable—though overwhelmed—in today's laboratories.

But even in the early days some investigators felt that laboratories were too artificial and instruments too limited to catch the broad, and presumably deeper, essence of human beings. William James was among the most outspoken advocates of a different road to discovery. He believed that careful observations of human events, involving normal individuals (such as himself) enmeshed in daily life, would produce more valid information about significant human characteristics. In spite of its methodological difficulties, this "humanistic" approach remains popular today, especially among many therapists and those who are concerned with the whole person (e.g. Lewin and Maslow).

As we saw in the first three encounters, during the early years both the laboratory and the observational approaches employed the same procedure—introspection. Wundt asked his subjects, James asked himself, and Freud asked his patients, what they thought, felt, or remembered. Wundt, however, was more systematic and also used instruments. He carefully trained his subjects in introspection, employed objective measures as much as possible, and repeated his experiments many times. Later experimenters eliminated introspection and minimized inferences, relying instead on objective indicators from increasingly sophisticated instruments. Today, those who use introspection in the tradition of James and Freud typically do not train their subjects and show little interest in systematic replication.

For many years, the advocates of these two paths to psychological knowledge engaged in rather caustic debates. Each side disparaged the methods and results of the other. James' derogatory words "brass instrument psychology" are among the milder examples of verbal missiles that continue to be hurled—although perhaps with less frequency.

The complexity of psychology's subject matter suggests that one should use whatever methods are appropriate for any given investigation. It makes sense to use the methods that are most likely to produce valid answers to our questions. We should expect that effective methods are likely to vary with the level on which the investigation occurs. For example, if we are interested in matters involving overt actions, such as the learning of complex skills, an experimental approach is most likely to provide valid answers. If we are interested in psychodynamic issues, for example the role of "meaning" in the lives of normal and troubled individuals, we may not be able to use instruments and probably want to go outside the laboratory. Some questions, finally, can be answered best by using a combination of methods. Certain problems of cognition, for example the kinds of errors that people typically make when they assess the probabilities of future events, can be investigated best by combining experiments with careful observations and inferences.

In the following sections I outline a framework for organizing the twelve psychologists' discoveries, and discuss several examples from their work. I begin with the most concrete level—overt activities. Then I examine the cognitive level and the internal processes involved in human action. Finally, I consider the psychodynamic level with its focus on the broader aspects of human beings. On all three levels I start with the empirically most solidly founded propositions, go on to less certain statements, and end up with interesting, plausible hypotheses. The scale of human significance may well run the other way, but at present it is best to begin with firmly established principles.

LEVEL ONE:
OBSERVABLE ACTIVITIES

At the turn of the century, most psychologists explained human activities in terms of rather complex processes which were presumed to operate within a person. Typically, researchers inferred the nature and operation of internal processes from observed behaviors of various people, and relied on their own or their subjects' introspections.

Major problems with inferences and introspection, however, soon became apparent. It is difficult to analyze the inner processes which are discovered by these methods. If Wundt's subject could recognize a luminous pattern after half a second, for example, or Freud's patient remembered a long forgotten childhood event, there was no objective way to determine what was actually going on. It was impossible to tell whether similar or different processes were occurring when other people described their sensations or reported past events. Thus it was hard to test propositions about internal processes, and researchers frequently disagreed. The argument between Adler and Freud (in chapter 5) is a typical example.

Because of these difficulties, some psychologists decided to follow a radically different path. Several early experimenters, especially in the United States, sought to avoid these methodological problems entirely: a focus on overt actions and measurable events should eliminate the need for inferences. These researchers wondered whether human behavior might be explained in terms of preceding or simultaneous events in a person's context that could be measured objectively.

As laboratories developed in many countries, experiments became more sophisticated and new instruments were invented to measure subtler and more intricate aspects of human behavior. The careful description of experimental procedures and the increasing use of ever more sophisticated statistical techniques made it possible to replicate experiments and compare results. Before long a large number of academic psychologists were convinced that subtle and complex human actions could be explained without reliance on internal processes. Watson, for example, championed the view that external events are at the root of human actions, and that introspection is not a necessary procedure for their analysis.

The early behaviorists applied the principles of classical conditioning, which had been discovered in Pavlov's experiments with dogs. The automatic link between a stimulus (e.g. meat powder, in the original experiment) and the natural response (e.g. salivation) can lead to the learning of new relationships. When the original stimulus (the meat) is paired often enough with a new stimulus (e.g the sound of a bell), the latter eventually will produce the original response: the dog salivates after the bell rings, even without the meat powder. By the mid-1920s there were hundreds of experiments demonstrating the power and range of classical conditioning.

As we saw in the encounter with Watson, many of the early experimenters assumed that these conditioning principles operated in humans as well as in animals, and could be used to explain a great variety of human activities—perhaps all. Thus many researchers exulted that psychology had just about completed its task of explaining the essential components of daily life, and probably of civilization.

Such claims weakened, however, when it became increasingly evident that classical conditioning is not the only process at work when individuals learn new actions or go through their daily routines. Beginning in the 1930s, Skinner noted in his experiments that many activities of rats and pigeons are affected by the consequences they had experienced earlier. In the years since then, hundreds of studies by a host of researchers have demonstrated that the same relationships operate in people as well.

Human beings engage in a much wider range of activities than do animals, and most of these activities are considerably more complex. Hence we need to consider some additional dimensions. First, just about all actions involve some physical and/or mental effort—and many require the expenditure of much energy for a long time. This is true not only in one's job but also in recreational activities such as cross-country skiing or playing chess. We may not always be aware of the effort we expend, but we do consider them quite frequently.

Second, many activities are intrinsically enjoyable or unpleasant for the individual. Some of these are natural to a person (for example, some sports for the "born athlete"), others are learned (e.g. playing chess). Needless to say, few actions are intrinsically positive or negative for everyone. Some people love to play tennis or cook, others dislike chess or hate to play the piano.

It is useful to think of these two factors as part of the behavior itself:

$$B_E^{I\ +\ or\ -}$$

Here B stands for any behavior, I for the intrinsic characteristics which may be positive (+) or negative (-) and vary in magnitude (indicated by the size of the letter I). The effort E may be large or small, again indicated by the size of the letter E.

There are, of course, great individual differences, which reflect capacities and past events. If one likes to play chess, for example, there is some mental effort (hence a small E), and the playing itself is very pleasant (thus a large I+). If one does not like to play chess and has a hard time remembering the moves, the E would be large and the I might be negative. Some individual differences are due to experiences, for example in driving a car. A beginner feels awkward and uncertain, tenses in traffic, and thinks about every move. The basic actions of "driving" require considerable effort (hence a large E), while the outing itself may be nerve-wracking and somewhat unpleasant (thus a small I–). An experienced driver, however, is likely to put much less effort into handling the car (hence a smaller E) and enjoy the drive itself much more (thus a large I+). Situational differences also play a role: driving through a rain storm takes more effort and gives less pleasure than driving on a sunny day.

One of the fundamental propositions psychologists have discovered is that people are more likely to repeat an action that has been rewarded in the past than another action which was not. Generally speaking, activities are learned and maintained when they are reinforced, and actions fade away when positive consequences disappear. Since behavior always occurs in a context, certain aspects of the environment eventually become "signals" which indicate the likely consequences that are apt to follow various actions (based on past events).

The several principles involved in this process of learning and behaving are collectively known as operant conditioning—because the action operates on the context. The relationship between activities and events in the context can be summarized in this paradigm of the basic behavior triad:

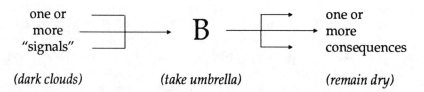

one or more "signals"	B	one or more consequences
(dark clouds)	*(take umbrella)*	*(remain dry)*

DIAGRAM 1: *The Basic Behavior Triad*

In this example we assume that the several activities involved in "bringing an umbrella" are intrinsically neutral (hence no I) and requires practically no effort (thus no E). The consequence "remaining dry" is therefore the only factor we need to consider. From past experiences we know that the signal "dark clouds" indicates we will get wet unless we have an umbrella. If I play tennis, on the other hand, there is some intrinsic pleasure and some effort which I will probably combine with the later consequences I anticipate on the basis of past experiences—such as other people's esteem (if I win) or disdain (if I lose).

As we saw in the encounter with Skinner, behavioral (or learning) principles explain a great variety of activities. Furthermore, these principles have been successfully applied in many areas, ranging from programmed learning to behavior modification (e.g. in therapies).

The basic behavior triad is also the fundamental component of social interaction (diagram 2). In essence, one person's action is equivalent to another person's "signal" and/or consequence, as indicated by the dotted vertical lines. When Joe and Josephine meet, for example, Joe's words and gestures (e.g. "Hi!" and a smile) are the signals which prompt Josephine to return the greeting. Her smile and words are positive consequences for Joe and also signals for further interactions (e.g. "How are you?"). In this way, social relations can persist for quite some time, as long as the participants reward each other.

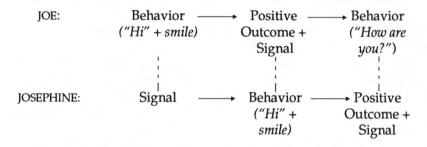

DIAGRAM 2: Behavior Triads in Social Interaction

The fundamental proposition—human activities are largely determined by the consequences a person experienced in the past—raises an interesting question. Why do previous outcomes have such powerful effect? Basically there are three main factors: 1) the nature of an action's consequences, 2) the action itself, and 3) the individual's anticipation that past events will be repeated. In this section we will consider only the first two; the third will be discussed in the next section (on cognitive processes).

First, consequences are reinforcing (positive) or aversive (negative) depending on the individual's momentary condition. A consequence is reinforcing because it reduces a person's deprivation or because it enables him to avoid or escape noxious events. Thus a meal is a positive consequence for a person who has not eaten for some time, and turning off an overly loud radio is rewarding because that reduces the stress of noise. A consequence is aversive because it produces pain or discomfort, leads to deprivation, or prevents individuals from doing what they like. Since deprivations play more significant roles in human behavior than punishment, we will concentrate on the former.

Human beings are subject to a great variety of deprivations and their associated reinforcers. Some deprivations have a physiological basis, such as hunger, thirst, and being cold—we will call them "primary." But humans are even more affected by another kind of deprivation (and its associated reinforcers): "secondary" deprivations are learned and reflect a culture's definitions and customs. For example, some individuals feel deprived when they do not have the "proper" clothes for a dance or do not have the "right" recorded music in their collection. In that case, the positive outcome of an activity chain (such as work) would be the purchase of "proper" clothes and the "right" music.

Until the 1930s it was thought that primary (e.g. hunger) and secondary (e.g. no "proper" clothes) deprivations were the principal roots of human motivation, and thus the major determinants of behavior. But then it was discovered that monkeys, for example, could be rewarded simply by allowing them to watch new things (such as a toy train); evidently there was no "deprivation" at work.

The second factor became apparent in the ensuing years, when psychologists discovered that many people prefer to engage in a wide range of new, interesting, or otherwise satisfying experiences. Mountain climbing, playing chess or tennis, and performing on a musical instrument, are examples of rather complex, difficult, and arduous activities which an individual may perform for their own sake. Since deprivation does not operate here, psychologists now speak of intrinsically reinforcing (or aversive) actions—as indicated earlier by the symbol I.

Over the years, the "behavioral perspective" in psychology has increasingly come to mean the analysis of operant conditioning principles and their applications. Today we know that both sets of conditioning (or learning) principles operate. It appears that most human actions involve operant principles rather than respondent (classical) principles. The dividing line between the two sets is fuzzy, however, and remains to be fully determined.

Today, radical behaviorists are apt to maintain an uncompromising stance regarding the methods and substance of their work. These researchers focus on the careful, systematic study of overt actions and their relations to contextual events. Internal processes are disregarded because these are deemed to be irrelevant or beyond the scope of current methodology.

As we saw in the encounters, however, the radical position is probably an overstatement. While many actions can be explained by classical and operant conditioning, it is quite evident that most people, most of the time, do not react automatically to external stimuli (as rats and pigeons apparently do). In daily life, human beings often confront choices, ranging from "how much coffee?" in the morning to "which TV program?" at night. Most choices, even mundane ones, involve the evaluation of alternatives in terms of immediate and longer-term consequences ("I like this program, even though it's dumb, but I have to get up early tomorrow"). This third factor has received considerable attention by cognitive psychologists.

In much of daily life, and especially when we find ourselves at significant cross roads, we are aware that each possible action has several consequences: some are positive, others are negative; some happen right away, others come later (and a few very much later). Some results are just about guaranteed, others are not very likely. And then there is the possi-

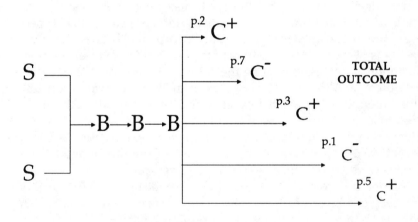

3 days   1 week   1 month   1 year   5 years

B: In this illustration, the activities require no effort (hence no E), and they are intrinsically neutral (thus no I).

C: Consequences. The size of the letter indicates the consequence's significance for the individual in terms of the momentary and anticipated deprivations.

P: The probabilities, perceived or real (depending on the perspective) that the consequences (C) will occur.

S: Signals, various aspects of a person's context which serve as cues regarding likely consequences of various activities (on the basis of past experiences).

DIAGRAM 3: *Example of A Complete Behavior Triad*

bility that we do not know all of the consequences—or indeed all of the alternatives. Furthermore, there are likely to be several "signals" in the environment, and the final outcome will probably not occur until a long chain of actions has been completed (e.g. the weekly pay check).

A more complete paradigm of human activities, therefore, would include the following elements: a chain of behaviors (B–B–B), several "signals" (S), a number of positive (C+) and negative (C–) consequences which vary in importance, and the probabilities (P) and time scales of their occurrence. In Diagram 3, which combines all of these components, the time scale of each consequence is shown by the length of the arrow, and the significance of the various effects is indicated by the size of the symbol (the larger the C, the more important it is to the individual).

LEVEL TWO:
COGNITIVE PROCESSES

Behavioral principles indicate that actions are linked to environmental signals and, through past experiences, to likely consequences. But the basic paradigm ("Signal" → Behavior → Consequences) does not give us a complete picture of human activities. Behavioral principles do not specify the nature of the linkages (how the arrows operate) between any two components of the triad. In fact, most linkages involve a variety of mental operations, such as evaluating the nature and probabilities of a particular outcome. Although many of these cognitive processes ultimately must be inferred, sophisticated experimental procedures have been developed to analyze quite a few of them.

When an individual selects a particular behavior, the choice is based on several factors: perceived competence to perform this or another action, perceived consequences, and the perceived probabilities and time scales of their occurrence. These perceptions can be in accord with reality or not, they can be carefully constructed or haphazard recollections. A person may be aware of consequences or follow a habitual course, make objective assessments or be emotionally involved.

We can see the importance of such cognitive processes in the dilemma faced by many dedicated smokers: to continue smoking or not? As objective observers we are immediately aware that there are two perspectives of relevant factors, each structured as we see in diagram 3. First, there is the real world, filled with actual consequences that occur with specific probabilities and within particular time frames. Second, there is the individual's world, full of perceptions, feelings, and beliefs. In this cognitive world there may be misconceptions, ignorance, and illusions, fear as well as hope. How many smokers think that they are not likely to get lung cancer; a cure will be found before they come down with it; cigarettes have little to do with emphysema; only other smokers' breath smells; and other people don't mind second-hand smoke, even in restaurants? When these beliefs are combined with the immediate pleasures of smoking (I+), it is not surprising that people find it difficult to quit.

The existence of mental operations does not invalidate behavioral principles. Rather, such operations add vital components to the basic paradigm. Cognitive processes help us understand the complex reciprocal relationships between environmental events and behavior.

As a minimum, individuals are aware (even if only subconsciously) of the "signals" in the context which indicate the likely consequences of various activities. Those signals were learned, of course, and can be effective only as long as they are remembered and perceived. People usually consider the range of activities in which they are competent. They usually select the action they believe they can perform well, which they think is most appropriate, and which they hope will have the desired consequences.

Human beings assess the magnitude of their actual and anticipated deprivations, and estimate how well the several consequences they can expect will reduce those deprivations. Here they take into account the immediate costs of various actions (e.g. time and effort) as well as expected later consequences. Finally, individuals combine all of these immediate and eventual consequences, magnitudes, and probabilities into one "total outcome" (diagram 3). In our example, the dedicated smoker is likely to view the "total outcome" of smoking as positive or at least neutral, while the non-smoker considers the "total outcome" as being negative.

Such calculations are foregone only when actions are simple and short or have been repeated many times—habits usually require little if any deliberate "mental effort." In recent years, cognitive psychology has become a major force in the field. Bandura's work exemplifies this transition from a strictly behavioral approach to a broader emphasis on a wide range of internal factors. Today, a host of researchers are investigating the nature and operation of the intricate processes involved in even simple activities.

To illustrate the complexities involved, consider a drive through the countryside. In the past we learned to recognize certain aspects of our context as signals (e.g. a speed limit sign), and we remember the positive and negative consequences of our subsequent actions (e.g. avoiding a speeding ticket when we slowed down). At any one moment, we can recall many of our own and other people's experiences in which various activities were related to various signals and positive or negative consequences. Therefore, when these signals (or similar elements) reappear in our environment we recognize them and, remembering past events, are likely to anticipate various consequences (e.g. we slow down when we see a speed limit sign because we do not want a ticket).

On the basis of our own or other people's experiences we attach probabilities to the occurrence of the several consequences we expect (e.g. "this town is known as a speed trap, but I don't see any police cars"). Furthermore, we are aware of a wide range of present deprivations whose magnitude depends on their significance for us (e.g. "I really can't be late for this crucial appointment"). We are also likely to look ahead and anticipate other deprivations and consequences in the near or distant future (e.g. "but getting a ticket will take more time than slowing down"). Whether or not we adhere to the speed limit, therefore, will depend on the convergence of several factors, some of them quite personal.

When we face a choice of actions, for example whether to see a movie with friends or to visit boring but wealthy relatives, we perform these often intricate calculations for each alternative. After our decision, however, we may well have second thoughts. In order to reduce dissonance feelings, we may then—retroactively, so to speak—rearrange some elements of our calculations to bring our mental supporting structure into line with our actual behavior. Upon deciding on the visit, for instance, we may convince ourselves that the movie is not all that good anyway, or that the relatives sometimes can be reasonably interesting.

Behavior change in particular is often more complex than the early behaviorists realized. People are likely to alter their activities when the perceived consequences change from positive to negative, when the perceived probabilities change, or when the new behavior is followed by sufficient positive consequences. Thus smokers will have great difficulty quitting until their perceptions of likely consequences undergo a fundamental change. Indeed, the essence of reality therapy, as well as of some other procedures, is the systematic attempt to change an individual's perceptions so that they will correspond more closely to actual events.

As we saw in our encounters with Adler and others, the importance of anticipated consequences (i.e. goals) for present behavior has been recognized for some time. It is also interesting to note that when psychologists today speak of an individual's behavioral repertoire and cognitive routines, they are describing essentially what Adler called a person's "style of life."

Individuals receive information relevant for these mental calculations mainly from 1) their own and other people's experiences, and 2) symbolic information from various sources (e.g. the mass media, books, and people). But one's analysis of anticipated consequences is not a simple, straightforward process. In recent years, considerable research has been devoted to the study of common errors that frequently intrude upon decision making. Today it is well known, for instance, that people frequently are not aware of environmental signals and do not always attribute events to the actual causes. Experiments have also shown that people tend to pay more attention to information with which they agree, and often underestimate the likelihood of negative effects. The processes which underlie activities and social interaction, then, are much more complex, not to say convoluted, than strictly behavioral principles suggest.

Most psychological propositions describe processes that occur in normal adults. Indeed, the implication that the "individuals" whom researchers talk about are physiologically normal adults is so pervasive that the characteristics "normal" and "adult" are rarely specified. Yet the question arises: does it matter in whom behavioral and cognitive processes occur?

It matters indeed.

As mentioned earlier, the principles that describe overt behavior and cognitive factors are ultimately the manifestations of physiological structures and neurological processes that are beyond the scope of this book. So-called "abnormal" individuals would be subject to these principles within the limitations of the particular physiological abnormality. But as long as such individuals are only a small part of the population, it is sufficient to describe the general principles.

The other characteristic—adult—is more problematic.

It has been evident for quite some time that children think differently than do adults. But it was not until Jean Piaget began to describe the development of cognitive processes that the differences between children and adults were understood. Today we know much about the ways in which children of various ages think and reason, and how adult ways of processing information emerge and develop.

During the early years of life, maturing neurological structures gradually enable the child to remember more, to think abstractly and look farther ahead, to deduce general principles and causes from several observations, and to make complex calculations of costs and benefits. As we saw in the encounter with Piaget, however, the child's active manipulation of objects in the physical environment appears to be the crucial aspect of cognitive development. Deliberate interactions with the world transform the merely possible into actual knowledge.

Few human beings see their context as a disparate collection of stimuli. Rather, most people organize their sensory impressions into larger units that are meaningful to them. Originally, such a unit that brings some sense to amorphous stimuli was called a "gestalt" (German for figure or form). Today, psychologists have expanded the original idea and usually speak of a "schema." As the encounter with Piaget indicates, once we have developed schemas of things, people, and events, we tend to behave in terms of them; schemas become part of the reality in which we live.

In daily life we interact with many people and are influenced by (and influence) numerous people, objects and events. Indeed, even a relatively quiet day is filled with a host of "signal"—behavior—consequence triads which usually include past events and present circumstances as well. As we saw in the encounter with Kurt Lewin, people organize these significant aspects of their surroundings into rather large units, which he called "life space." When Lewin describes a person's "life space" within which an activity occurs, he is basically talking about an individual's— and observer's—perceptions of the complicated first ("signal") and last ("consequence") elements of the typical behavior triad. Diagram 3, for example, illustrates the interrelations of several important components of a person's life space. For a more comprehensive "life space" we should add the people whose actions provide so many of an individual's signals and consequences (cf. diagram 2).

LEVEL THREE:
PSYCHODYNAMIC ELEMENTS

As good experimenters, Bandura, Piaget and Lewin were primarily interested in those internal processes which involve measurable variables and therefore can be analyzed objectively. Hence their studies focused primarily on the rather mundane aspects of an individual's daily life. But human existence also involves phenomena that are rather difficult to analyze in a laboratory. Most people—and perhaps all—prefer to live in reasonably predictable and secure surroundings over which they can exert some control; they like to have friends and want to be loved. Many individuals seek answers to questions such as "what is the purpose of my life?", and they may worry about death.

These phenomena occur on the psychodynamic level.

Just as cognitive processes augment the fundamental learning principles, so psychodynamic elements (such as motives, feelings, and needs) add human dimensions to the basic behavioral paradigm. The result is the full-bodied individual whose possibilities and limitations are the hallmark of human nature. It is only when we combine the elements of all three levels that we behold the human being who becomes manifest in the arts and sciences, in philosophy and religion.

The analysis of psychodynamic processes is complicated by preferences in terminology which reflect the theoretical position of the researcher and the focus of a study. Many psychologists, for example, would rather speak of "motivation" and "needs" than "deprivation," while some reject all three.

The major difference among the three concepts is the perspective involved. "Deprivation" implies certain relations between the individual and the context (e.g. nothing to eat since an early breakfast), and focuses on the individual's (recent) past. Just as an experimenter might deprive a rat of food and water, so humans may be deprived of what they define as "proper" food, clothes, recordings, etc. The term "motivation" changes the perspective to the individual's feelings and potential actions regarding a deprivation. Thus a person might be motivated to eat lunch early because he skipped breakfast, or to work overtime so he can purchase "proper" clothes. While most deprivations are temporary and can easily increase or decrease, the term "needs" suggests permanent human requirements (which may or may not be met at any particular moment).

As we saw in the two preceding sections, most activities of daily life involve primary and secondary deprivations, intrinsically reinforcing behaviors, and a variety of cognitive processes. But some actions do not seem to follow this general pattern. Additional factors evidently are at work, and perhaps these further attributes are what sets us off from other animals.

Social-psychological studies as well as observations of daily life indicate that most people strive toward a world view that is internally consistent and corresponds to (their conception of) reality. Furthermore, most individuals prefer situations in which they are treated fairly and are in control of their lives. Some of us devote much time and effort to solving problems of nature or answering questions about the universe. Many individuals seek new information, more knowledge, or extraordinary experiences. At one time or another most people have asked themselves: who am I? what is the purpose of my life? and: am I living up to my capacities?

There seem to be other, more amorphous qualities as well, which are most clearly evident in some of the great artists. Mozart, for example, often seemed "driven" to compose, even when he did not have to worry about money. The modern poet Rainer Maria Rilke felt compelled to write, even during personally very difficult times. Gauguin left a good and secure life to become a painter in Tahiti. Today, quite a few individuals devote considerable time to a search for an often elusive sense of fulfillment.

Psychology must deal with all of these phenomena. While many researchers limit their work to the explanation of overt behavior and the associated cognitive processes, the actions and questions just mentioned are equally significant aspects of human beings—and thus legitimate subjects of scientific inquiry.

Several well known psychologists have devoted much time and effort to the careful study of these phenomena. For example, beginning in the 1920s, Carl Jung postulated that people have a natural desire to develop their potential. As we saw in our encounter with him, Jung believed that individuals who are not in the process of fulfilling their capacities would become neurotic. Abraham Maslow devoted a major part of his life during the 1950s and 1960s to the study of this highest human need—to develop one's potential. And when Piaget described schemas, accommodation, and cognitive equilibrium, he complemented other researchers who analyzed the human preference for consistency.

Hence it is useful to hypothesize a third type of deprivation. "Tertiary" deprivations, and thus also tertiary reinforcers, reflect intellectual, philosophical, and spiritual requirements which are just as real and significant to some people as physiological deprivations are to others. Individuals have different concerns, of course; for some, questions regarding life and death are extremely important, for others they matter less. When such questions are significant, we are likely to do whatever is necessary to find satisfying answers. The search for answers may lead us to read philosophical books, to look for the "right" religion, or to have discussions with other seekers.

There exists, then, a broad class of reinforcers that appear to be quite different from those we considered earlier. A thoughtful person may feel rewarded by a satisfying answer to a philosophical question, and a distraught individual may feel relieved after a religious experience. We feel comfortable when our ideas about daily events and the world fit together, we are content when we are treated fairly, and we are happy when we are in control of significant portions of our daily life. The writing of a symphony or poem, even if no one is likely to hear the work, can be a powerful and exhilarating experience. An astronomer may feel deeply rewarded by a new explanation of black holes.

As we saw in the encounter with Maslow, it makes considerable sense to hypothesize a hierarchy of needs and to suppose that lower needs must be minimally satisfied before higher needs become significant—for most people. Maslow's "lower" needs have an immediate physiological basis, and when they are not met they essentially take the form of the "primary deprivations" discussed earlier. These needs are reduced or satisfied by whatever activities bring about the appropriate outcome, such as adequate food, clothing, and comfort.

While most of the needs discussed by Maslow and others are assumed to be universal, they vary in magnitude and specific content. The need for food is innate, for example, but hunger can be expressed and reduced in several ways. Some people have to eat much, others get by on little, depending on their metabolism. An individual's definition of a "proper" meal and criteria of "adequate" comfort are learned, and the degrees of consistency and control one seeks reflect one's experiences, culture and times.

We may assume, then, that the satisfaction of most needs, including the "higher" ones, is equivalent to the positive outcomes discussed by Bandura and the reinforcers mentioned by Skinner. These satisfactions strengthen the preceding activity chains—as when we work for a living, try to make and keep friends, maintain a marriage, and seek answers to philosophical questions.

The highest need in Maslow's hierarchy, and an important aspect of Jung's theory developed thirty years earlier, is the need to develop one's potential. Whenever it is not met—for people who are aware of it—life seems to lack meaning. In our encounters with Jung, Binswanger, and Maslow it became apparent that the "higher" needs are just as important as the "lower" ones, although experimenters have not systematically studied them in their laboratories.

As we saw in these and other encounters, psychodynamic factors such as the need for meaning or to develop one's potential are extremely difficult to analyze. We should not be surprised that today the major tools of scientific psychology, especially the laboratory experiment, seem to be inadequate. Perhaps they are inappropriate. Furthermore, it may be hard to find subjects. Maslow discovered that this need is not felt by everyone (especially in youth), and Jung believed that individuals have to reach middle age before they might be concerned with their potential.

Some people may find it easy to dismiss the hypothesis of higher needs as far-fetched and irrelevant. But Jung, Binswanger, and Maslow present strong arguments for the existence and significance of such needs. Indeed, it is possible that these amorphous and hard to measure phenomena are closer to the essence of human nature than some of the activities usually studied in laboratories. We see here what may be psychology's greatest dilemma: the more comprehensive a conception of human nature is, the more difficult its validation is likely to be.

We should not conclude that intellectual and creative aspects of human beings, including people's philosophical concerns, are outside the realm—or competence—of scientific psychology. In our first encounter, Wundt expressed his conviction that psychologists would never be able to analyze what he called the "higher faculties," those human aspects he was not able to investigate in his rather primitive laboratory. How wrong he was! Today, psychology encompasses specialties Wundt never dreamed of. The sophisticated equipment of modern laboratories, combined with the ingenuity and skills of researchers, have given us a host of insights regarding motives, feelings, and cognition. It would be equally foolhardy to suppose today that cognitive and psychodynamic processes are beyond the scope of systematic and objective inquiry. Indeed, the analysis of such complex and uniquely human processes is the great challenge of psychology's future.

Notes

The sources of specific ideas and propositions which appear in this chapter have already been mentioned in the "Notes" sections of the preceding chapters. The diagrams have been adapted from my *Behavior, Social Problems, and Change* (Englewood Cliffs: Prentice-Hall, 1975). Four general books that describe the wide range of perspectives in modern scientific psychology are especially noteworthy.

Ernest R. Hilgard and Gordon H. Bower describe and assess the most important theories of learning—and, by implication, the major sets of behavior principles—in their famous *Theories of Learning*, 5th edition (Englewood Cliffs: Prentice-Hall, 1981).

In *Human Inference: Strategies and Shortcomings of Informal Judgment* (Englewood Cliffs: Prentice-Hall, 1980) Robert E. Nisbet and Lee D. Ross discuss many of the significant cognitive processes and errors that influence behavior and pervade much of everyday life.

The *Handbook of Motivation and Cognition*, edited by Richard M. Sorrentino and E. Tory Higgins (New York: The Guilford Press, 1986) provides a comprehensive treatment of cognitive principles and perspectives. The book also summarizes research and outlines methodological problems.

Although Ernest R. Hilgard focuses on psychology in only one country, his monumental *Psychology in America: A Historical Survey* (San Diego: Harcourt Brace Jovanovich, 1987) ranges far beyond national boundaries. The book covers many of the perspectives, topics, and problems we have met in the preceding encounters. Modern psychology's diversity of views—as well as the underlying continuity of effort by scores of investigators—are lovingly described in considerable detail.

Finally, those who are interested in the factors that contribute to psychology's diversity and who wonder about the possibility of unification will find an interesting discussion in Arthur W. Staats's *Psychology's Crisis of Disunity: Philosophy and Method for a Unified Science* (New York: Praeger, 1983).